Critique of Pure Reason

(Abridged)

Immanuel Kant

Critique of Pure Reason

Abridged

Translated by

WERNER S. PLUHAR

Abridged, with an Introduction, by

ERIC WATKINS

Hackett Publishing Company
Indianapolis/Cambridge

Immanuel Kant: 1724–1804

Translation copyright © 1996 by Hackett Publishing Company, Inc.

Abridgment and new material copyright © 1999 by Hackett Publishing Company, Inc.

05 04 03 02 01 00 99   1 2 3 4 5 6 7 8 9

Cover design by Listenberger Design & Associates

Interior design by Meera Dash

For further information, please address
        Hackett Publishing Company, Inc.
        P.O. Box 44937
        Indianapolis, IN 46244-0937

Library of Congress Cataloging-in-Publication Data

Kant, Immanuel, 1724–1804.
        [Kritik der reinen Vernunft. English. Selections]
        Critique of pure reason (abridged) / by Immanuel Kant; translated by
Werner S. Pluhar; abridged, with an introduction by Eric Watkins.
              p.   cm.
        Includes bibliographical references and index.
        ISBN 0-87220-449-9. — ISBN 0-87220-448-0 (pbk.)
        1. Knowledge, Theory of. 2. Causation. 3. Reason. I. Pluhar,
Werner S., 1940–   . II. Title.
        B2778.E5P57   1999   98-47078
        121—dc21   CIP

CONTENTS

INTRODUCTION

1. Education, Career, and Publications

Immanuel Kant was born in 1724 in Königsberg, at the time a city of about fifty thousand inhabitants, located near the Baltic Sea in East Prussia, Germany. With his revolutionary work in metaphysics, epistemology, ethics, philosophy of science, and aesthetics, he became one of the most important philosophers of the eighteenth century. Kant was educated first at the Collegium Fridericianum (1732–40) and then at the Albertus Universität (1740–44), both in Königsberg. After graduating in 1744, he was a tutor to a number of families in the Königsberg area, until he became a lecturer at the university in 1755. Though Kant published a number of works on a variety of topics while he was a lecturer, it was only at the age of forty-five, in 1770, that he became a professor of logic and metaphysics at the Albertus Universität, a position he held until his retirement in 1796. He died eight years later in 1804.

Kant's life is often divided into three periods: his pre-Critical period, his "silent" period, and his Critical period. His pre-Critical period began in 1747 with the publication of his first work, *Thoughts on the True Estimation of Living Forces,* which focused on a hotly debated question in physics (whether "dead" or "living" forces are conserved in nature). In 1755 he published *New Elucidation of the First Principles of Metaphysical Cognition,* a critique of Leibnizian-Wolffian metaphysics, and *Universal Natural History and Theory of the Heavens,* a cosmology according to Newtonian principles that anticipated Laplace's cosmology in its fundamentals. In addition to numerous smaller pieces in the 1750s and 1760s on physics, metaphysics, mathematics, geography, theology, and aesthetics, his most significant works included the *Physical Monadology* (1756), which attempted to reconcile mathematics' demand for infinite divisibility with metaphysics' requirement of unity, and *The Only Possible Argument in Support of a Demonstration of the Existence of God* (1763), which contained many of his later criticisms of the traditional theistic proofs—though at this point he maintained the possibility of a theoretical proof of God's existence. The pre-Critical period concluded in 1770 with his Inaugural Dissertation (a work required for acceptance of the professorship he was offered) titled *Concerning the Form and Principles of the Sensible and Intelligible World*. During his "silent" period, which reaches from 1770 to 1780, Kant published only a few minor essays.

Kant initiated his Critical period in 1781 with the first of his truly great works, the *Critique of Pure Reason*. In order to clarify and simplify his position as it was presented in the *Critique of Pure Reason*, he subsequently issued the *Prolegomena to Any Future Metaphysics* in 1783. He then published a major treatise in ethics, the *Groundwork of the Metaphysics of Morals*, in 1785 and an important work in the foundations of physics, *Metaphysical First Principles of Natural Science*, in 1786. In 1787 he issued a second edition of the *Critique of Pure Reason*, with a considerable number of important revisions.[1] In 1788 he published his second Critique, the *Critique of Practical Reason*, and in 1790, less than a decade after the first, his third and final Critique, the *Critique of Judgment*. Though Kant continued to be productive throughout the rest of his career, these three Critiques (along with the other publications of this decade) constituted the core of his Critical period and revolutionized how philosophy would be done ever after.

2. Main Theses of the *Critique of Pure Reason*

Although one can approach Kant's revolutionary philosophy from a variety of different perspectives, it is perhaps appropriate to make a start by considering one of Kant's own ways (as developed in the Introduction to the *Critique of Pure Reason*) of characterizing the difference between his philosophy and that of his predecessors. His claim is that he is the first one to understand that the traditional claims of metaphysics consist of synthetic a priori judgments, a claim which, if correct, has extraordinarily rich consequences.

Kant first distinguishes between judgments that depend for their justification on particular experiences, i.e., a posteriori knowledge claims, and judgments that can be justified independently of any particular experience, i.e., a priori knowledge claims. He also distinguishes between truths known by the meanings of the terms involved

---

1. For the purposes of this abridged edition, only major variations between editions will be indicated, where the second edition formulation is typically preferred.

in the proposition in question, i.e., analytic truths, and those that require something beyond these meanings in order to be known, i.e., synthetic truths. Now it is clear enough that an analytic truth can be known a priori, since one needs to know only the meanings of the terms involved in the proposition in question in order to know its truth. And it is equally clear that a synthetic truth can be known a posteriori, since particular experiences can provide evidence not supplied by the meanings of the terms. However—and this is the question Kant focuses on—can we have synthetic a priori knowledge? If so, how is such knowledge possible? Since such knowledge is synthetic, something beyond the mere meanings of the terms is required. But since it is a priori, particular experiences are excluded. So, if we make synthetic a priori knowledge claims, by what right can we make such claims? To put the question differently: How can we know any nontrivial (i.e., synthetic) features of an object even before we look at it (i.e., a priori)?

The problem of synthetic a priori knowledge is highlighted by the fact that the claims that Kant thinks fall in this problematic class of judgments are nothing less than the claims of traditional metaphysics, that is, claims that are of tremendous importance to us, such as "God exists," "the soul is immortal," "we have free will," and "the world as a whole has no beginning in space or time and does not consist of simple particles." Given this analysis of the synthetic a priori status of metaphysical claims, Kant sees his task as twofold: first, he must reveal the conditions that make synthetic a priori knowledge possible; and second, he must consider whether the claims of traditional metaphysics satisfy those conditions and can thus be known.

Kant discovers two general kinds of conditions that make synthetic a priori knowledge possible. The first kind of condition pertains to the way in which we become acquainted with objects, that is, the way in which objects act on us so that we can receive sensory information about them. Kant argues that all objects must be given to us in space and time; space and time are the sensible forms through which we intuit objects (that is, as Kant sometimes puts it, space and time are "forms of intuition"). He then argues that geometry, as a body of synthetic a priori truths, is possible only on the basis of our primitive representation of space. (Kant employs a similar argument for time as well, so that mathematics as a whole is possible only by means of both space and time.) In this way Kant hopes to establish that space and time are conditions of synthetic a priori knowledge.[2] The second kind of condition pertains to the way in which we actively conceptualize our sensory information. Kant first argues that there is a set of primitive and nonempirical concepts (which he often calls "categories") that we must use in order to understand or grasp the world. Prominent examples of such concepts are substance and causality. He then argues that these concepts are necessarily involved in certain synthetic a priori judgments about the world (such as "every event has a cause"). Once again, Kant's idea is that synthetic a priori knowledge is possible only if these primitive concepts are used.[3] Moreover, not only must these primitive concepts be used; they also must be applied to objects given in space and time. Thus, these two kinds of conditions are necessarily related.

At this point, Kant is in a position to consider the second part of his overall task. Given these two kinds of conditions, he asks whether the traditional claims of metaphysics satisfy these conditions and thus can purport to be knowledge. Kant argues that traditional (or dogmatic) metaphysical claims do not in fact satisfy these conditions. They do employ the fundamental nonempirical concepts he has isolated, but their distinguishing feature is that they do not involve objects that we could encounter in space and time. (That is, they satisfy

2. More specifically, Kant argues that mathematical knowledge is possible only if space and time are simply subjective forms through which objects are given to us in experience. In other words, space and time are not properties of objects *per se*, but are rather our own subjective forms for perceiving objects. Since space and time are *subjective* forms (rather than properties of objects), our access to them can be a priori. Further, since mathematical knowledge depends on these spatial and temporal forms (by means of which objects are given to us) rather than a mere analysis of concepts, such knowledge can be synthetic. Accordingly, it is only if space and time are subject-dependent or ideal in this way that synthetic a priori knowledge of mathematics is possible.

3. To be more specific, it is the synthetic a priori knowledge of natural science that is made possible by the application of primitive concepts such as causality to spatio-temporal objects. Since these concepts are not derived from experience, such knowledge can be a priori, and since this knowledge is not obtained through an analysis of experience, but rather stems from the application of these pure concepts to spatio-temporal objects, it can be synthetic. Further, as in the case of space and time, we can know a priori that the world we perceive is spatio-temporal and governed by, for example, causal rules because it is we who contribute these features to our experience of the world.

only the second, not the first, kind of condition.) God and the soul are certainly not spatial. God is not temporal in the way that "normal" sensory objects are—in fact, one traditional conception of God maintains that God is completely outside of time—and the soul's immortality, which proceeds to infinity, is not something we can confirm in our limited experience either. The world as a whole (including our freedom) is also not something we can experience in space and time, since all we ever perceive in space and time are parts of the world, never the whole thing. Given this analysis, the claims of traditional metaphysics cannot amount to knowledge. In fact, this negative conclusion is directly connected to the title of the book. Kant calls it a *critique* of pure reason because he is criticizing pure reason's attempt to establish synthetic a priori claims that do not satisfy the conditions that must be met for synthetic a priori knowledge. More specifically, the claims of traditional metaphysics are asserted on the basis of *pure* reason (and thus must be rejected), precisely because they do not apply our fundamental nonempirical concepts to spatio-temporal objects and thus do not involve the sensible conditions of space and time.

At this stage in Kant's argument, one might think that his point is primarily negative. His main goal might appear to be simply that of criticizing the viewpoint of dogmatic metaphysics. Yet this is to neglect the broader context of his critical project. For his ultimate goal is to make room for morality and all that such a proper practical standpoint would require. However, before one can accept the demands of morality, one must be certain that our theoretical knowledge of the world does not preclude the possibility of morality. Such certainty can be obtained only be restricting the scope of what we can know. Kant hopes to have achieved this certainty by rejecting the claims of pure reason.

3. The Structure of the *Critique of Pure Reason*

The first Critique begins with a preface and an introduction—sections that, despite their differences in the first and second editions (referred to in the margins by A and B, respectively), explain Kant's project in metaphysics, briefly outline his novel approach, and develop the distinctions necessary for posing the question of synthetic a priori propositions. In the Transcendental Aesthetic, which is devoted to our passive faculty of sensibility by which objects are given to us,

Kant argues that space and time are a priori intuitions. (An intuition is a representation that refers to a single object immediately and contrasts primarily with a concept, which is a representation that can refer to many objects and does so mediately, that is, via other representations.) He then argues that space and time can be a priori intuitions (which is necessary for them to make synthetic a priori knowledge possible) only if they are merely forms of intuition, that is, purely subjective ways in which objects are given to us. This argument represents one of Kant's most distinctive contributions to philosophy, a doctrine he calls transcendental idealism. The important aspect of that doctrine being emphasized here is that space, time, and the entire spatio-temporal world are simply appearances, that is, objects that depend on subjects that have space and time as sensible forms of intuition. Space, time, and the spatio-temporal world are not objective entities that exist independently "in the things themselves." If they were, we could have neither our synthetic a priori knowledge of mathematics nor our a priori intuitions of space and time.

In the Transcendental Logic Kant turns to our faculty of concepts, namely the understanding. He undertakes the twofold task of showing that the understanding's pure or nonempirical concepts are necessary for knowledge and that these concepts do not generate knowledge if they are not applied to objects given through sensibility, that is, if they are used to think what Kant calls "things in themselves," e.g., God, the soul, and the world as a totality. The former, positive task is undertaken in the Transcendental Analytic. In the Analytic of Concepts Kant first attempts (in the so-called "Metaphysical Deduction") to derive an exhaustive list of the most basic pure concepts, i.e. categories, that we must use in thinking about objects of any sort. Then, in the famous Transcendental Deduction, he tries to show that we are justified in using the categories to obtain knowledge if and only if we apply them to objects of a particular sort, namely those given through sensible intuition. In the Analytic of Principles, Kant first provides spatio-temporal meanings for the categories (in the Schematism chapter) and then attempts to develop a series of arguments that show how each particular category is required for a different kind of experience. It is in this context (more specifically, the Analogies of Experience) that Kant argues (against Hume) that the categories of substance and causality are required for knowledge of duration and objective succession. (Hume famously rejects substance and thinks that we can have knowledge of succession without using a strong notion of causality like Kant's.) Towards the end of the Analytic of Principles (in the Refutation of Idealism) Kant also provides an interesting argument against idealism as it is understood by Berkeley (and, in an odd way, Descartes).

Kant's negative task of showing that we cannot have knowledge of things in themselves (in particular, God, the soul, and freedom) is undertaken in the Transcendental Dialectic. The Paralogisms are devoted to exposing the faulty inferences pure reason is tempted to make about the soul based on nothing more than "I think." The Antinomies (that is, the "Conflicts of Transcendental Ideas") develop pairs of arguments for contradictory claims about the world, contradictions that can be resolved only if one first distinguishes between the sensible and intelligible worlds—a distinction that is fundamental to transcendental idealism—and then denies that the intelligible world is spatio-temporal. Given this distinction and denial, it is then clear that we can know only the sensible world, not the intelligible world. Further, since we know from the Second Analogy of Experience that the sensible world is governed by causal laws without exception, freedom and thus morality as well are possible only in the unknowable intelligible world. Finally, the Ideal of Pure Reason considers the three traditional arguments for the existence of God. Since Kant argues that the cosmological and teleological (or what Kant calls the physico-theological) arguments for the existence of God depend on the ontological argument, Kant's famous objections to the ontological argument are of crucial importance in establishing his negative thesis that theoretical knowledge of God is not possible. Taken together, the Paralogisms, Antinomies, and Ideal of Pure Reason establish that pure reason cannot have knowledge of things in themselves. However, as Kant points out in the second edition preface to the first Critique, the fact that he restricts our knowledge to the sensible world does not mean that our representation of things in themselves (including God, the soul, and our freedom) can play no role in our lives. For our ideas of these things are regulative ideals, that is, they regulate our cognitive activities by forcing us to search for further conditions for any conditioned object. More important, restricting knowledge opens up room for faith, that is, for the idea that freedom, God, and immortality could be required not by theoretical reason, but rather by the practical standpoint of morality—an idea Kant explores in detail in the second Critique.

ERIC WATKINS

SELECTED BIBLIOGRAPHY

The following bibliography contains select lists of Kant's own writings as well as literature that focuses on Kant's theoretical philosophy. It is not intended to be exhaustive, but rather should simply give the interested reader a place to look to see how others have read the *Critique of Pure Reason*. The most helpful biography of Kant has been written by Manfred Kuehn and will be published shortly by Cambridge University Press.

KANT'S WRITINGS
Pre-Critical Writings

Thoughts on the True Estimation of Living Forces (1747).

Universal Natural History and Theory of the Heavens (1755).

New Elucidation of the First Principles of Metaphysical Cognition (1755).

Physical Monadology (1756).

The Only Possible Argument in Support of a Demonstration of the Existence of God (1763).

Observations on the Feeling of the Beautiful and the Sublime (1764).

Inquiry Concerning the Distinctness of the Principles of Natural Theology and Morals (1764).

Dreams of a Spirit-Seer Elucidated by Dreams of Metaphysics (1766).

Concerning the Form and Principles of the Sensible and Intelligible World (Inaugural Dissertation; 1770).

Critical Writings

Critique of Pure Reason (1781/1787).

Prolegomena to Any Future Metaphysics (1783).

Groundwork for the Metaphysics of Morals (1785).

Metaphysical First Principles of Natural Science (1786).

Critique of Practical Reason (1788).

Critique of Judgment (1790).

Religion within the Bounds of Reason Alone (1793).

Perpetual Peace (1795).

Metaphysics of Morals (1797).

The Conflict of the Faculties (1798).
Anthropology from a Pragmatic Standpoint (1798).

WORKS ON KANT

Allison, Henry. *Kant's Transcendental Idealism. An Interpretation and Defense* (New Haven: Yale University Press, 1983).

Ameriks, Karl. *Kant's Theory of Mind* (Oxford: Oxford University Press, 1982).

Beck, Lewis White. *Studies in the Philosophy of Kant* (Indianapolis: Bobbs-Merrill, 1965).

Beiser, Frederick. *The Fate of Reason: German Philosophy from Kant to Fichte* (Cambridge: Harvard University Press, 1987).

Broad, Charles Dunbar. *Kant. An Introduction* (Cambridge: Cambridge University Press, 1978).

Friedman, Michael. *Kant and the Exact Sciences* (Cambridge: Harvard University Press, 1992).

Guyer, Paul. *Kant and the Claims of Knowledge* (Cambridge: Cambridge University Press, 1987).

Guyer, Paul, ed. *The Cambridge Companion to Kant* (Cambridge: Cambridge University Press, 1992).

Kuehn, Manfred. *Scottish Common Sense Philosophy in Germany, 1768–1800: A Contribution to the History of Critical Philosophy* (Montreal: McGill-Queen's University Press, 1987).

Melnick, Arthur. *Kant's Analogies of Experience* (Chicago: University of Chicago Press, 1973).

Strawson, Peter F. *The Bounds of Sense* (London: Methuen, 1966).

TRANSLATOR'S PREFACE

This volume contains an abridged version of my translation of the *Critique of Pure Reason (Kritik der reinen Vernunft)*, Kant's *magnum opus* on epistemology and metaphysics. The table of contents indicates which portions of the work have been retained. Selections were made by Eric Watkins, who also compiled an index especially suited to this abridgment.

The translation is based on the *Critique's* first and second editions—respectively of 1781 and 1787 and known as editions A and B—as these appear in the standard edition of Kant's works, *Kants gesammelte Schriften* (Berlin: Königlich Preußische Akademie der Wissenschaften, 1908–1913). In that *Akademie* edition, B occupies volume 3, and A insofar as it deviates from B is contained in volume 4; the editor for both is Benno Erdmann.

In this translation I have sought to maximize accuracy by maintaining a high degree of terminological consistency. Thus wherever possible I have translated technical terms in the original by the same English term and have refrained from using this English term, without alerting the reader, to render some other expression. The same applies to technical distinctions in the original.[1]

To enhance readability, I have divided up Kant's notoriously long sentences, replaced Kant's frequently ambiguous uses of "the former . . . the latter" or "the first . . . the second" by the appropriate

---

The complete version—Immanuel Kant, *Critique of Pure Reason* (Indianapolis: Hackett Publishing Company, 1996)—includes an introduction by Patricia Kitcher, a comprehensive index, a detailed select bibliography, a glossary of the most important German terms, and acknowledgments of the various contributions made by others.

1. For example, the English word "real" (similarly for the noun) is used only for Kant's technical term *real*, never for his likewise technical but far from synonymous term *wirklich*, which means "actual." Likewise, Kant's *Erkenntnis* (similarly for the verb) is translated always as "cognition," never as "knowledge," which renders *Wissen*. The two German terms are by no means synonymous, and hence translating both as "knowledge" leads to grave inaccuracies, including illusory contradictions.

referents, and provided interpolations that in my view are plainly part of Kant's intended meaning. All the *philosophically important* interpolations, and only these, are marked by brackets.

WERNER SCHRUTKA PLUHAR

THE PENNSYLVANIA STATE UNIVERSITY
FAYETTE CAMPUS, UNIONTOWN

Critique of Pure Reason (1781/1787)[1]

PREFACE [FIRST EDITION]

Human reason has a peculiar fate in one kind of its cognitions: it is troubled by questions that it cannot dismiss, because they are posed to it by the nature of reason itself, but that it also cannot answer, because they surpass human reason's every ability.

Our reason falls into this perplexity through no fault of its own. Reason starts from principles that it cannot avoid using in the course of experience, and that this experience at the same time sufficiently justifies it in using. By means of these principles our reason (as indeed its nature requires it to do) ascends ever higher, to more remote condi- tions. But it becomes aware that in this way, since the questions never cease, its task must remain forever uncompleted. Thus it finds itself compelled to resort to principles that go beyond all possible use in experience, and that nonetheless seem so little suspect that even common human reason agrees with them. By doing this, however, human reason plunges into darkness and contradictions; and although it can indeed gather from these that they must be based on errors lying hidden somewhere, it is unable to discover these errors. For the principles that it employs go beyond the boundary of all experience and hence no longer acknowledge any touchstone of experience. The combat arena of these endless conflicts is what we call metaphysics.

[...] It [the indifference that ultimately ensues] is evidently the ef- fect not of the heedlessness but of the matured *judgment*[2] of our age,

---

1. Translated from the German by Werner S. Pluhar (Indianapolis: Hackett Publishing Company, 1996), abridged by Eric Watkins. In this selection the translator's notes are indicated by brackets, except for indications of abridged passages. All subsequent footnotes not in brackets are Kant's.

2. Now and then one hears complaints about the shallow way of thinking in our age and the decline of thorough science. But I fail to see how the sciences that

which is no longer willing to be put off with seeming knowledge.
And it is a call to reason to take on once again the most difficult of all
its tasks—viz., that of self-cognition—and to set up a tribunal that
Axii will make reason secure in its rightful claims and will dismiss all
baseless pretensions, not by fiat but in accordance with reason's eternal and immutable laws. This tribunal is none other than the critique
of reason itself: the *critique of pure reason.*

By critique of pure reason, however, I do not mean a critique of
books and systems, but I mean the critique of our power of reason as
such, in regard to all cognitions after which reason may strive *independently of all experience.* Hence I mean by it the decision as to
whether a metaphysics as such is possible or impossible, and the determination of its sources as well as its range and bounds—all on the
basis of principles.

Now, this is the path—the only one that remained—which I have
pursued, and I flatter myself to have found on it the elimination of
all the errors that had thus far set reason, as used independently of
experience, at variance with itself. I have certainly not evaded reason's questions, by pleading the incapacity of human reason. Rather,
I have made a complete specification of them according to principles,
and, upon discovering the locus of reason's disagreement with itself,
Axiii have resolved them to its full satisfaction. To be sure, my answers to
these questions have not turned out to be such as a raving dogma-
tist's thirst for knowledge might expect. Nothing but magical powers—at which I am no adept—could satisfy that kind of thirst for
knowledge. Presumably, however, this was also not the aim of our
reason's natural vocation. The duty of philosophy was, rather, to remove the deception arising from misinterpretation, even at the cost

---

rest on a well-built foundation—such as mathematics, natural science, etc.—in
the least deserve this reproach. On the contrary, they are upholding their an-
cient reputation for thoroughness, and in the case of natural science even surpass it. Now, the same spirit would be found operative in other kinds of cognition as well, if care had first been taken to correct their principles. In the absence
of such correction, indifference, doubt, and—finally—strict critique are, rather,
proofs of a thorough way of thinking. Our age is properly the age of critique, and
to critique everything must submit. *Religion* and *legislation* commonly seek to
exempt themselves from critique, religion through its *sanctity* and legislation
through its *majesty*. But in doing so they arouse well-deserved suspicion and
cannot lay claim to unfeigned respect; such respect is accorded by reason only to
what has been able to withstand reason's free and open examination.

of destroying the most highly extolled and cherished delusion. In that activity, I have made comprehensiveness my major aim, and I venture to say that there should not be a single metaphysical problem that has not been solved here, or for whose solution the key has not at least been provided. In fact, pure reason is so perfect a unity that, if its principle were insufficient for the solution of even a single one of all the questions assigned to reason by its own nature, then we might just as well throw the principle away; for then we could not fully rely on its being adequate to any of the remaining questions either. [...]

PREFACE [SECOND EDITION]

Bvii   Whether someone's treatment of the cognitions pertaining to reason's business does or does not follow the secure path of a science—
this we can soon judge from the result. If, after many preparations
and arrangements have been made, the treatment falters as soon as it
turns to its purpose; or if, in order to reach that purpose, it repeatedly has to retrace its steps and enter upon a different path; or, again,
if the various collaborators cannot be brought to agree on the manner in which their common aim is to be achieved—then we may rest
assured that such an endeavor is still far from having entered upon
the secure path of a science, but is a mere groping about. We shall indeed be rendering a service to reason if we can possibly discover that
path, even if we should have to give up as futile much that was included in the purpose which we had previously adopted without deliberation.

Bviii   *Logic* has been following that secure path from the earliest times.
This is evident from the fact that since *Aristotle* it has not needed to
retrace a single step, unless perhaps removing some of its dispens-
able subtleties, or setting it forth in a more distinct and determinate
way, were to be counted as improvements of logic, even though they
pertain more to the elegance of that science than to its being secure.
Another remarkable fact about logic is that thus far it also has not
been able to advance a single step, and hence is to all appearances
closed and completed. It is true that some of the more recent
[philosophers] have meant to expand logic. Some of them have inserted into it *psychological* chapters on the different cognitive powers
(e.g., on our power of imagination, or on ingenuity). Others have inserted *metaphysical* chapters on the origin of cognition, or the origin
of the different kinds of certainty according to the difference in the
objects (i.e., chapters on idealism, skepticism, etc.). Still others have
inserted into logic *anthropological* chapters on prejudices (as well as
their causes and remedies). But all these attempts to expand logic are
the result of ignorance concerning the peculiar nature of this science. We do not augment sciences, but corrupt them, if we allow
Bix   their boundaries to overlap. But the boundary of logic is determined
quite precisely by the fact that logic is a science that provides noth-

ing but a comprehensive exposition and strict proof of the formal rules of all thought. (Such thought may be a priori or empirical, may have any origin or object whatsoever, and may encounter in our minds obstacles that are accidental or natural.)

That logic has been so successful in following the secure path of a science is an advantage that it owes entirely to its limitations. They entitle it, even obligate it, to abstract from all objects of cognition and their differences; hence in logic the understanding deals with nothing more than itself and its form. Reason naturally had to find it far more difficult to enter upon the secure path of science when dealing not just with itself, but also with objects. By the same token, logic is a propaedeutic and forms, as it were, only the vestibule of the sciences; and when knowledge is at issue, while for the judging of such knowledge we do indeed presuppose a logic, yet for its acquisition we must look to what are called sciences properly and objectively.

Now insofar as there is to be reason in these sciences, something in them must be cognized a priori. Moreover, reason's cognition can be Bx referred to the object of that cognition in two ways: either in order merely to *determine* the object and its concept (which must be supplied from elsewhere), or in order to *make it actual* as well. The first is reason's *theoretical,* the second its *practical cognition.* In both the pure part, i.e., the part in which reason determines its object entirely a priori, must be set forth all by itself beforehand, no matter how much or how little it may contain. We must not mix with this part what comes from other sources. For we follow bad economic procedure if we blindly spend what comes in and are afterwards unable, when the procedure falters, to distinguish which part of the income can support the expenditure and which must be cut from it.

Two [sciences involving] theoretical cognitions by reason are to determine their *objects* a priori: they are *mathematics* and *physics.* In mathematics this determination is to be entirely pure; in physics it is to be at least partly pure, but to some extent also in accordance with sources of cognition other than reason.

Mathematics has been following the secure path of a science since the earliest times to which the history of human reason extends; it did so already among that admirable people, the Greeks. But we Bxi must not think that it was as easy for mathematics to hit upon that royal road—or, rather, to build it on its own—as it was for logic, where reason deals only with itself. Rather, I believe that for a long time (above all, it was still so among the Egyptians) mathematics did

no more than grope about, and that its transformation into a science
was due to a *revolution* brought about by the fortunate idea that occurred to one man during an experiment. From that time onward,
the route that mathematics had to take could no longer be missed,
and the secure path of a science had been entered upon and traced out
for all time and to an infinite distance. This revolution in the way of
thinking was much more important than the discovery of the passage
around the celebrated Cape. Its history, and that of the fortunate man
who brought this revolution about, is lost to us. But *Diogenes Laërtius*
always names the reputed authors of even the minutest elements of
geometrical demonstration, elements that in ordinary people's judgment do not even stand in need of proof; and Diogenes hands down to
us a story concerning the change that was brought about by the first
indication of this new path's discovery. This story shows that the
memory of this change must have seemed exceedingly important to
Bxii mathematicians, and thus became indelible. When the *isosceles triangle*
was first demonstrated, something dawned on the man who did so.
(He may have been called *Thales*, or by some other name.) He found
that what he needed to do was not to investigate what he saw in the
figure, nor—for that matter—to investigate the mere concept of that
figure, and to let that inform him, as it were, of the figure's properties. He found, rather, that he must bring out (by constructing the figure) the properties that the figure had by virtue of what he himself
was, according to concepts, thinking into it a priori and exhibiting.
And he found that in order for him to know anything a priori and with
certainty about the figure, he must attribute to this thing nothing but
what follows necessarily from what he has himself put into it in accordance with his concept.

Natural science took much longer to hit upon the high road of science. For only about a century and a half have passed since the inge-
nious *Bacon*, Baron Verulam, made the proposal that partly prompted
this road's discovery, and partly—insofar as some were already on the
trail of this discovery—invigorated it further. This discovery, too, can
be explained only by a sudden revolution in people's way of thinking. I
shall here take account of natural science only insofar as it is founded on
empirical principles.

Something dawned on all investigators of nature when *Galileo* let
balls, of a weight chosen by himself, roll down his inclined plane; or
when *Torricelli* made the air carry a weight that he had judged beforehand to be equal to the weight of a water column known to him;

or when, in more recent times, *Stahl* converted metals into calx and $\qquad$ Bxiii
that in turn into metal, by withdrawing something from the metals
and then restoring it to them.[3] What all these investigators of nature
comprehended was that reason has insight only into what it itself
produces according to its own plan; and that reason must not allow
nature by itself to keep it in leading strings, as it were, but reason
must—using principles that underlie its judgments—proceed according to constant laws and compel nature to answer reason's own
questions. For otherwise our observations, made without following
any plan outlined in advance, are contingent, i.e., they have no coherence at all in terms of a necessary law—even though such a law is
what reason seeks and requires. When approaching nature, reason
must hold in one hand its principles, in terms of which alone concor-
dant appearances can count as laws, and in the other hand the experiment that it has devised in terms of those principles. Thus reason
must indeed approach nature in order to be instructed by it; yet it
must do so not in the capacity of a pupil who lets the teacher tell him
whatever the teacher wants, but in the capacity of an appointed judge
who compels the witnesses to answer the questions that he puts to $\qquad$ Bxiv
them. Thus even physics owes that very advantageous revolution in
its way of thinking to this idea: the idea that we must, in accordance
with what reason itself puts into nature, seek in nature (not attribute
to it fictitiously) whatever reason must learn from nature and would
know nothing of on its own. This is what put natural science, for the
very first time, on the secure path of a science, after it had for so
many centuries been nothing more than a mere groping about.

Metaphysics is a speculative cognition by reason that is wholly isolated and rises entirely above being instructed by experience. It is
cognition through mere concepts (not, like mathematics, cognition
through the application of concepts to intuition), so that here reason
is to be its own pupil. But although metaphysics is older than all the
other sciences, and would endure even if all the others were to be en-
gulfed utterly in the abyss of an all-annihilating barbarism, fate thus
far has not favored it to the point of enabling it to enter upon the secure path of a science. For in metaphysics reason continually falters,
even when the laws into which it seeks to gain (as it pretends) a priori
insight are those that are confirmed by the commonest experience.

3. I am not here following with precision the course of the history of the exper-
imental method; indeed, the first beginnings of that history are not well known.

Bxv Countless times, in metaphysics, we have to retrace our steps, because we find that our path does not lead us where we want to go. As regards agreement in the assertions made by its devotees, metaphysics is very far indeed from such agreement. It is, rather, a combat arena which seems to be destined quite specifically for practicing one's powers in mock combat, and in which not one fighter has ever been able to gain even the smallest territory and to base upon his victory a lasting possession. There can be no doubt, therefore, that the procedure of metaphysics has thus far been a mere groping about, and—worst of all—a groping about among mere concepts.

Why is it, then, that in metaphysics we have thus far been unable to find the secure path of science? Might this path be impossible here? Why, then, has nature inflicted on reason, as one of reason's most important concerns, the restless endeavor to discover that path? What is more: how little cause have we to place confidence in our reason, when in one of the most important matters where we desire knowledge reason not merely forsakes us, but puts us off with mere pretenses and in the end betrays us! Or if we have only missed the path thus far, what indication do we have that if we renew our search, we may hope to be more fortunate than others before us have been?

I would think that the examples of mathematics and natural sci-

Bxvi ence, which have become what they now are by a revolution accomplished all at once, are sufficiently remarkable to [suggest that we should] reflect on the essential component in that revolution, viz., the transformation of the way of thinking that became so advantageous for them; and as far as is permitted by the fact that they, as rational cognitions, are analogous to metaphysics, we should [there] imitate them with regard to that transformation, at least by way of an experiment. Thus far it has been assumed that all our cognition must conform to objects. On that presupposition, however, all our attempts to establish something about them a priori, by means of concepts through which our cognition would be expanded, have come to nothing. Let us, therefore, try to find out by experiment whether we shall not make better progress in the problems of metaphysics if we assume that objects must conform to our cognition.—This assumption already agrees better with the demanded possibility of an a priori cognition of objects—i.e., a cognition that is to ascertain something about them before they are given to us. The situation here is the same as was that of *Copernicus* when he first thought of explaining the motions of celestial bodies. Having found it difficult to make progress there when he assumed that the entire host of stars revolved around the spectator, he tried to find out by experiment whether he might not be more successful if he had the spectator revolve and the Bxvii stars remain at rest. Now, we can try a similar experiment in metaphysics, with regard to our *intuition* of objects. If our intuition had to conform to the character of its objects, then I do not see how we could know anything a priori about that character. But I can quite readily conceive of this possibility if the object (as object of the senses) conforms to the character of our power of intuition. However, if these intuitions are to become cognitions, I cannot remain with them but must refer them, as presentations, to something or other as their object, and must determine this object by means of them. [Since for this determination I require concepts, I must make one of two assumptions.] I can assume that the *concepts* by means of which I bring about this determination likewise conform to the object; and in that case I am again in the same perplexity as to how I can know anything a priori about that object. Or else I assume that the objects, or—what amounts to the same—the *experience* in which alone they (as objects that are given to us) can be cognized, conform to those concepts. On this latter assumption, I immediately see an easier way out. For experience is itself a way of cognizing for which I need understanding. But understanding has its rule, a rule that I must presuppose within me even before objects are given to me, and hence Bxviii must presuppose a priori; and that rule is expressed in a priori concepts. Hence all objects of experience must necessarily conform to these concepts and agree with them. Afterwards, however, we must also consider objects insofar as they can merely be thought, though thought necessarily, but cannot at all be given in experience (at least not in the way in which reason thinks them). Our attempts to think these objects (for they must surely be thinkable) will afterwards provide us with a splendid touchstone of what we are adopting as the changed method in our way of thinking, viz., that all we cognize a priori about things is what we ourselves put into them.

This experiment is as successful as was desired. It promises that metaphysics will be on the secure path of a science in its first part, viz., the part where it deals with those a priori concepts for which Bxix corresponding objects adequate to these concepts can be given in experience. For on the changed way of thinking we can quite readily explain how a priori cognition is possible; what is more, we can provide satisfactory proofs for the laws that lie a priori at the basis of

nature considered as the sum of objects of experience. Neither of
these accomplishments was possible on the kind of procedure used
thus far. On the other hand, this deduction—provided in the first
part of metaphysics—of our power to cognize a priori produces a
disturbing result that seems highly detrimental to the whole purpose
of metaphysics as dealt with in the second part: viz., that with this
power to cognize a priori we shall never be able to go beyond the
Bxx   boundary of possible experience, even though doing so is precisely
the most essential concern of this science. Yet this very [situation
permits] the experiment that will countercheck the truth of the result that we obtained from the first assessment of our a priori rational cognition: viz., that our rational cognition applies only to appearances, and leaves the thing in itself uncognized by us, even though
inherently actual. For what necessarily impels us to go beyond the
boundary of experience and of all appearances is the unconditioned
that reason demands in things in themselves; reason—necessarily
and quite rightfully—demands this unconditioned for everything
conditioned, thus demanding that the series of conditions be completed by means of that unconditioned. Suppose, now, we find that
the unconditioned *cannot be thought at all without contradiction* if we
assume that our experiential cognition conforms to objects as things
in themselves, yet that *the contradiction vanishes* if we assume that our
presentation of things, as these are given to us, does not conform to
them as things in themselves, but that these objects are, rather, appearances that conform to our way of presenting. Suppose that we
find, consequently, that the unconditioned is not to be met with in
things insofar as we are acquainted with them (i.e., insofar as they
are given to us), but is to be met with in them [only] insofar as we are
not acquainted with them, viz., insofar as they are things in themselves. If this is what we find, it will show that what we assumed ini-
Bxxi   tially only by way of an experiment does in fact have a foundation.[4]
Now, once we have denied that speculative reason can make any

4. This experiment of pure reason is very similar to that done in *chemistry*,
which is called sometimes the experiment of *reduction*, but generally the *synthetic procedure*. The *analysis* of the *metaphysician* has divided pure a priori cognition into two very heterogeneous elements, namely, that of things as appearances and then of things in themselves. The [metaphysician's] *dialectic*
recombines the two so as to yield *agreement* with reason's necessary idea of the
unconditioned, and finds that this agreement can never be obtained except
through that distinction, which is therefore [a] true one.

progress in that realm of the suprasensible, we still have an option available to us. We can try to discover whether perhaps in reason's practical cognition data can be found that would allow us to determine reason's transcendent concept of the unconditioned. Perhaps in this way our a priori cognition, though one that is possible only from a practical point of view, would still allow us to get beyond the boundary of all possible experience, as is the wish of metaphysics. Moreover, when we follow this kind of procedure, still speculative reason has at least provided us with room for such an expansion [of our cognition], even if it had to leave that room empty. And hence Bxxii there is as yet nothing to keep us from filling in that room, if we can, with practical *data* of reason; indeed, reason summons us to do so.[5]

The task, then, of this critique of pure speculative reason consists in the described attempt to transform the procedure previously followed in metaphysics, by subjecting metaphysics to a complete revolution, thus following the example set by the geometricians and investigators of nature. The critique is a treatise on the method [of the science of metaphysics], not a system of the science itself. Yet it does Bxxiii set down the entire outline of metaphysics, including the bounds of this science as well as its entire internal structure. [...]

[...] Now in the analytic part of the critique I shall prove that space Bxxv and time are only forms of our sensible intuition and hence are only conditions of the existence of things as appearances, and that, furthermore, we have no concepts of understanding, and hence also no elements whatever for the cognition of things, except insofar as intu- Bxxvi ition can be given corresponding to these concepts. That will prove,

---

5. In the same way, the central laws governing the motions of the celestial bodies provided with established certainty what *Copernicus* had initially assumed only as a hypothesis, and at the same time provided proof of the invisible force (*Newtonian* attraction) that links together the world edifice. That force would have remained forever undiscovered if Copernicus had not dared, in a manner that conflicted with the senses but yet was true, to seek the observed motions not in the celestial objects but in the spectator. The transformation in the way of thinking which I set forth in the *Critique* is analogous to the Copernican hypothesis. Here in the preface I likewise put it forth only as a hypothesis, even though in the treatise itself it will be proved, not hypothetically but apodeictically, from the character of our representations of space and time and from the elementary concepts of the understanding. Here I put it forth as a hypothesis in order merely to draw attention to the first attempts at such a transformation; and such attempts are always hypothetical.

consequently, that we cannot have [speculative] cognition of any object as thing in itself, but can have such cognition only insofar as the object is one of sensible intuition, i.e., an appearance. And from this it does indeed follow that any possible speculative cognition of reason is restricted to mere objects of *experience*. On the other hand, it must be noted carefully that this [conclusion] is always subject to
Bxxvii this reservation: that we must be able at least to *think*, even if not [speculatively] *cognize*, the same objects also as things in themselves.[6] For otherwise an absurd proposition would follow, viz., that there is appearance without anything that appears. Now let us suppose that the distinction, necessitated by our critique, between objects of experience and these same objects as things in themselves, had not been made at all. In that case the principle of causality, and hence nature's mechanism as governing the determination of [the exercise of] that causality, would definitely have to hold for all things as such [construed] as efficient causes. Hence I could not, without manifest contradiction, say of the same being, for example the human soul, that its will is free and yet is subject to natural necessity, i.e., not free. For I would be taking the soul *in the same sense* in the two propositions, viz., as a thing as such (thing in itself); nor, without prior critique, could I help taking it so. Suppose, on the other hand, that the *Critique* is not in error when it teaches us to take the object in *two different senses*, viz., as appearance and as thing in itself; and that the deduction of the *Critique*'s concepts of understanding is correct, so that the principle of causality applies to things only in the first sense, viz., insofar as they are objects of experience, but that these same ob-
Bxxviii jects are not subject to that principle when taken in the second sense. On these suppositions, no contradiction arises when we think the same will in both these ways: in its appearance (i.e., in its visible acts), as conforming necessarily to natural law and as to that extent

6. In order for me to *cognize* an object I must be able to prove its [real] possibility (either from its actuality as attested by experience, or a priori by means of reason). But I can *think* whatever I want to, even if I am unable to commit myself to there being, in the sum of all [logical] possibilities, an object corresponding to the concept. All that is required in order for me to think something is that I do not contradict myself, i.e., that my concept be a [logically] possible thought. But I require something further in order to attribute objective reality to a concept (i.e., real possibility, as distinguished from the merely logical possibility just mentioned). However—and this is my point—this something further need not be sought in theoretical sources of cognition, but may also lie in practical ones.

not free; yet on the other hand, *qua* belonging to a thing in itself, as
not subject to that law, and hence as *free.* Now as regards my soul
when considered from this second standpoint, I cannot *cognize* it
through any [use of] speculative reason (let alone through empirical
observation); nor, therefore, can I in this way cognize freedom as the
property of a being to which I attribute effects in the world of sense.
For otherwise I would have to cognize such a being as a being determined with regard to its existence and yet as not determined in time
(which is impossible, because I cannot base such a concept on any intuition). Nevertheless, [although I cannot in this way cognize my
freedom,] I can still *think* freedom. I.e., at least my presentation of
freedom contains no contradiction, if we make our critical distinction between the two ways of presenting (sensible and intellectual),
and restrict accordingly the pure concepts of understanding and
hence also the principles that flow from them. Now let us suppose
that morality necessarily presupposes freedom (in the strictest sense)
as a property of our will; for morality adduces a priori, as *data* of reason, original practical principles residing in reason, and these princi-   Bxxix
ples would be absolutely impossible without the presupposition of
freedom. But then suppose that speculative reason had proved that
freedom cannot be thought at all. In that case the moral presupposition would have to yield to the other [supposition]. For this other
[supposition]'s opposite involves a manifest contradiction (whereas
the opposite of freedom and morality involves no contradiction, unless freedom has already been presupposed). Hence *freedom,* and
with it morality, would have to give way to the *mechanism of nature.*
But in fact the situation is different. All I need for morality is that
freedom does not contradict itself and hence can at least be thought;
I do not need to have any further insight into it. In other words, all I
need is that freedom [in my act] puts no obstacle whatever in the way
of the natural mechanism [that governs] the same act (when the act is
taken in a different reference). Thus the doctrine of morality maintains its own place, and so does natural science. But this would not
have happened if the critique had not instructed us beforehand
about our unavoidable ignorance regarding things in themselves, restricting to mere appearances what we can *cognize* theoretically. This
same exposition of the positive benefit found in critical principles of
pure reason can be produced again in regard to the concept of *God*
and of the *simple nature* of our *soul;* but for the sake of brevity I shall
omit it. Thus I cannot even *assume God, freedom,* and *immortality,* [as   Bxxx

I must] for the sake of the necessary practical use of my reason, if I do not at the same time *deprive* speculative reason of its pretensions to transcendent insight. For in order to reach God, freedom, and immortality, speculative reason must use principles that in fact extend merely to objects of possible experience; and when these principles are nonetheless applied to something that cannot be an object of experience, they actually do always transform it into an appearance, and thus they declare all *practical expansion* of reason to be impossible. I therefore had to annul *knowledge* in order to make room for *faith*. And the true source of all the lack of faith which conflicts with morality—and is always highly dogmatic—is dogmatism in metaphysics, i.e., the prejudice according to which we can make progress in metaphysics without a [prior] critique of pure reason. [...]

INTRODUCTION
[SECOND EDITION]

I. ON THE DISTINCTION BETWEEN PURE AND EMPIRICAL COGNITION

There can be no doubt that all our cognition begins with experience. For what else might rouse our cognitive power to its operation if objects stirring our senses did not do so? In part these objects by themselves bring about presentations. In part they set in motion our understanding's activity, by which it compares these presentations, connects or separates them, and thus processes the raw material of sense impressions into a cognition of objects that is called experience. *In terms of time,* therefore, no cognition in us precedes experience, and all our cognition begins with experience.

But even though all our cognition **starts** with experience, that does not mean that all of it **arises** from experience. For it might well be that even our experiential cognition is composite, consisting of what we receive through impressions and what our own cognitive power supplies from itself (sense impressions merely prompting it to do so). If our cognitive power does make such an addition, we may not be able to distinguish it from that basic material until long practice has made us attentive to it and skilled in separating it from the basic material.

This question, then, whether there is such a cognition that is independent of experience and even of all impressions of the senses, is one that cannot be disposed of as soon as it comes to light, but that at least still needs closer investigation. Such cognitions are called *a priori cognitions;* they are distinguished from empirical cognitions, whose sources are a posteriori, namely, in experience. [. . .]

In what follows, therefore, we shall mean by a priori cognitions not those that occur independently of this or that experience, but those that occur *absolutely* independently of all experience. They contrast with empirical cognitions, which are those that are possible only a posteriori, i.e., through experience. But we call a priori cognitions *pure* if nothing empirical whatsoever is mixed in with them. Thus, e.g., the proposition, Every change has its cause, is an a priori proposition; yet it is not pure, because change is a concept that can be obtained only from experience [. . .]

IV. ON THE DISTINCTION BETWEEN ANALYTIC AND SYNTHETIC JUDGMENTS

A6/
B10
In all judgments in which we think the relation of a subject to the predicate (I here consider affirmative judgments only, because the application to negative judgments is easy afterwards), this relation is possible in two ways. Either the predicate B belongs to the subject A as something that is (covertly) contained in this concept A; or B,
A7 though connected with concept A, lies quite outside it. In the first case I call the judgment *analytic;* in the second, *synthetic.* Hence (affirmative) analytic judgments are those in which the predicate's connection with the subject is thought by [thinking] identity, whereas
B11 those judgments in which this connection is thought without [thinking] identity are to be called synthetic. Analytic judgments could also be called *elucidatory.* For they do not through the predicate add anything to the concept of the subject; rather, they only dissect the concept, breaking it up into its component concepts which had already been thought in it (although thought confusedly). Synthetic judgments, on the other hand, could also be called *expansive.* For they do add to the concept of the subject a predicate that had not been thought in that concept at all and could not have been extracted from it by any dissection. For example, if I say: All bodies are extended—then this is an analytic judgment. For I do not need to go beyond the concept that I link with the word body in order to find that extension is connected with it. All I need to do in order to find this predicate in the concept is to dissect the concept, i.e., become conscious of the manifold that I always think in it. Hence the judgment is analytic. By contrast, if I say: All bodies are heavy—then the predicate is something quite different from what I think in the mere concept of a body as such. Hence adding such a predicate yields a synthetic judgment.

Experiential judgments, as such, are one and all synthetic. For to base an analytic judgment on experience would be absurd, because in its case I can formulate my judgment without going outside my concept, and hence do not need for it any testimony of experience. Thus the [analytic] proposition that bodies are extended is one that holds a
B12 priori and is not an experiential judgment. For before I turn to experience, I already have in the concept [of body] all the conditions re-

quired for my judgment. I have only to extract from it, in accordance with the principle of contradiction, the predicate [of extension]; in doing so, I can at the same time become conscious of the judgment's necessity, of which experience would not even inform me. On the other hand, though in the concept of a body as such I do not at all include the predicate of heaviness, yet the concept designates an object of experience by means of part of this experience; hence I can [synthetically] add to this part further parts, of the same experience, in addition to those that belonged to the concept of a body as such. I can begin by cognizing the concept of a body *analytically* through the characteristics of extension, impenetrability, shape, etc., all of which are thought in this concept. But then I expand my cognition: by looking back to the experience from which I have abstracted this concept of body, I also find heaviness to be always connected with the above characteristics; and so I add it, as a predicate, to that concept *synthetically*. Hence experience is what makes possible the synthesis of the predicate of heaviness with the concept of body. For although neither of the two concepts is contained in the other, yet they belong to each other, though only contingently, as parts of a whole; that whole is experience, which is itself a synthetic combination of intuitions.

In synthetic judgments that are a priori, however, this remedy is entirely lacking. If I am to go beyond the concept A in order to cognize another concept B as combined with it, I rely on something that makes the synthesis possible: what is that something, considering that here I do not have the advantage of looking around for it in the realm of experience? Take the proposition: Everything that happens has its cause.—In the concept of something that happens I do indeed think an existence preceded by a time, etc., and from this one can obtain analytic judgments. But the concept of a cause lies quite outside that earlier concept and indicates something different from what happens; hence it is not part of what is contained in this latter presentation. In speaking generally of what happens, how can I say about it something quite different from it, and cognize as belonging to it—indeed, belonging to it necessarily—the concept of cause, even though this concept is not contained in the concept of what happens? What is here the unknown = X on which the understanding relies when it believes that it discovers, outside the concept A, a predicate B that is foreign to concept A but that the understanding considers nonetheless to be connected with that concept? This unknown cannot be experience. For in adding the presentation of cause

A9/
B13

to the presentation of what happens, the above principle does so not
only with greater universality than experience can provide, but also
with the necessity's being expressed; hence it does so entirely a priori
and on the basis of mere concepts. Now, on such synthetic, i.e., ex-
A10/ pansive, principles depends the whole final aim of our speculative a
B14   priori cognition. For, analytic principles are indeed exceedingly important and needed, but only for attaining that distinctness in concepts which is required for a secure and extensive synthesis that, as
such, will actually be a new acquisition [of cognition].

V. ALL THEORETICAL SCIENCES OF REASON CONTAIN SYNTHETIC A PRIORI JUDGMENTS AS PRINCIPLES

1. *Mathematical judgments are one and all synthetic.* Although this
proposition is incontestably certain and has very important consequences, it seems thus far to have escaped the notice of those who have
analyzed human reason; indeed, it seems to be directly opposed to all
their conjectures. For they found that all the inferences made by mathematicians proceed (as the nature of all apodeictic certainty requires)
according to the principle of contradiction; and thus they came to be
persuaded that the principle of contradiction is also the basis on which
we cognize the principles [of mathematics]. In this they were mistaken. For though we can indeed gain insight into a synthetic proposition according to the principle of contradiction, we can never do so [by
considering] that proposition by itself, but can do so only by presupposing another synthetic proposition from which it can be deduced.

We must note, first of all, that mathematical propositions, properly
so called, are always a priori judgments rather than empirical ones;
B15   for they carry with them necessity, which we could never glean from
experience. But if anyone refuses to grant that all such propositions
are a priori—all right: then I restrict my assertion to *pure mathematics,* in the very concept of which is implied that it contains not empirical but only pure a priori cognition.

It is true that one might at first think that the proposition 7 + 5 = 12
is a merely analytic one that follows, by the principle of contradiction,
from the concept of a sum of seven and five. Yet if we look more
closely, we find that the concept of the sum of 7 and 5 contains nothing more than the union of the two numbers into one; but in [think-
ing] that union we are not thinking in any way at all what that single

number is that unites the two. In thinking merely that union of seven
and five, I have by no means already thought the concept of twelve;
and no matter how long I dissect my concept of such a possible sum,
still I shall never find in it that twelve. We must go beyond these concepts and avail ourselves of the intuition corresponding to one of the
two: e.g., our five fingers, or (as *Segner* does in his *Arithmetic*) five
dots. In this way we must gradually add, to the concept of seven, the
units of the five given in intuition. For I start by taking the number
7. Then, for the concept of the 5, I avail myself of the fingers of my
hand as intuition. Thus, in that image of mine, I gradually add to the   B16
number 7 the units that I previously gathered together in order to
make up the number 5. In this way I see the number 12 arise. That 5
were to be added to 7, this I had indeed already thought in the concept
of a sum = 7+5, but not that this sum is equal to the number 12.
Arithmetic propositions are therefore always synthetic. We become
aware of this all the more distinctly if we take larger numbers. For
then it is very evident that, no matter how much we twist and turn
our concepts, we can never find the [number of the] sum by merely
dissecting our concepts, i.e., without availing ourselves of intuition.

    Just as little are any principles of pure geometry analytic. That the
straight line between two points is the shortest is a synthetic proposition. For my concept of *straight* contains nothing about magnitude,
but contains only a quality. Therefore the concept of shortest is entirely added to the concept of a straight line and cannot be extracted
from it by any dissection. Hence we must here avail ourselves of intuition; only by means of it is the synthesis possible.

    It is true that a few propositions presupposed by geometricians are
actually analytic and based on the principle of contradiction. But, like   B17
identical propositions, they serve not as principles but only [as links
in] the chain of method. Examples are a = a; the whole is equal to itself; or (a+b) > a, i.e., the whole is greater than its part. And yet even
these principles, although they hold according to mere concepts, are
admitted in mathematics only because they can be exhibited in intuition. [As for mathematics generally,] what commonly leads us to believe that the predicate of its apodeictic judgments is contained in our
very concept, and that the judgment is therefore analytic, is merely the
ambiguity with which we express ourselves. For we say that we *are to*
add in thought a certain predicate to a given concept, and this necessity adheres indeed to the very concepts. But here the question is not
what we *are to* add in thought to the given concept, but what we *actu-*

ally think in the concept, even if only obscurely; and there we find that, although the predicate does indeed adhere necessarily to such concepts, yet it does so not as something thought in the concept itself, but by means of an intuition that must be added to the concept.

2. *Natural science (physica) contains synthetic a priori judgments as principles.* Let me cite as examples just a few propositions: e.g., the proposition that in all changes in the corporeal world the quantity of matter remains unchanged; or the proposition that in all communica-

B18 tion of motion, action and reaction must always be equal to each other. Both propositions are clearly not only necessary, and hence of a priori origin, but also synthetic. For in the concept of matter I do not think permanence, but think merely the matter's being present in space insofar as it occupies space. Hence I do actually go beyond the concept of matter, in order to add to it a priori in thought something that I have not thought *in it*. Hence the proposition is thought not analytically but synthetically and yet a priori, and the same occurs in the remaining propositions of the pure part of natural science.

3. *Metaphysics is to contain synthetic a priori cognitions.* This holds even if metaphysics is viewed as a science that thus far has merely been attempted, but that because of the nature of human reason is nonetheless indispensable. Metaphysics is not at all concerned merely to dissect concepts of things that we frame a priori, and thereby to elucidate them analytically. Rather, in metaphysics we want to expand our a priori cognition. In order to do this, we must use principles which go beyond the given concept and which add to it something that was not contained in it; and, by means of such synthetic a priori judgments, we must presumably go so far beyond such concepts that even experience can no longer follow us; as in the proposition: The world must have a first beginning—and others like that. And hence metaphysics consists, at least *in terms of its purpose,* of nothing but synthetic a priori propositions.

B19 ## VI. THE GENERAL PROBLEM OF PURE REASON

Much is gained already when we can bring a multitude of inquiries under the formula of a single problem. For we thereby facilitate not only our own business by defining it precisely, but also—for anyone else who wants to examine it—the judgment as to whether or not we have carried out our project adequately. Now the proper problem of pure reason is contained in this question:

How are synthetic judgments possible a priori?

That metaphysics has thus far remained in such a shaky state of uncertainty and contradictions is attributable to a sole cause: the fact that this problem, and perhaps even the distinction between *analytic* and *synthetic* judgments, has not previously occurred to anyone. Whether metaphysics stands or falls depends on the solution of this problem, or on an adequate proof that the possibility which metaphysics demands to see explained does not exist at all. *David Hume* at least came closer to this problem than any other philosopher. Yet he did not think of it nearly determinately enough and in its universality, but merely remained with the synthetic proposition about the B20 connection of an effect with its causes *(principium causalitatis)*. He believed he had discovered that such a proposition is quite impossible a priori. Thus, according to his conclusions, everything that we call metaphysics would amount to no more than the delusion of a supposed rational insight into what in fact is merely borrowed from experience and has, through habit, acquired a seeming necessity. This assertion, which destroys all pure philosophy, would never have entered Hume's mind if he had envisaged our problem in its universality. For he would then have seen that by his argument there could be no pure mathematics either, since it certainly does contain synthetic a priori propositions; and from such an assertion his good sense would surely have saved him.

In solving the above problem we solve at the same time another one, concerning the possibility of the pure use of reason in establishing and carrying out all sciences that contain theoretical a priori cognition of objects; i.e., we also answer these questions:

How is pure mathematics possible?
How is pure natural science possible?

Since these sciences are actually given [as existent], it is surely proper for us to ask **how** they are possible; for that they must be pos- B21 sible is proved by their being actual.[7] As regards *metaphysics*, however, there are grounds on which everyone must doubt its possibility: its progress thus far has been poor; and thus far not a single metaphysics has been put forth of which we can say, as far as the essential purpose of metaphysics is concerned, that it is actually at hand.

---

7. This actuality may still be doubted by some in the case of pure natural science. Yet we need only examine the propositions that are to be found at the beginning of physics proper (empirical physics), such as those about the perma-

Yet in a certain sense this *kind of cognition* must likewise be regarded as given; and although metaphysics is not actual as a science,
yet it is actual as a natural predisposition (i.e., as a *metaphysica natu-
ralis*). For human reason, impelled by its own need rather than
moved by the mere vanity of gaining a lot of knowledge, proceeds ir-
resistibly to such questions as cannot be answered by any experiential use of reason and any principles taken from such use. And thus
all human beings, once their reason has expanded to [the point where
it can] speculate, actually have always had in them, and always will
have in them, some metaphysics. Now concerning it, too, there is this
question:

B22   **How is metaphysics as a natural predisposition possible?**
i.e., how, from the nature of universal human reason, do the questions arise that pure reason poses to itself and is impelled, by its own
need, to answer as best it can?

Thus far, however, all attempts to answer these natural questions—e.g., whether the world has a beginning or has been there
from eternity, etc.—have met with unavoidable contradictions.
Hence we cannot settle for our mere natural predisposition for metaphysics, i.e., our pure power of reason itself, even though some metaphysics or other (whichever it might be) always arises from it.
Rather, it must be possible, by means of this predisposition, to attain
certainty either concerning our knowledge or lack of knowledge of
the objects [of metaphysics], i.e., either concerning a decision about
the objects that its questions deal with, or certainty concerning the
ability or inability of reason to make judgments about these objects.
In other words, it must be possible to expand our pure reason in a reliable way, or to set for it limits that are determinate and safe. This
last question, which flows from the general problem above, may
rightly be stated thus:

How is metaphysics as science possible?

Ultimately, therefore, critique of pure reason leads necessarily to
B23   science; the dogmatic use of pure reason without critique, on the

---

nence of the quantity of matter, about inertia, about the equality of action and
reaction, etc., in order to be quickly convinced that these propositions themselves amount to a *physica pura* (or *physica rationalis*). Such a physics, as a science in its own right, surely deserves to be put forth separately and in its whole
range, whether this range be narrow or broad.

other hand, to baseless assertions that can always be opposed by others that seem equally plausible, and hence to *skepticism*.

This science, moreover, cannot be overly, forbiddingly voluminous. For it deals not with objects of reason, which are infinitely diverse, but merely with [reason] itself. [Here reason] deals with problems that issue entirely from its own womb; they are posed to it not by the nature of things distinct from it, but by its own nature. And thus, once it has become completely acquainted with its own ability regarding the objects that it may encounter in experience, reason must find it easy to determine, completely and safely, the range and the bounds of its use [when] attempted beyond all bounds of experience.

Hence all attempts that have been made thus far to bring a metaphysics about *dogmatically* can and must be regarded as if they had never occurred. For whatever is analytic in one metaphysics or another, i.e., is mere dissection of the concepts residing a priori in our reason, is only a prearrangement for metaphysics proper, and is not yet its purpose at all. That purpose is to expand our a priori cognition synthetically, and for this purpose the dissection of reason's a priori concepts is useless. For it shows merely what is contained in these concepts; it does not show how we arrive at such concepts a priori, so that we could then also determine the valid use of such concepts in regard to the objects of all cognition generally. Nor do B24 we need much self-denial to give up all these claim; for every metaphysics put forth thus far has long since been deprived of its reputation by the fact that it gave rise to undeniable, and in the dogmatic procedure indeed unavoidable, contradictions of reason with itself. A different treatment, completely opposite to the one used thus far, must be given to metaphysics—a science, indispensable to human reason, whose every new shoot can indeed be lopped off but whose root cannot be eradicated. We shall need more perseverance in order to keep from being deterred—either from within by the difficulty of this science or from without by people's resistance to it—from thus finally bringing it to a prosperous and fruitful growth.

VII. IDEA AND DIVISION OF A SPECIAL SCIENCE UNDER THE NAME OF CRITIQUE OF PURE REASON

From all of the above we arrive at the idea of a special science that may be called the *critique of pure reason*. For reason is the power that A11

provides us with the *principles* of a priori cognition. Hence pure reason is that reason which contains the principles for cognizing something absolutely a priori. An *organon* of pure reason would be the
B25   sum of those principles by which all pure a priori cognitions can be
acquired and actually brought about. Comprehensive application of
such an organon would furnish us with a system of pure reason.
Such a system, however, is a tall order; and it remains to be seen
whether indeed an expansion of our cognition is possible here at all,
and in what cases it is possible. Hence a science that merely judges
pure reason, its sources, and its bounds may be regarded as the
propaedeutic to the system of pure reason. Such a propaedeutic
would have to be called not a *doctrine* but only a *critique* of pure reason. Its benefit, in regard to speculation, would actually only be negative. For such a critique would serve only to purify our reason, not
to expand it, and would keep our reason free from errors, which is a
very great gain already. I call *transcendental* all cognition that deals
A12   not so much with objects as rather with our way of cognizing objects
in general insofar as that way of cognizing is to be possible a priori. A
system of such concepts would be called *transcendental philosophy*.
But, once again, this [system of] transcendental philosophy is too
much for us as yet, here at the beginning. For since such a science
would have to contain both analytic cognition and synthetic a priori
cognition, in their completeness, it has too broad a range as far as our
aim is concerned. For we need to carry the analysis only as far as it is
indispensably necessary for gaining insight, in their entire range,
into the principles of a priori synthesis, which is all that we are concerned with. [...]
A15/   [...] Human cognition has two stems, viz., *sensibility* and *under-*
B29   *standing*, which perhaps spring from a common root, though one
B30   unknown to us. Through sensibility objects are *given* to us; through
understanding they are *thought*. Now if sensibility were to contain a
priori presentations constituting the condition under which objects
A16   are given to us, it would to that extent belong to transcendental
philosophy. And since the conditions under which alone the objects
of human cognition are given to us precede the conditions under
which these objects are thought, the transcendental doctrine of
sense would have to belong to the *first* part of the science of elements.

TRANSCENDENTAL DOCTRINE OF ELEMENTS

PART I
TRANSCENDENTAL AESTHETIC

§ 1

In whatever way and by whatever means a cognition may refer to objects, still *intuition* is that by which a cognition refers to objects directly, and at which all thought aims as a means. Intuition, however, takes place only insofar as the object is given to us; but that, in turn, is possible only—for us human beings, at any rate—by the mind's being affected in a certain manner. The capacity (a receptivity) to acquire presentations as a result of the way in which we are affected by objects is called **sensibility**. Hence by means of sensibility objects are *given* to us, and it alone supplies us with *intuitions*. Through understanding, on the other hand, objects are *thought*, and from it arise *concepts*. But all thought must, by means of certain characteristics, refer ultimately to intuitions, whether it does so straightforwardly *(directe)* or circuitously *(indirecte)*; and hence it must, in us [human beings], refer ultimately to sensibility, because no object can be given to us in any other manner than through sensibility.

The effect of an object on our capacity for presentation, insofar as we are affected by the object, is *sensation*. Intuition that refers to the object through sensation is called *empirical* intuition. The undetermined object of an empirical intuition is called *appearance*.

Whatever in an appearance corresponds to sensation I call its *matter;* but whatever in an appearance brings about the fact that the manifold of the appearance can be ordered in certain relations I call the *form* of appearance. Now, that in which alone sensations can be ordered and put into a certain form cannot itself be sensation again. Therefore, although the matter of all appearance is given to us only a posteriori, the form of all appearance must altogether lie ready for the sensations a priori in the mind; and hence that form must be capable of being examined apart from all sensation.

All presentations in which nothing is found that belongs to sensation I call *pure* (in the transcendental sense of the term). Accordingly, the pure form of sensible intuitions generally, in which everything manifold in experience is intuited in certain relations, will be found

B35 in the mind a priori. This pure form of sensibility will also itself be called *pure intuition*. Thus, if from the presentation of a body I separate what the understanding thinks in it, such as substance, force, divisibility, etc., and if I similarly separate from it what belongs to sen-

A21 sation in it, such as impenetrability, hardness, color, etc., I am still left with something from this empirical intuition, namely, extension and shape. These belong to pure intuition, which, even if there is no actual object of the senses or of sensation, has its place in the mind a priori, as a mere form of sensibility.

There must, therefore, be a science of all principles of a priori sen-

B36 sibility; I call such a science *transcendental aesthetic*. It constitutes the first part of the transcendental doctrine of elements, and stands in contrast to that [part of the] transcendental doctrine of elements which contains the principles of pure thought and is called transcendental logic.

A22 Hence in the transcendental aesthetic we shall, first of all, *isolate* sensibility, by separating from it everything that the understanding through its concepts thinks [in connection] with it, so that nothing other than empirical intuition will remain. Second, we shall also segregate from sensibility everything that belongs to sensation, so that nothing will remain but pure intuition and the mere form of appearances, which is all that sensibility can supply a priori. In the course of that inquiry it will be found that there are two pure forms of sensible intuition, which are principles for a priori cognition: viz., space and time. We now proceed to the task of examining these.

TRANSCENDENTAL AESTHETIC

Section I
Space

§ 2
METAPHYSICAL EXPOSITION OF THIS CONCEPT

By means of outer sense (a property of our mind) we present objects as outside us, and present them one and all in space. In space their shape, magnitude, and relation to one another are determined or determinable. By means of inner sense the mind intuits itself, or its inner state. Although inner sense provides no intuition of the soul itself as an object, yet there is a determinate form under which alone [as condition] we can intuit the soul's inner state. [That form is time.] Thus everything belonging to our inner determinations is presented in relations of time. Time cannot be intuited outwardly, any more than space can be intuited as something within us. What, then, are space and time? Are they actual beings? Are they only determinations of things, or, for that matter, relations among them? If so, are they at least determinations or relations that would belong to things intrinsically also, i.e., even if these things were not intuited? Or are they determinations and relations that adhere only to the form of intuition and hence to the subjective character of our mind, so that apart from that character these predicates cannot be ascribed to any thing at all? In order to inform ourselves on these points, let us first of all give an exposition of the concept of space. Now, by *exposition (expositio)* I mean clear (even if not comprehensive) presentation of what belongs to a concept; and such exposition is *metaphysical* if it contains what exhibits the concept as *given a priori*.

1. Space is not an empirical concept that has been abstracted from outer experiences. For the presentation of space must already lie at the basis in order for certain sensations to be referred to something outside me (i.e., referred to something in a location of space other

than the location in which I am). And it must similarly already lie at the basis in order for me to be able to present [the objects of] these sensations as outside and *alongside* one another, and hence to present them not only as different but as being in different locations. Accordingly, the presentation of space cannot be one that we take from the relations of outer appearance by means of experience; rather, only through the presentation of space is that outer experience possible in the first place.

A24   2. Space is a necessary a priori presentation that underlies all outer
B39   intuitions. We can never have a presentation of there being no space, even though we are quite able to think of there being no objects encountered in it. Hence space must be regarded as the condition for the possibility of appearances, and not as a determination dependent on them. Space is an a priori presentation that necessarily underlies outer appearances.

        3. Space is not a discursive or, as we say, universal concept of
A25   things as such; rather, it is a pure intuition. For, first, we can present only one space; and when we speak of many spaces, we mean by that only parts of one and the same unique space. Nor, second, can these parts precede the one all-encompassing space, as its constituents, as it were (from which it can be assembled); rather, they can be thought only as *in it*. Space is essentially one; the manifold in it, and hence also the universal concept of spaces as such, rests solely on [our bringing in] limitations. It follows from this that, as far as space is concerned, an a priori intuition of it (i.e., one that is not empirical) underlies all concepts of space. By the same token, no geometric principles—e.g., the principle that in a triangle two sides together are greater than the third—are ever derived from universal concepts of *line* and *triangle;* rather, they are all derived from intuition, and are derived from it moreover a priori, with apodeictic certainty.

        4. We present space as an infinite *given* magnitude. Now it is true
B40   that every concept must be thought as a presentation that is contained in an infinite multitude of different possible presentations (as their common characteristic) and hence the concept contains these presentations *under itself.* But no concept, as such, can be thought as containing an infinite multitude of presentations *within itself.* Yet that is how we think space (for all parts of space, *ad infinitum*, are simultaneous). Therefore the original presentation of space is an a priori *intuition*, not a *concept*.

§ 3
TRANSCENDENTAL EXPOSITION
OF THE CONCEPT OF SPACE

By a *transcendental exposition* I mean the explication of a concept as a principle that permits insight into the possibility of other synthetic a priori cognitions. Such explication requires (1) that cognitions of that sort do actually flow from the given concept, and (2) that these cognitions are possible only on the presupposition of a given way of explicating that concept.

Geometry is a science that determines the properties of space synthetically and yet a priori. What, then, must the presentation of space be in order for such cognition of space to be possible? Space B41 must originally be intuition. For from a mere concept one cannot obtain propositions that go beyond the concept; but we do obtain such propositions in geometry (Introduction, V). This intuition must, however, be encountered in us a priori, i.e., prior to any perception of an object; hence this intuition must be pure rather than empirical. For geometric propositions are one and all apodeictic, i.e., linked with the consciousness of their necessity—e.g., the proposition that space has only three dimensions. But propositions of that sort cannot be empirical judgments or judgments of experience; nor can they be inferred from such judgments (Introduction, II).

How, then, can the mind have an outer intuition which precedes the objects themselves, and in which the concept of these objects can be determined a priori? Obviously, this can be so only insofar as this intuition resides merely in the subject, as the subject's formal character of being affected by objects and of thereby acquiring from them *direct presentation,* i.e., *intuition,* and hence only as form of outer *sense* in general.

Our explication of the concept of space is, therefore, the only one that makes comprehensible the *possibility of geometry* as a [kind of] synthetic a priori cognition. Any way of explicating the concept that fails to make this possibility comprehensible, even if it should otherwise seem to have some similarity to ours, can be distinguished from it most safely by these criteria.

CONCLUSIONS FROM THE ABOVE CONCEPTS   A26/B42

(a) Space represents no property whatever of any things in themselves, nor does it represent things in themselves in their relation to one another. That is, space represents no determination of such things, no determination that adheres to objects themselves and that would remain even if we abstracted from all subjective conditions of intuition. For determinations, whether absolute or relative, cannot be intuited prior to the existence of the things to which they belong, and hence cannot be intuited a priori.

(b) Space is nothing but the mere form of all appearances of outer senses; i.e., it is the subjective condition of sensibility under which alone outer intuition is possible for us. Now, the subject's receptivity for being affected by objects precedes necessarily all intuitions of these objects. Thus we can understand how the form of all appearances can be given in the mind prior to all actual perceptions, and hence given a priori; and we can understand how this form, as a pure intuition in which all objects must be determined, can contain, prior to all experience, principles for the relations among these objects.

Only from the human standpoint, therefore, can we speak of space, of extended beings, etc. If we depart from the subjective condition under which alone we can—viz., as far as we may be affected by objects—acquire outer intuition, then the presentation of space means nothing whatsoever. This predicate is ascribed to things only insofar as they appear to us, i.e., only insofar as they are objects of sensibility. The constant form of this receptivity which we call sensibility is a necessary condition of all relations in which objects are intuited as outside us; and if we abstract from these objects, then the form of that receptivity is a pure intuition that bears the name of space. We cannot make the special conditions of sensibility to be conditions of the possibility of things, but only of the possibility of their appearances. Hence we can indeed say that space encompasses all things that appear to us externally, but not that it encompasses all things in themselves, intuited or not, or intuited by whatever subject. For we can make no judgment at all about the intuitions of other thinking beings, as to whether they are tied to the same conditions that limit our intuition and that are valid for us universally. If the limitation on a judgment is added to the concept of the subject [term], then the judgment holds unconditionally. The proposition, All things are side by side in space, holds under the limitation: if these things are taken as objects of our sensible intuition. If I here add the condition to the concept and say, All things considered as outer appearances are side by side in space, then this rule holds universally and without limitation. Accordingly, our exposition teaches

A27/
B43

A28/
B44

that space is *real* (i.e., objectively valid) in regard to everything that we can encounter externally as object, but teaches at the same time that space is *ideal* in regard to things when reason considers them in themselves, i.e., without taking into account the character of our sensibility. Hence we assert that space is *empirically real* (as regards all possible outer experience), despite asserting that space is *transcendentally ideal*, i.e., that it is nothing as soon as we omit [that space is] the condition of the possibility of all experience and suppose space to be something underlying things in themselves.

Besides space, on the other hand, no other subjective presentation that is referred to something external could be called an a priori objective presentation. For from none of them can we derive synthetic a priori propositions, as we can from intuition in space (§ 3). Hence, strictly speaking, ideality does not apply to them, even though they agree with the presentation of space inasmuch as they belong merely to the subjective character of the kind of sense involved. They may belong, e.g., to the sense of sight, of hearing, or of touch, by [being] sensations of colors, sounds, or heat. Yet because they are mere sensations rather than intuitions, they do not allow us to cognize any object at all, let alone a priori.

The only aim of this comment is to forestall an error: it might B45 occur to someone to illustrate the ideality of space asserted above by means of examples such as colors or taste, etc. These are thoroughly insufficient for this, because they are rightly regarded not as properties of things, but merely as changes in ourselves as subjects, changes that may even be different in different people. For in this case, something that originally is itself only appearance—e.g., a rose—counts A30 as a thing in itself in the empirical meaning of this expression, a thing in itself that in regard to color can nonetheless appear differently to every eye. The transcendental concept of appearances in space, on the other hand, is a critical reminder. It reminds us that nothing whatever that is intuited in space is a thing in itself, and that space is not a form of things, one that might belong to them as they are in themselves. Rather, what we call external objects are nothing but mere presentations of our sensibility. The form of this sensibility is space; but its true correlate, i.e., the thing in itself, is not cognized at all through these presentations, and cannot be. Nor, on the other hand, is the thing in itself ever at issue in experience.

TRANSCENDENTAL AESTHETIC

Section II
Time

§ 4
METAPHYSICAL EXPOSITION
OF THE CONCEPT OF TIME

1. Time is not an empirical concept that has been abstracted from any experience. For simultaneity or succession would not even enter our perception if the presentation of time did not underlie them a priori. Only on the presupposition of this presentation can we present this and that as being at one and the same time (simultaneously) or at different times (sequentially).

A31   2. Time is a necessary presentation that underlies all intuitions. As regards appearances in general, we cannot annul time itself, though we can quite readily remove appearances from time. Hence time is given a priori. All actuality of appearances is possible only in time. Appearances, one and all, may go away; but time itself (as the universal condition of their possibility) cannot be annulled.

B47   3. This a priori necessity, moreover, is the basis for the possibility of apodeictic principles about relations of time, or for the possibility of axioms about time in general. Time has only one dimension; different times are not simultaneous but sequential (just as different spaces are not sequential but simultaneous). These principles cannot be obtained from experience. For experience would provide neither strict universality nor apodeictic certainty; we could say only that common perception teaches us that it is so, but not that it must be so. These principles hold as rules under which alone experiences are possible at all; and they instruct us prior to experience, not through it.

4. Time is not a discursive or, as it is called, universal concept; A32   rather, it is a pure form of sensible intuition. Different times are only

parts of one and the same time; and the kind of presentation that can be given only through a single object is intuition. Moreover, the proposition that different times cannot be simultaneous could not be derived from a universal concept. The proposition is synthetic, and [therefore] cannot arise from concepts alone. Hence it is contained directly in the intuition and presentation of time.

5. To say that time is infinite means nothing more than that any determinate magnitude of time is possible only through limitations [put] on a single underlying time. Hence the original presentation *time* must be given as unlimited. But if something is such that its parts themselves and any magnitude of an object in it can be presented determinately only through limitation, then the whole presentation of it cannot be given through concepts (for they contain only partial presentations), but any such presentation must be based on direct intuition.

B48

§ 5
TRANSCENDENTAL EXPOSITION
OF THE CONCEPT OF TIME

I may refer for this exposition to No. 3, where, for the sake of brevity, I put among the items of the metaphysical exposition what in fact is transcendental. Let me add here that the concept of change, and with it the concept of motion (as change of place), is possible only through and in the presentation of time; and that if this presentation were not (inner) a priori intuition, no concept whatsoever could make comprehensible the possibility of a change, i.e., of a combination, in one and the same object, of contradictorily opposed predicates (e.g., one and the same thing's being in a place and not being in that same place). Only in time can both of two contradictorily opposed determinations be met with in one thing: viz., *sequentially*. Hence our concept of time explains the possibility of all that synthetic a priori cognition which is set forth by the—quite fertile— general theory of motion.

B49

§ 6
CONCLUSIONS FROM THESE CONCEPTS

(a) Time is not something that is self-subsistent or that attaches to things as an objective determination, and that hence would remain if one abstracted from all subjective conditions of our intuition of it. For if time were self-subsistent, then it would be something that A33 without there being an actual object would yet be actual. But if, on the second alternative, time were a determination or order attaching to things themselves, then it could not precede the objects as their condition, and could not a priori be cognized through synthetic propositions and intuited. But this a priori cognition and intuition can take place quite readily if time is nothing but the subjective condition under which alone any intuition can take place in us. For in that case this form of inner intuition can be presented prior to the objects, and hence presented a priori.

(b) Time is nothing but the form of inner sense, i.e., of the intuit-B50 ing we do of ourselves and of our inner state. For time cannot be a determination of outer appearances, [because] it does not belong to any shape or position, etc., but rather determines the relation of presentations in our inner state. And precisely because this inner intuition gives us no shape, do we try to make up for this deficiency by means of analogies. We present time sequence by a line progressing *ad infinitum,* a line in which the manifold constitutes a series of only one dimension. And from the properties of that line we infer all the properties of time, except for the one difference that the parts of the line are simultaneous whereas the parts of time are always sequential. This fact, moreover, that all relations of time can be expressed by means of outer intuition, shows that the presentation of time is itself intuition.

A34   (c) Time is the formal a priori condition of all appearances generally. Space is the pure form of all outer appearances; as such it is limited, as a priori condition, to just outer appearances. But all presentations, whether or not they have outer things as their objects, do yet in themselves, as determinations of the mind, belong to our inner state; and this inner state is subject to the formal condition of inner intuition, and hence to the condition of time. Therefore time is an a priori condition of all appearance generally: it is the direct condition B51 of inner appearances (of our souls), and precisely thereby also, indirectly, a condition of outer appearances. If I can say a priori that all outer appearances are in space and are determined a priori according to spatial relations, then the principle of inner sense allows me to say, quite universally, that all appearances generally, i.e., all objects of the senses, are in time and stand necessarily in relations of time.

If we take objects as they may be in themselves—i.e., if we abstract from the way in which we intuit ourselves inwardly, and in which by means of this intuition we also take into our power of presentation all outer intuitions—then time is nothing. Time has objective validity only with regard to appearances, because these are already things considered *as objects of our senses*. But time is no longer objective if we abstract from the sensibility of our intuition, and hence from the way of presenting peculiar to us, and speak of *things as such*. Hence time is merely a subjective condition of our (human) intuition (an intuition that is always sensible—i.e., inasmuch as we are affected by objects); in itself, i.e., apart from the subject, time is nothing. Nevertheless, time is necessarily objective in regard to all appearances, and hence also in regard to all things that we can encounter in experience. We cannot say that all things [as such] are in time; for in the concept of things as such we abstract from all ways of intuiting them, while yet this intuition is the very condition under which time belongs in the presentation of objects. If now we add the condition to the concept, and say that all things as appearances (objects of sensible intuition) are in time, then this principle has all its objective correctness and a priori universality.

Hence the doctrine we are asserting is that time is *empirically real,* i.e., objectively valid in regard to all objects that might ever be given to our senses. And since our intuition is always sensible, no object that is not subject to the condition of time can ever be given to us in experience. On the other hand, we dispute that time has any claim to absolute reality; i.e., we dispute any claim whereby time would, quite without taking into account the form of our sensible intuition, attach to things absolutely, as a condition or property. Nor indeed can such properties, properties belonging to things in themselves, ever be given to us through the senses. In this, then, consists the *transcendental ideality* of time. According to this view, if we abstract from the subjective conditions of sensible intuition, then time is nothing, and cannot be included among objects in themselves (apart from their relation to our intuition) either as subsisting [as such an object] or as inhering [in one]. But this ideality of time is not to be compared, any more than is the ideality of space, with the subreptions of sensations. For in their case we presuppose that the appearance itself in which these predicates [allegedly] inhere has objective reality. In the case of time, such objective reality is entirely absent, except insofar as this reality is merely empirical, i.e., except insofar as we regard the object itself as merely appearance. See, on this, the above comment, in SECTION I.

A35

B52

A36

B53

§ 7
ELUCIDATION

Against this theory, which grants that time is empirically real but disputes that it is real absolutely and transcendentally, I have heard men of insight raise quite unanimously an objection. I gather from this great unanimity that the objection must occur naturally to every A37 reader who is not accustomed to contemplations such as these. The objection is the following. Changes are actual. (This is proved by the variation on the part of our own presentations—even if one were to deny all outer appearances, along with their changes.) Now changes are possible only in time. Therefore time is something actual. There is no difficulty in replying to the objection. I concede the whole argument. Time is indeed something actual, viz., the actual form of B54 inner intuition. It therefore has subjective reality in regard to inner experience; i.e., I actually have the presentation of time and of my determinations in time. Hence time is to be regarded as actual, though not as an object but as the way of presenting that I myself have as an object. Suppose, on the other hand, that I could intuit myself without being subject to this condition of sensibility, or that another being could so intuit me; in that case the very same determinations that we now present as changes would provide a cognition in which the presentation of time, and hence also that of change, would not occur at all. Hence time retains its empirical reality as condition of all our experiences. Only absolute reality must, by the reasons adduced above, be denied to time. Time is nothing but the form of our inner intuition.[8] If we take away from time [the qualification that it A38 is] the special condition of our sensibility, then the concept of time vanishes as well; time attaches not to objects themselves, but merely to the subject intuiting them.

But what causes this objection to be raised so unanimously, and B55 raised, moreover, by those who nonetheless cannot think of any plausible objection against the doctrine that space is ideal, is the following. They had no hope of establishing apodeictically that space is real absolutely; for they are confronted by idealism, according to which

---

8. I can indeed say: My presentations follow one another. But that means only that we are conscious of them as being in a time sequence—in accordance, i.e., with the form of inner sense. Time is not, on that account, something in itself, nor is it a determination attaching to things objectively.

the actuality of external objects is incapable of strict proof. By contrast, the actuality of the object of our inner sense (the actuality of myself and of my state) is directly evident through consciousness. External objects might be a mere illusion; but the object of inner sense is, in their opinion, undeniably something actual. They failed to bear in mind, however, that both of them, though their actuality as presentations is indisputable, still belong only to appearance. Appearance always has two sides. One is the side where the object is regarded in itself (without regard to the way in which it is intuited, which is precisely why its character always remains problematic). The other is the side where we take account of the form of the intuition of this object. This form must be sought not in the object in itself, but in the subject to whom the object appears. Yet this form belongs to the appearance of this object actually and necessarily.

Time and space are, accordingly, two sources of cognition. From these sources we can draw a priori different synthetic cognitions—as $\quad$ A39 is shown above all by the splendid example that pure mathematics provides in regard to our cognitions of space and its relations. For time and space, taken together, are pure forms of all sensible intu- $\quad$ B56 ition, and thereby make synthetic propositions possible a priori. But precisely thereby (i.e., by being merely conditions of sensibility), these a priori sources of cognition determine their own bounds; viz., they determine that they apply to objects merely insofar as these are regarded as appearances, but do not exhibit things in themselves. Appearances are the sole realm where these a priori sources of cognition are valid; if we go outside that realm, there is no further objective use that can be made of them. This [limited] reality of space and time leaves the reliability of experiential cognition otherwise untouched; for we have equal certainty in that cognition, whether these forms necessarily attach to things in themselves or only to our intuition of these things. Those, on the other hand, who assert that space and time—whether they assume these as subsistent or as only inherent—are real absolutely must be at variance with the principles of experience itself. For suppose they decide to assume space and time as subsistent (thus taking what is usually the side of the mathematical investigators of nature): then they must assume two eternal and infinite self-subsistent nonentities (space and time), which exist (yet without there being anything actual) only in order to encompass everything actual. Or suppose they assume space and time as only in- $\quad$ A40 herent (thus taking the side to which some metaphysical natural

scientists belong). Here space and time count for them as relations of appearances (occurring concurrently or sequentially)—relations ab-
B57 stracted from experience but, as thus separated, presented confus-edly. If they take this second side, then they must dispute that the mathematical a priori doctrines are valid for actual things (e.g., things in space), or at least that they are apodeictically certain. For a posteri-ori there is no such certainty at all. According to this second opinion, the a priori concepts of space and time are only creatures of the imag-ination, and their source must actually be sought in experience: the relations are abstracted from experience; and the imagination has made from them something that, while containing what is universal in these relations, yet cannot occur without the restrictions that na-ture has connected with them. Those who assume space and time as [real absolutely and] subsistent do gain this much: they make the realm of appearances free for mathematical assertions. On the other hand, these very conditions create great confusion for them when the understanding wants to go beyond the realm of appearances. Those, on the other hand, who assume space and time as [real absolutely but as] only inherent gain on this latter point. I.e., they do not find the presentations of space and time getting in their way when they want to judge objects not as appearances but merely as they relate to the understanding. But they can neither indicate a basis for the possibil-ity of mathematical a priori cognitions (since they lack a true and ob-
A41 jectively valid a priori intuition), nor bring the propositions of experi-ence into necessary agreement with those a priori mathematical
B58 assertions. Our theory of the true character of these two original forms of sensibility provides the remedy for both [sets of] difficulties.

    Finally, transcendental aesthetic cannot contain more than these two elements, i.e., space and time. This is evident from the fact that all other concepts belonging to sensibility presuppose something em-pirical. This holds even for the concept of motion, which unites the two components. For [the concept of] motion presupposes the per-ception of something movable. But in space, considered in itself, there is nothing movable; therefore the movable must be something that we find *in space only through experience*, and hence must be an em-pirical datum. Similarly, transcendental aesthetic cannot include among its a priori data the concept of change. For time itself does not change; rather, what changes is something that is in time. Therefore the concept of change requires the perception of some existent and of the succession of its determinations; hence it requires experience.

TRANSCENDENTAL DOCTRINE OF ELEMENTS

PART II
TRANSCENDENTAL LOGIC

Introduction
Idea of a Transcendental Logic

I. ON LOGIC AS SUCH

Our cognition arises from two basic sources of the mind. The first is [our ability] to receive presentations (and is our receptivity for impressions); the second is our ability to cognize an object through these presentations (and is the spontaneity of concepts). Through receptivity an object is *given* to us; through spontaneity an object is *thought* in relation to that [given] presentation (which [otherwise] is a mere determination of the mind). Intuition and concepts, therefore, constitute the elements of all our cognition. Hence neither concepts without an intuition corresponding to them in some way or other, nor intuition without concepts can yield cognition. Both intuition and concepts are either pure or empirical. They are *empirical* if they contain sensation (sensation presupposes the actual presence of the object); they are *pure* if no sensation is mixed in with the presentation. Sensation may be called the matter of sensible cognition. Hence pure intuition contains only the form under which something is intuited, and a pure concept contains solely the form of the thought of an object as such. Only pure intuitions or concepts are possible a priori; empirical ones are possible only a posteriori.

Let us give the name *sensibility* to our mind's *receptivity*, [i.e., to its ability] to receive presentations insofar as it is affected in some manner. *Understanding,* on the other hand, is our ability to produce presentations ourselves, i.e., our *spontaneity* of cognition. Our *intuition,* by our very nature, can never be other than *sensible* intuition; i.e., it contains only the way in which we are affected by objects. *Understanding,* on the other hand, is our ability to *think* the object of sensible intuition. Neither of these properties is to be preferred to the other. Without sensibility no object would be given to us; and without understanding no object would be thought. Thoughts without content are empty; intuitions without concepts are blind. Hence it is just as necessary that we make our concepts sensible (i.e., that we add the object to them in intuition) as it is necessary that we make our intuitions understandable (i.e., that we bring them under concepts). Moreover, this capacity and this ability cannot exchange their func-

B76 tions. The understanding cannot intuit anything, and the senses cannot think anything. Only from their union can cognition arise. This fact, however, must not lead us to confuse their respective contribu-

A52 tions; it provides us, rather, with a strong reason for carefully separating and distinguishing sensibility and understanding from each other. Hence we distinguish the science of the rules of sensibility as such, i.e., aesthetic, from the science of the rules of the understanding as such, i.e., logic. [...]

TRANSCENDENTAL LOGIC

DIVISION I
TRANSCENDENTAL ANALYTIC

Transcendental analytic consists in the dissection of our entire a priori cognition into the elements of understanding's pure cognition. The following points are what matters in this dissection: (1) The concepts must be pure rather than empirical. (2) They must belong not to intuition and sensibility, but to thought and understanding. (3) They must be elementary concepts, and must be distinguished carefully from concepts that are either derivative or composed of such elementary concepts. (4) Our table of these concepts must be complete, and the concepts must occupy fully the whole realm of pure understanding. Now, this completeness [characteristic] of a science cannot be assumed reliably by gauging an aggregate of concepts that was brought about merely through trials. Hence this completeness is possible only by means of an *idea of the whole* of understanding's a priori cognition, and through the division, determined by that idea, of the concepts amounting to that cognition; and hence A65 this completeness is possible only through the *coherence* of these concepts *in a system*. Pure understanding differentiates itself fully not only from everything empirical, but even from all sensibility [gener- B90 ally]. Therefore it is a unity that is self-subsistent, sufficient to itself, and that cannot be augmented by supplementing it with any extrinsic additions. Hence the sum of pure understanding's cognition will constitute a system that can be encompassed and determined by an idea. The system's completeness and structure can at the same time serve as a touchstone of the correctness and genuineness of whatever components of cognition fit into the system. This entire part of the Transcendental Logic consists, however, of two *books;* one of these contains the *concepts,* the other the *principles,* of pure understanding.

Transcendental Analytic

Book I
Analytic of Concepts

By *analytic of concepts* I do not mean the analysis of concepts, i.e., the usual procedure in philosophical inquiries of dissecting already available concepts in terms of their content and bringing them to distinctness; rather, I mean the hitherto rarely attempted *dissection of* A66 *the power of understanding itself.* The purpose of this dissection is to explore the possibility of a priori concepts, by locating them solely in the understanding, as their birthplace, and by analyzing the under- B91 standing's pure use as such. For this exploration is the proper task of a transcendental philosophy; the rest is the logical treatment of concepts in philosophy generally. Hence we shall trace the pure concepts all the way to their first seeds and predispositions in the human understanding, where these concepts lie prepared until finally, on the occasion of experience, they are developed and are exhibited by that same understanding in their purity, freed from the empirical conditions attaching to them.

Analytic of Concepts

Chapter I
On the Guide for the Discovery of All Pure Concepts of Understanding

When we bring into play a cognitive power, then, depending on the various ways in which we may be prompted to do so, different concepts come to the fore that allow us to recognize this power. These concepts can be collected in an essay that will be more or less comprehensive, once the concepts have been observed fairly long or with significant mental acuity. But by this—as it were, mechanical—procedure we can never reliably determine at what point that inquiry A67 will be completed. Moreover, if concepts are discovered only on

given occasions, then they reveal themselves in no order or system- B92
atic unity; instead they are ultimately only paired according to simi-
larities, and arranged in series according to the quantity of their content, from the simple concepts on to the more composite. The way in
which these series are brought about, despite being methodical in a
certain manner, is anything but systematic.

Transcendental philosophy has the advantage, but also the obligation, of locating its concepts according to a principle. For these concepts arise, pure and unmixed, from the understanding, which is an
absolute unity; and hence these concepts themselves must cohere
with each other according to one concept or idea. Such coherence,
however, provides us with a rule by which we can determine a priori
the proper place for each pure concept of understanding, and the
completeness of all of them taken together—whereas otherwise all of
this would be subject to one's own discretion or to chance.

Transcendental Guide for the Discovery of All Pure Concepts of Understanding

Section I
On the Understanding's Logical Use As Such

The understanding was explicated merely negatively above, viz., as a
nonsensible cognitive power. And since independently of sensibility A68
we cannot partake of any intuition, it follows that the understanding B93
is not a power of intuition. Apart from intuition, however, there is
only one way of cognizing, viz., through concepts. Hence the cognition of any understanding, or at least of the human understanding, is
a cognition through concepts; it is not intuitive, but discursive. All
our intuitions, as sensible, rest on our being affected; concepts, on
the other hand, rest on functions. By *function* I mean the unity of the
act of arranging various presentations under one common presentation. Hence concepts are based on the spontaneity of thought,
whereas sensible intuitions are based on the receptivity for impressions. Now the only use that the understanding can make of these

concepts is to judge by means of them. But in such judging, a concept is never referred directly to an object, because the only kind of presentation that deals with its object directly is intuition. Instead the concept is referred directly to some other presentation of the object (whether that presentation be an intuition or itself already a concept). Judgment, therefore, is the indirect cognition of an object, viz., the presentation of a presentation of it. In every judgment there is a concept that [comprises and thus] holds for many [presentations], and, among them, comprises also a given presentation that is referred directly to the object. E.g., in the judgment, *All bodies are divisible,* the concept of the divisible refers to various other concepts; but, among these, it is here referred specifically to the concept of body, and the concept of body is referred in turn to certain appearances that we encounter. Hence these objects are presented indirectly through the concept of divisibility. Accordingly, all judgments are functions of unity among our presentations. For instead of cognizing the object by means of a direct presentation, we do so by means of a higher presentation comprising both this direct presentation and several other presentations; and we thereby draw many possible cognitions together into one. Now since all acts of the understanding can be reduced to judgments, the *understanding* as such can be presented as a *power of judgment.* For, according to what we said above, the understanding is a power of thought. But thought is cognition through concepts; and concepts, as predicates of possible judgments, refer to some presentation of an as yet undetermined object. Thus the concept of body signifies something—e.g., metal—that can be cognized through that concept. Hence it is a concept only because there are contained under it other presentations by means of which it can refer to objects. Therefore the concept of body is the predicate for a possible judgment, e.g., the judgment that every metal is a body. Therefore we can find all of the functions of the understanding if we can exhibit completely the functions of unity in judgments. This, however, can be accomplished quite readily, as the following section will show.

A69/
B94

[Transcendental] Guide for the Discovery of All Pure Concepts of Understanding
Section II

§ 9
ON THE UNDERSTANDING'S LOGICAL FUNCTION IN JUDGMENTS

If we abstract from all content of a judgment as such and pay attention only to the mere form of understanding in it, then we find that the function of thought in judgment can be brought under four headings, each containing under it three moments. They can conveniently be presented in the following table.

1
Quantity of Judgments
Universal
Particular
Singular

2		3
Quality		*Relation*
Affirmative		Categorical
Negative		Hypothetical
Infinite		Disjunctive

4
Modality
Problematic
Assertoric
Apodeictic

[...]

[Transcendental] Guide for the Discovery of All Pure Concepts of Understanding
Section III

§ 10
ON THE PURE CONCEPTS OF
UNDERSTANDING, OR CATEGORIES

General logic, as we have said several times already, abstracts from all content of cognition. It expects presentations to be given to it from somewhere else—no matter where—in order then to transform these presentations into concepts in the first place. This it does analytically. Transcendental logic, on the other hand, has lying before it a

manifold of a priori sensibility, offered to it by transcendental aesthetic. Transcendental aesthetic offers it this manifold in order to provide it with a material for the pure concepts of understanding. Without this material, transcendental logic would have no content, and hence would be completely empty. Now space and time contain a manifold of pure a priori intuition. But they belong nonetheless to the conditions of our mind's receptivity under which alone the mind can receive presentations of objects, and which, by the same token, must always affect the concept of these objects. Yet the spontaneity of our thought requires that this manifold, in order to be turned into a cognition, must first be gone through, taken up, and combined in a certain manner. This act I call synthesis.

By *synthesis,* in the most general sense of the term, I mean the act of putting various presentations with one another and of comprising their manifoldness in one cognition. Such synthesis is *pure* if the manifold is given not empirically but a priori (as is the manifold in space and time). Before any analysis of our presentations can take place, these presentations must first be given, and hence in terms of *content* no concepts can originate analytically. Rather, synthesis of a manifold (whether this manifold is given empirically or a priori) is what first gives rise to a cognition. Although this cognition may still

be crude and confused at first and hence may require analysis, yet synthesis is what in fact gathers the elements for cognition and unites them to [form] a certain content. Hence if we want to make a judgment about the first origin of our cognition, then we must first direct our attention to synthesis.

Synthesis as such, as we shall see hereafter, is the mere effect produced by the imagination, which is a blind but indispensable function of the soul without which we would have no cognition whatsoever, but of which we are conscious only very rarely. Bringing this synthesis *to concepts*, on the other hand, is a function belonging to the understanding; and it is through this function that the understanding first provides us with cognition in the proper meaning of the term.

Now *pure synthesis, conceived of generally,* yields the pure concept of understanding. By pure synthesis I mean the synthesis that rests on a basis of synthetic a priori unity. E.g., our act of counting (as is more noticeable primarily with larger numbers) is a *synthesis according to concepts,* because it is performed according to a common basis of unity (such as the decimal system). Hence under this concept the unity of the manifold's synthesis becomes necessary. B104

Bringing various presentations *under* a concept (a task dealt with by general logic) is done analytically. But bringing, not presentations but the *pure synthesis* of presentations, *to* concepts is what transcendental logic teaches. The first [thing] that we must be given a priori in order to cognize any object is the *manifold* of pure intuition. The second [thing] is the *synthesis* of this manifold by the imagination. But this synthesis does not yet yield cognition. The third [thing we need] in order to cognize an object that we encounter is the concepts which give *unity* to this pure synthesis and which consist solely in the presentation of this necessary synthetic unity. And these concepts rest on the understanding. A79

The same function that gives unity to the various presentations *in a judgment* also gives unity to the mere synthesis of various presentations *in an intuition*. This unity—speaking generally—is called pure concept of understanding. Hence the same understanding—and indeed through the same acts whereby it brought about, in concepts, the logical form of a judgment by means of analytic unity—also brings into its presentations a transcendental content, by means of the synthetic unity of the manifold in intuition as such; and because of this, these presentations are called pure concepts of understanding applying a priori to objects. Bringing such a transcendental content into these presentations is something that general logic cannot accomplish. B105

Thus there arise precisely as many pure concepts of understanding applying a priori to objects of intuition as such, as in the preceding table there were logical functions involved in all possible judgments. For these functions of the understanding are completely
A80 exhaustive and survey its power entirely. Following Aristotle, we shall
B106 call these functions *categories*. For our aim is fundamentally the same as his, even though it greatly deviates from his in its execution.

Table of Categories

1
Of Quantity
Unity
Plurality
Totality

2
Of Quality
Reality
Negation
Limitation

3
Of Relation
of *Inherence* and Subsistence
(substantia et accidens)
of *Causality* and Dependence
(Cause and Effect)
of *Community*
(Interaction between
Agent and Patient)

4
Of Modality
Possibility—Impossibility
Existence—Nonexistence
Necessity—Contingency

This, then, is the list of all the original pure concepts of synthesis that the understanding contains a priori. Indeed, it is a pure understanding only because of these concepts; for through them alone can it understand something in the manifold of intuition, i.e., think an object of intuition. This division of the categories has been generated
A81 systematically from a common principle, viz., our ability to judge (which is equivalent to our ability to think). It has not been gener-
B107 ated rhapsodically, by locating pure concepts haphazardly, where we can never be certain that the enumeration of the concepts is complete. For we then infer the division only by induction, forgetting

that in this way we never gain insight into why precisely these concepts, rather than others, reside in the pure understanding. Locating these basic concepts was a project worthy of an acute man like Aristotle. But having no principle, he snatched them up as he came upon them. He hunted up ten of them at first, and called them *categories* (predicaments). He later believed that he had discovered five more categories, and added them under the name of postpredicaments. But his table remained deficient even then. Moreover, we also find in it some modes of pure sensibility *(quando, ubi, situs, and prius, simul)*, as well as an empirical mode *(motus)*, none of which belong at all in this register of the root [concepts] of the understanding. Again, derivative concepts *(actio, passio)* are also included among the original concepts, while some of the original concepts are missing entirely.

Hence for the sake of [distinguishing] the original concepts, we must note also that the categories, as the true *root concepts* of pure understanding, have also their equally pure *derivative concepts*. In a complete system of transcendental philosophy these derivative concepts can by no means be omitted. In a merely critical essay, on the other hand, I can settle for merely mentioning them. A82

Let me call these pure but derivative concepts of understanding B108 the *predicables* of pure understanding (in contrast to the predicaments). Once we have the original and primitive concepts, we can easily add the derivative and subsidiary ones and thus depict completely the genealogical tree of pure understanding. Since I am here concerned with the completeness not of the system but only of the principles for a system, I am reserving that complementary work for another enterprise. We can, however, come close to achieving that aim of completing the tree if we pick up a textbook on ontology and subordinate the predicables to the categories: e.g., to the category of causality, the predicables of force, action, undergoing; to the category of community, the predicables of presence, resistance; to the predicaments of modality, the predicables of arising, passing away, change; and so on. When the categories are combined either with the modes of pure sensibility or with one another, they yield a great multitude of derivative a priori concepts. Mentioning these concepts and, if possible, listing them completely would be a useful and not disagreeable endeavor, but one that we can here dispense with.

In this treatise I deliberately refrain from offering definitions of these categories, even though I may possess them. I shall hereafter A83 dissect these concepts only to a degree adequate for the doctrine of B109 method that I here produce. Whereas definitions of the categories could rightly be demanded of me in a system of pure reason, here they would only make us lose sight of the main point of the inquiry. For they would give rise to doubts and charges that we may readily relegate to another activity without in any way detracting from our essential aim. Still, from what little I have mentioned about this, we can see distinctly that a complete lexicon with all the requisite explications not only is possible but could easily be brought about. The compartments are now at hand. They only need to be filled in; and a systematic [transcendental] topic, such as the present one, will make it difficult to miss the place where each concept properly belongs, and at the same time will make it easy to notice any place that is still empty. [... in second edition only]

Chapter II
On the Deduction of the
Pure Concepts of Understanding

Section I

§ 13
ON THE PRINCIPLES OF A
TRANSCENDENTAL DEDUCTION AS SUCH

When teachers of law talk about rights and claims, they distinguish in a legal action the question regarding what is legal *(quid iuris)* from the question concerning fact *(quid facti)*, and they demand proof of both. The first proof, which is to establish the right, or for that matter the legal entitlement, they call the *deduction*. [This term also applies to philosophy.] We employ a multitude of empirical concepts without being challenged by anyone. And we consider ourselves justified, even without having offered a deduction, to assign to these B117 empirical concepts a meaning and imagined signification, because we always have experience available to us to prove their objective reality. But there are also concepts that we usurp, as, e.g., *fortune, fate*. And although these concepts run loose, with our almost universal for- A85 bearance, yet they are sometimes confronted by the question [of their legality], *quid iuris*. This question then leaves us in considerable perplexity regarding the deduction of these concepts; for neither from experience nor from reason can we adduce any distinct legal basis from which the right to use them emerges distinctly.

But there are, among the various concepts making up the highly mixed fabric of human cognition, some that are determined for pure a priori use as well (i.e., for a use that is completely independent of all experience); and their right to be so used always requires a deduction. For proofs based on experience are insufficient to establish the legitimacy of using them in that way; yet we do need to know how these concepts can refer to objects even though they do not take these objects from any experience. Hence when I explain in what way concepts can refer to objects a priori, I call that explanation the *transcendental deduction* of these concepts. And I distinguish transcendental deduction from *empirical* deduction, which indicates in what way a concept has been acquired through experience and through reflection upon experience, and which therefore concerns not the concept's legitimacy but only the fact whereby we came to possess it.

B118   We already have, at this point, two types of concepts that, while being wholly different in kind, do yet agree inasmuch as both of them refer to objects completely a priori: viz., on the one hand, the concepts of space and time as forms of sensibility; and, on the other hand, the categories as concepts of understanding. To attempt an empirical deduction of these two types of concepts would be a futile job. For what is distinctive in their nature is precisely the fact that

A86   they refer to their objects without having borrowed anything from experience in order to present these objects. Hence if a deduction of these concepts is needed, then it must always be transcendental.

But even for these concepts, as for all cognition, we can locate in experience, if not the principle of their possibility, then at least the occasioning causes of their production. Thus the impressions of the senses first prompt [us] to open up the whole cognitive power in regard to them, and to bring about experience. Experience contains two quite heterogeneous elements: viz., a *matter* for cognition, taken from the senses; and a certain *form* for ordering this matter, taken from the inner source of pure intuition and thought. It is on the occasion of the impressions of the senses that pure intuition and thought are first brought into operation and produce concepts. Such exploration of our cognitive power's first endeavors to ascend from

B119   singular perceptions to universal concepts is doubtless highly beneficial, and we are indebted to the illustrious *Locke* for first opening up the path to it. Yet such exploration can never yield a *deduction* of the pure a priori concepts, which does not lie on that path at all. For in view of these concepts' later use, which is to be wholly independent of experience, they must be able to display a birth certificate

A87   quite different from that of descent from experiences. The attempted physiological derivation concerns a *quaestio facti*, and therefore cannot properly be called a deduction at all. Hence I shall name it the explanation of our *possession* of a pure cognition. Clearly, then, the only possible deduction of this pure cognition is a transcendental and by no means an empirical one, and empirical deductions regarding the pure a priori concepts are nothing but futile attempts—

attempts that only those can engage in who have not comprehended the quite peculiar nature of these cognitions.

Yet even if it be granted that the only possible kind of deduction of pure a priori cognition is one along the transcendental path, that still does not show that this deduction is inescapably necessary. We did earlier trace the concepts of space and time to their sources by means of a transcendental deduction, and we explained and determined their a B120 priori objective validity. Yet geometry, using nothing but a priori cognitions, follows its course securely without needing to ask philosophy for a certificate of the pure and legitimate descent of geometry's basic concept of space. On the other hand, the use of the concept of space in this science does apply only to the external world of sense. Space is the pure form of the intuition of that world. In that world, therefore, all geometric cognition is directly evident, because it is based on a priori intuition; and, through cognition itself, objects are (as regards their A88 form) given a priori in intuition. With the *pure concepts of understanding,* on the other hand, begins the inescapable requirement to seek a transcendental deduction—not only of these concepts themselves, but also of space. For these concepts speak of objects through predicates of pure a priori thought, not through predicates of intuition and sensibility; hence they refer to objects universally, i.e., apart from all conditions of sensibility. They are, then, concepts that are not based on experience; and in a priori intuition, too, they cannot display any object on which they might, prior to all experience, base their synthesis. Hence these concepts not only arouse suspicion concerning the objective validity and limits of their use, but they also make ambiguous the B121 *concept of space;* for they tend to use it even beyond the conditions of sensible intuition—and this indeed is the reason why a transcendental deduction of this concept was needed above. I must therefore convince the reader, before he has taken a single step in the realm of pure reason, that such a deduction is inescapably necessary. For otherwise he proceeds blindly, and after manifold wanderings must yet return to the ignorance from which he started. But the reader must also distinctly see in advance the inevitable difficulty of providing such a deduction. For otherwise he might complain of obscurity when in fact the matter itself is deeply shrouded, or might be too quickly discouraged during the removal of obstacles. For we either must entirely abandon all A89 claims to pure rational insights into the realm that we care about most, viz., the realm beyond the bounds of all possible experience, or else must bring this critical inquiry to completion.

We had little trouble above in making comprehensible how the concepts of space and time, despite being a priori cognitions, must yet refer necessarily to objects, and how they make possible, independently of any experience, a synthetic cognition of objects. For only by means of such pure forms of sensibility can an object appear to us, B122 i.e., can it be an object of empirical intuition. Hence space and time are pure intuitions containing a priori the condition for the possibility of objects as appearances, and the synthesis in space and time has objective validity.

The categories of understanding, on the other hand, do not at all present to us the conditions under which objects are given in intuition. Therefore objects can indeed appear to us without having to refer necessarily to functions of understanding, and hence without the understanding's containing a priori the conditions of these objects. Thus we find here a difficulty that we did not encounter in the realm of sensibility: viz., how *subjective conditions of thought* could have *objective validity*, i.e., how they could yield conditions for the possibility A90 of all cognition of objects. For appearances can indeed be given in intuition without functions of understanding. Let me take, e.g., the concept of cause. This concept signifies a special kind of synthesis where upon [the occurrence of] something, A, something quite different, B, is posited according to a rule. Why appearances should contain anything like that is not evident a priori. (I say *a priori* because experience cannot be adduced as proof, since we must be able to establish this concept's objective validity a priori.) Hence there is doubt a priori whether perhaps such a concept might not even be empty and en- B123 counter no object at all among appearances. For while it is evident that objects of sensible intuition must conform to the formal conditions of sensibility lying a priori in the mind, since otherwise they would not be objects for us, it is not so easy to see the inference whereby they must in addition conform to the conditions that the understanding requires for the synthetic unity of thought. For, I suppose, appearances might possibly be of such a character that the understanding would not find them to conform at all to the conditions of its unity. Everything might then be so confused that, e.g., the sequence of appearances would offer us nothing providing us with a rule of synthesis and A91 thus corresponding to the concept of cause and effect, so that this concept would then be quite empty, null, and without signification. But appearances would nonetheless offer objects to our intuition; for intuition in no way requires the functions of thought.

Suppose that we planned to extricate ourselves from these troublesome inquiries by saying that examples of such regularity among appearances are offered to us incessantly by experience, and that these examples give us sufficient prompting to isolate from them the concept of cause and thus to verify at the same time the objective validity of such a concept. In that case we would be overlooking the fact that the concept of cause cannot arise in that way at all; rather, it either must have its basis completely a priori in the understanding, B124 or must be given up entirely as a mere chimera. For this concept definitely requires that something, A, be of such a kind that something else, B, follows from it *necessarily* and according to an *absolutely universal rule*. Although appearances do provide us with cases from which we can obtain a rule whereby something usually happens, they can never provide us with a rule whereby the result is *necessary*. This is, moreover, the reason why the synthesis of cause and effect is imbued with a dignity that cannot at all be expressed empirically: viz., that the effect is not merely added to the cause, but is posited *through* the cause and results *from* it. And the strict universality of the rule is indeed no property whatever of empirical rules; empirical rules can, A92 through induction, acquire none but comparative universality, i.e., extensive usability. But if we treated the pure concepts of understanding as merely empirical products, then our use of them would change entirely.

§ 14
Transition to the Transcendental Deduction of the Categories

Only two cases are possible where synthetic presentation and its objects can concur, can necessarily refer to each other, and can—as it were—meet each other: viz., either if the object makes the presenta- B125 tion possible, or if the presentation alone makes the object possible. If the object makes the presentation possible, then the reference is only empirical and the presentation is never possible a priori. This is what happens in the case of appearances, as regards what pertains to sensation in them. But suppose that the presentation alone makes the object possible. In that case, while presentation in itself does not produce its object *as regards existence* (for the causality that presentation has by means of the will is not at issue here at all), yet presentation is a priori determinative in regard to the object if *cognizing* something

as an object is possible only through it. Now there are two conditions
under which alone there can be cognition of an object. The first condition is *intuition;* through it the object is given, though only as ap-
A93   pearance. The second condition is the *concept;* through it an object is
thought that corresponds to this intuition. Now it is evident from
the above that the first condition, viz., the condition under which
alone objects can be intuited, does indeed, as far as their form is concerned, underlie objects a priori in the mind. Hence all appearances
necessarily agree with this formal condition of sensibility, because
only through it can they appear, i.e., be empirically intuited and
given. Now the question arises whether concepts do not also a priori
precede [objects], as conditions under which alone something can
be, if not intuited, yet thought as object as such. For in that case all
B126   empirical cognition of objects necessarily conforms to such concepts, because nothing is possible as *object of experience* unless these
concepts are presupposed. But all experience, besides containing the
senses' intuition through which something is given, does also contain a *concept* of an object that is given in intuition, or that appears.
Accordingly, concepts of objects as such presumably underlie all experiential cognition as its a priori conditions. Hence presumably the
objective validity of the categories, as a priori concepts, rests on the
fact that through them alone is experience possible (as far as the
form of thought in it is concerned). For in that case the categories
refer to objects of experience necessarily and a priori, because only
by means of them can any experiential object whatsoever be thought
at all.
A94   Hence the transcendental deduction of all a priori concepts has a
principle to which the entire investigation must be directed: viz., the
principle that these concepts must be cognized as a priori conditions
for the possibility of experience (whether the possibility of the intuition found in experience, or the possibility of the thought). If concepts serve as the objective basis for the possibility of experience,
then—precisely because of this—they are necessary. But to unfold
the experience in which these concepts are found is not to deduce
B127   them (but is only to illustrate them); for otherwise they would, after
all, be only contingent. Without that original reference of these concepts to possible experience wherein all objects of cognition occur,
their reference to any object whatever would be quite incomprehensible.
    The illustrious **Locke**, not having engaged in this contemplation,
and encountering pure concepts of understanding in experience, also

DIV I TRANS. ANALYTIC, BK I ANALYTIC OF CONCEPTS

derived them from experience. Yet he proceeded so *inconsistently* that he dared to try using these concepts for cognitions that go far beyond any boundary of experience. **David Hume** recognized that in order for us to be able to do this, the origin of these concepts must be a priori. But he was quite unable to explain how it is possible that concepts not in themselves combined in the understanding should nonetheless have to be thought by it as necessarily combined in the object. Nor did it occur to him that perhaps the understanding itself might, through these concepts, be the author of the experience wherein we encounter the understanding's objects. Thus, in his plight, he derived these concepts from experience (viz., from *habit,* a subjective necessity that arises in experience through repeated association and that ultimately is falsely regarded as objective). But he proceeded quite consistently after that, for he declared that we cannot use these concepts and the principles that they occasion in order to go beyond the boundary of experience. Yet the *empirical* derivation of these concepts which occurred to both cannot be reconciled with the scientific a priori cognitions that we actually have, viz., our a priori cognitions of *pure mathematics* and *universal natural science,* and hence this empirical derivation is refuted by that fact.

B128

Of these two illustrious men, Locke left the door wide open for *fanaticism;* for once reason has gained possession of such rights, it can no longer be kept within limits by indefinite exhortations to moderation. Hume, believing that he had uncovered so universal a delusion—regarded as reason—of our cognitive power, surrendered entirely to *skepticism.* We are now about to try to find out whether we cannot provide for human reason safe passage between these two cliffs, assign to it determinate bounds, and yet keep open for it the entire realm of its appropriate activity.

The only thing that I still want to do before we start is to *explicate the categories:* they are concepts of an object as such whereby the object's intuition is regarded as *determined* in terms of one of the *logical functions* in judging. Thus the function of the *categorical* judgment—e.g., All bodies are divisible—is that of the relation of subject to predicate. But the understanding's merely logical use left undetermined to which of the two concepts we want to give the function of the subject, and to which the function of the predicate. For we can also say, Something divisible is a body. If, on the other hand, I bring the concept of a body under the category of substance, then through this category is determined the fact that the body's empirical

B129

intuition in experience must be considered always as subject only, never as mere predicate. And similarly in all the remaining categories.

Deduction of the Pure Concepts of Understanding

Section II
[Second Edition]
Transcendental Deduction of the Pure Concepts of Understanding

§ 15
ON THE POSSIBILITY OF A COMBINATION AS SUCH

The [uncombined] manifold of presentations can be given in an intuition that is merely sensible, i.e., nothing but receptivity; and the form of this intuition can lie a priori in our power of presentation without being anything but the way in which the subject is affected. But a manifold's *combination (coniunctio)* as such can never come to us through B130 the senses; nor, therefore, can it already be part of what is contained in the pure form of sensible intuition. For this combination is an act of spontaneity by the power of presentation; and this power must be called understanding, in order to be distinguished from sensibility. Hence all combination is an act of understanding—whether or not we become conscious of such combination; whether it is a combination of the manifold of intuition or of the manifold of various concepts; and whether, in the case of intuition, it is a combination of sensible or of nonsensible intuition. I would assign to this act of understanding the general name *synthesis*, in order to point out at the same time: that we cannot present anything as combined in the object without ourselves' having combined it beforehand; and that, among all presentations, *combination* is the only one that cannot be given through objects, but— being an act of the subject's self-activity —can be performed only by the subject himself. We readily become aware here that this act of synthesis must originally be a single act and must hold equally for all combination; and that resolution or *analysis*, which seems to be its opposite, yet always presupposes it. For where the understanding has not beforehand combined anything, there it also cannot resolve anything, because only *through the understanding* could the power of presentation have been given something as combined.

But the concept of combination carries with it, besides the concept of the manifold and of its synthesis, also the concept of the manifold's unity. Combination is presentation of the *synthetic* unity of the manifold. Hence the presentation of this unity cannot arise from the combination; rather, by being added to the presentation of the manifold, it makes possible the concept of combination in the first place. This unity, which thus precedes a priori all concepts of combination, is by no means the category of unity mentioned earlier (in § 10). For all categories are based on logical functions occurring in judgments; but in these functions combination, and hence unity of given concepts, is already thought. Hence a category already presupposes combination. We must therefore search for this unity (which is qualitative unity; see § 12)[9] still higher up, viz., in what itself contains the basis for the unity of different concepts in judgments, and hence contains the basis for the possibility of understanding, even as used logically.

B131

§ 16
ON THE ORIGINAL SYNTHETIC UNITY
OF APPERCEPTION

The *I think* must be *capable* of accompanying all my presentations. For otherwise something would be presented to me that could not be thought at all—which is equivalent to saying that the presentation either would be impossible, or at least would be nothing to me. Presentation that can be given prior to all thought is called *intuition*. Hence everything manifold in intuition has a necessary reference to the *I think* in the same subject in whom this manifold is found. But this presentation [i.e., the *I think*] is an act of spontaneity; i.e., it cannot be regarded as belonging to sensibility. I call it *pure apperception*, in order to distinguish it from *empirical* apperception. Or, again, I call it *original apperception;* for it is the self-consciousness which, because it produces the presentation *I think* that must be capable of accompanying all other presentations[,] and [because it] is one and the same in all consciousness, cannot be accompanied by any further presentation. I also call the *unity* of this apperception the *transcendental* unity

B132

---

9. [This section has not been included in this abridgment.]

of self-consciousness, in order to indicate that a priori cognition can be obtained from it. For the manifold presentations given in a certain intuition would not one and all be *my* presentations, if they did not one and all belong to one self-consciousness. I.e., as my presentations (even if I am not conscious of them as being mine), they surely must conform necessarily to the condition under which alone they
B133 *can* stand together in one universal self-consciousness, since otherwise they would not thoroughly belong to me. And from this original combination much can be inferred.

This same thoroughgoing identity of the apperception of a manifold given in intuition contains a synthesis of presentations, and is possible only through the consciousness of this synthesis. For the empirical consciousness that accompanies different presentations is intrinsically sporadic and without any reference to the subject's identity. Hence this reference comes about not through my merely accompanying each presentation with consciousness, but through my *adding* one presentation to another and being conscious of their synthesis. Hence only because I can combine a manifold of given presentations *in one consciousness,* is it possible for me to present the *identity itself of the consciousness in these presentations.* I.e., the *analytic*
B134 unity of apperception is possible only under the presupposition of some *synthetic* unity of apperception. The thought that these presentations given in intuition belong one and all to me is, accordingly, tantamount to the thought that I unite them, or at least can unite them, in one self-consciousness. And although that thought itself is not yet the consciousness of the *synthesis* of the presentations, it still presupposes the possibility of that synthesis. I.e., only because I can comprise the manifold of the presentations in one consciousness, do I call them one and all *my* presentations. For otherwise I would have a self as many-colored and varied as I have presentations that I am conscious of. Hence synthetic unity of the manifold of intuitions, as given a priori, is the basis of the identity itself of apperception, which precedes a priori all *my* determinate thought. But combination does not lie in objects, and can by no means be borrowed from
B135 them by perception and thus be taken up only then into the understanding. It is, rather, solely something performed by the understanding; and understanding itself is nothing more than the power to combine a priori and to bring the manifold of given intuitions under the unity of apperception—the principle of this unity being the supreme principle in all of human cognition.

Now, it is true that this principle of the necessary unity of apperception is itself merely an identical and hence an analytic proposition. Yet it does declare as necessary a synthesis of the manifold given in an intuition, a synthesis without which that thoroughgoing identity of self-consciousness cannot be thought. For through the I, as simple presentation, nothing manifold is given; only in intuition, which is distinct from this presentation, can a manifold be given, and only through *combination* can it be thought in one consciousness. An understanding wherein through self-consciousness alone everything manifold would at the same time be given would be an understanding that *intuits*. Our understanding can only *think*, and must seek intuition in the senses. I am, then, conscious of the self as identical, as regards the manifold of the presentations given to me in an intuition, because I call them one and all *my* presentations that make up *one* presentation. That, however, is tantamount to saying that I am conscious of a necessary a priori synthesis of them. This synthesis is called the original synthetic unity of apperception. All presentations given to me are subject to this unity; but they must also be brought under it through a synthesis. B136

§ 17
THE PRINCIPLE OF THE SYNTHETIC UNITY OF APPERCEPTION IS THE SUPREME PRINCIPLE FOR ALL USE OF THE UNDERSTANDING

The supreme principle for the possibility of all intuition in reference to sensibility was, according to the Transcendental Aesthetic, that everything manifold in intuition is subject to the formal conditions of space and time. The supreme principle for the possibility of all intuition in reference to understanding is that everything manifold in intuition is subject to conditions of the original synthetic unity of apperception.[10] All manifold presentations of intuition are subject to the first principle insofar as they are *given* to us. They are subject to the second principle insofar as they must be capable of being B137

---

10. Space and time, and all their parts, are *intuitions;* hence they, with the manifold that they contain, are singular presentations. (See the Transcendental Aesthetic). Hence space and time are not mere concepts, through which the very same consciousness is encountered as contained in many presentations. They are, rather, [presentations through which] many presentations are encountered

combined in one consciousness. For without that combination, nothing can be thought or cognized through such presentations, because the given presentations do then not have in common the act of apperception, *I think*, and thus would not be collated in one self-consciousness.

Understanding—speaking generally—is the power of *cognitions*. Cognitions consist in determinate reference of given presentations to an object. And an *object* is that in whose concept the manifold of a given intuition is *united*. But all unification of presentations requires that there be unity of consciousness in the synthesis of them. Consequently the reference of presentations to an object consists solely in this unity of consciousness, and hence so does their objective validity and consequently their becoming cognitions. On this unity, consequently, rests the very possibility of the understanding.

Hence the principle of the original *synthetic* unity of apperception is the primary pure cognition of understanding, on which the entire remaining use of the understanding is based; and this cognition is at the same time entirely independent of all conditions of sensible intuition. Thus the mere form of outer sensible intuition, i.e., space, is as yet no cognition at all; it provides only the manifold of a priori intuition for a possible cognition. Rather, in order to cognize something or other—e.g., a line—in space, I must *draw* it; and hence I must bring about synthetically a determinate combination of the given manifold, so that the unity of this act is at the same time the unity of consciousness (in the concept of a line), and so that an object (a determinate space) is thereby first cognized. The synthetic unity of consciousness is, therefore, an objective condition of all cognition. Not only do I myself need this condition in order to cognize an object, but every intuition must be subject to it *in order to become an object for me*. For otherwise, and without that synthesis, the manifold would *not* unite in one consciousness.

Although this last proposition makes the synthetic unity [of consciousness] a condition of all thought, it is—as I have said—itself analytic. For it says no more than that all *my* presentations in some given intuition must be subject to the condition under which alone I

B138

---

as contained in one presentation and in the consciousness thereof, and hence [they are presentations] encountered as composite; and consequently the unity of this consciousness is encountered as *synthetic,* but yet as original. This *singularity* of [intuition] is important in its application. (See § 25.)

can ascribe them—as my presentations—to the identical self, and hence under which alone I can collate them, as combined synthetically in one apperception, through the universal expression *I think*.

On the other hand, this principle is not one for every possible understanding as such, but is a principle only for that [kind of] understanding through whose pure apperception, in the presentation *I think*, nothing manifold whatever is yet given. An alternative [kind of] understanding would be that understanding through whose self-consciousness the manifold of intuition would at the same time be B139 given—i.e., an understanding through whose presentation the objects of this presentation would at the same time exist. Such an understanding would not require, for the unity of consciousness, a special act of synthesis of the manifold. The human understanding, which merely thinks but does not intuit, does need that synthesis. But still, for the human understanding the principle is unavoidably the first principle. And thus our understanding cannot even frame the slightest concept of a different possible understanding—whether of an understanding that itself would intuit; or of an understanding that would indeed have lying at its basis a sensible intuition, yet one of a different kind from that in space and time.

§ 18
WHAT OBJECTIVE UNITY OF
SELF-CONSCIOUSNESS IS

The *transcendental unity* of apperception is the unity whereby everything manifold given in an intuition is united in a concept of the object. Hence this unity is called *objective*, and must be distinguished from *subjective* unity of consciousness, which is a *determination of inner sense* whereby that manifold of intuition for such [objective] combination is given empirically. Whether I can be conscious *empirically* of the manifold as simultaneous or as sequential depends on circumstances or empirical conditions. Hence empirical unity of B140 consciousness, through association of presentations, itself concerns an appearance and is entirely contingent. On the other hand, the pure form of intuition in time, merely as intuition as such containing a given manifold, is subject to the original unity of consciousness. It is subject to that unity solely through the necessary reference of the manifold of intuition to the one [self], i.e., to the *I think*, and hence through the understanding's pure synthesis that lies a priori at the basis of the empirical synthesis. Only the original unity of consciousness is valid objectively. The empirical unity of apperception, which we are not examining here and which moreover is only derived from the original unity under given conditions *in concreto,* has only subjective validity. One person will link the presentation of a certain word with one thing, another with some other thing; and the unity of consciousness in what is empirical is not, as regards what is given, necessary and universally valid.

§ 19
THE LOGICAL FORM OF ALL JUDGMENTS CONSISTS IN THE OBJECTIVE UNITY OF APPERCEPTION OF THE CONCEPTS CONTAINED IN THEM

I have never been able to settle for the explication that logicians give of a judgment as such. A judgment, they say, is the presentation of a relation between two concepts. Now, I shall not here quarrel with them about one respect in which this explication is defective (although this oversight has given rise to many irksome consequences for logic): viz., that it fits at most *categorical* judgments only, but not hypothetical and disjunctive ones (since these contain a relation not of concepts but of further judgments). I shall point out only that this explication of a judgment leaves undetermined wherein this *relation* consists.

But suppose that I inquire more precisely into the [relation or] reference of given cognitions in every judgment, and that I distinguish it, as belonging to the understanding, from the relation in terms of laws of the reproductive imagination (a relation that has only subjective validity). I then find that a judgment is nothing but a way of bringing given cognitions to the objective unity of apperception. This is what the little relational word *is* in judgments intends [to indicate], in order to distinguish the objective unity of given presentations from the subjective one. For this word indicates the reference of the presentations to original apperception and its *necessary unity.* The reference to this necessary unity is there even if the judgment itself is empirical and hence contingent—e.g., Bodies are heavy. By this I do not mean that these presentations belong *necessarily to one another* in the empirical intuition. Rather, I mean that they belong to one another *by virtue of the necessary unity* of apperception in the synthesis of intuitions; i.e., they belong to one another according to

B141

B142

principles of the objective determination of all presentations insofar
as these presentations can become cognition—all of these principles
being derived from the principle of the transcendental unity of apperception. Only through this [reference to original apperception
and its necessary unity] does this relation [among presentations] become a *judgment*, i.e., a relation that is *valid objectively* and can be
distinguished adequately from a relation of the same presentations
that would have only subjective validity—e.g., a relation according
to laws of association. According to these laws, all I could say is:
When I support a body, then I feel a pressure of heaviness. I could
not say: It, the body, is heavy—which amounts to saying that these
two presentations are not merely together in perception (no matter
how often repeated), but are combined in the object, i.e., combined
independently of what the subject's state is.

§ 20

ALL SENSIBLE INTUITIONS ARE SUBJECT TO THE CATEGORIES, WHICH ARE CONDITIONS UNDER WHICH ALONE THEIR MANIFOLD CAN COME TOGETHER IN ONE CONSCIOUSNESS

B143

The manifold given [which is found] in a sensible intuition is subject
necessarily to the original synthetic unity of apperception; for solely
through this unity is the *unity* of intuition possible. (§ 17.) But the act
of understanding whereby the manifold of given presentations
(whether intuitions or concepts) are brought under one apperception
as such is the logical function of judgments. (§ 19.) Therefore everything manifold, insofar as it is given in one empirical intuition, is *determined* in regard to one of the logical functions of judging, inasmuch
as through this function it is brought to one consciousness as such.
The *categories*, however, are indeed nothing but precisely these functions of judging insofar as the manifold of a given intuition is determined in regard to them. (§ 13.) Hence, by the same token, the manifold in a given intuition is subject necessarily to the categories.

§ 21

COMMENT

B144

Through the synthesis of understanding, a manifold contained in an
intuition that I call mine is presented as belonging to the *necessary*

unity of self-consciousness, and this presenting is done by means of the category.[11] Hence the category indicates that the empirical consciousness of a given manifold of one intuition is just as subject to a pure a priori self-consciousness, as empirical intuition is subject to a pure sensible intuition that likewise takes place a priori. Hence in the above proposition I have made the beginning of a *deduction* of the pure concepts of understanding. Since the categories are *independent of sensibility* and arise in the understanding alone, I must still abstract, in this deduction, from the way in which the manifold for an empirical intuition is given, in order to take account solely of the unity that the understanding contributes to the intuition by means of the category. Afterwards (§ 26) I shall show, from the way in which

B145 the empirical intuition is given in sensibility, that the intuition's unity is none other than the unity that (by § 20, above) the category prescribes to the manifold of a given intuition as such; and that hence by my explaining the category's a priori validity regarding all objects of our senses, the deduction's aim will first be fully attained.

From one point, however, I could not abstract in the above proof: viz., from the fact that the manifold for the intuition must be given still prior to the understanding's synthesis, and independently of it; but how it is given remains undetermined here. For if I were to think of an understanding that itself intuited (as, e.g., a divine understanding that did not present given objects but through whose presentation the objects would at the same time be given or produced), then in regard to such cognition the categories would have no signification whatever. The categories are only rules for an understanding whose

B146 entire power consists in thought, i.e., in the act of bringing to the unity of apperception the synthesis of the manifold that has, in intuition, been given to it from elsewhere. Hence such an understanding by itself cognizes nothing whatever, but only combines and orders the material for cognition, i.e., the intuition, which must be given to it by the object. But why our understanding has this peculiarity, that it a priori brings about unity of apperception only by means of the categories, and only by just this kind and number of them—for this no further reason can be given, just as no reason can be given as to why we have

---

11. The basis of the proof for this rests on the presented *unity of intuition,* through which an *object* is given. This unity always implies a synthesis of the manifold given for an intuition and already contains this manifold given's reference to the unity of apperception.

just these and no other functions in judging, or why time and space are the only forms of our possible intuition.

§ 22
A Category Cannot Be Used for Cognizing Things Except When It Is Applied to Objects of Experience

Thinking an object and *cognizing* an object are, then, not the same. For cognition involves two components: first, the concept (the category), through which an object as such is thought; and second, the intuition, through which the object is given. For if no intuition corresponding to the concept could be given at all, then in terms of its form the concept would indeed be a thought; but it would be a thought without any object, and no cognition at all of any thing whatsoever would be possible by means of it. For as far as I would know, there would be nothing, and could be nothing, to which my thought could be applied. Now, all intuition that is possible for us is sensible (see the Transcendental Aesthetic). Hence in us, thinking an object as such by means of a pure concept of understanding can become cognition only insofar as this concept is referred to objects of the senses. Sensible intuition is either pure intuition (space and time) or empirical intuition of what, through sensation, is presented directly as actual in space and time. By determining pure intuition we can (in mathematics) acquire a priori cognition of objects as appearances, but only in terms of their form; that, however, still leaves unestablished whether there can be things that must be intuited in this form. Consequently all mathematical concepts are, by themselves, no cognitions—except insofar as one presupposes that there are things that can be exhibited to us only in accordance with the form of that pure sensible intuition. But *things in space and time* are given only insofar as they are perceptions (i.e., presentations accompanied by sensation), and hence are given only through empirical presentation. Consequently the pure concepts of understanding, even when they are (as in mathematics) applied to a priori intuitions, provide cognition only insofar as these intuitions—and hence, by means of them, also the concepts of understanding—can be applied to empirical intuitions. Consequently the categories also do not supply us, by means of intuition, with any cognition of things, except through their possible application to *empirical* intuition. I.e., the

B147

B148

categories serve only for the possibility of *empirical cognition*. Such cognition, however, is called *experience*. Consequently the categories cannot be used for cognizing things except insofar as these things are taken as objects of possible experience.

§ 23

The last proposition above is of the greatest importance. For it determines the bounds for the use of the pure concepts of understanding in regard to objects just as much as the Transcendental Aesthetic determined the bounds for the use of the pure form of our sensible intuition. Space and time, as conditions for the possibility as to how objects can be given to us, hold no further than for objects of the senses, and hence hold for objects of experience only. Beyond these bounds, space and time present nothing whatsoever; for they are only in the senses and have no actuality apart from them. The pure concepts of understanding are free from this limitation and extend to objects of intuition as such, whether this intuition is similar to ours or not, as long as it is sensible rather than intellectual. But this further extension of the concepts beyond *our* sensible intuition is of no benefit to us whatsoever. For they are then empty concepts of objects, i.e., concepts through which we cannot judge at all whether or not these objects are so much as possible. I.e., the pure concepts of understanding are then mere forms of thought, without objective reality; for we then have available no intuition to which the synthetic B149   unity of apperception—which is all that those concepts contain— could be applied so that the concepts could determine an object. Solely *our* sensible and empirical intuition can provide them with meaning and significance.

Hence if we suppose an object of a *nonsensible* intuition as given, then we can indeed present it through all the predicates that are already contained in the presupposition *that the object has as a property nothing belonging to sensible intuition:* hence we can present that it is not extended or in space, that its duration is not a time, that no change (i.e., succession of determinations in time) is to be found in it, etc. But yet I have no proper cognition if I merely indicate how the intuition of the object *is not*, without being able to say what the intuition does contain. For I have not then presented the possibility of there being an object for my pure concept of understanding, since I was unable to give an intuition corresponding to the concept, but was able only to say that our intuition does not hold for it. However, the foremost point here is that to such a something not even one single category could be applied. E.g., one could not apply to it the concept of a substance, i.e., the concept of something that can exist as subject but never as mere predicate. For I do not know at all, concerning this concept, whether there can be anything whatever corresponding to this conceptual determination [of substance], unless empirical intuition gives me the instance for applying it. But more about this later.

§ 24
ON APPLYING THE CATEGORIES TO OBJECTS OF THE SENSES AS SUCH

B150

The pure concepts of understanding refer, through mere understanding, to objects of intuition as such—i.e., we leave undetermined whether this intuition is ours or some other, although it must be sensible intuition. But the concepts are, precisely because of this, mere *forms of thought*, through which as yet no determinate object is cognized. We saw that the synthesis or combination of the manifold in them referred merely to the unity of apperception, and was thereby the basis for the possibility of a priori cognition insofar as such cognition rests on the understanding; and hence this synthesis was not just transcendental but was also purely intellectual only. But there lies at the basis in us a priori a certain form of sensible intuition, a form that is based on the receptivity of our capacity to present (i.e., based on our sensibility). Hence the understanding (as spontaneity) can, by means of the manifold of given presentations, determine inner sense in accordance with the synthetic unity of apperception; and thus it can think synthetic unity of the apperception of the manifold of a priori *sensible intuition*—this unity being the condition to which all objects of our (i.e., human) intuition must necessarily be subject. And thereby the categories, as themselves mere forms of thought, acquire objective reality. I.e., they acquire B151 application to objects that can be given to us in intuition. But they apply to these objects only as appearances; for only of appearances are we capable of having a priori intuition.

This *synthesis* of the manifold of sensible intuition, which is a priori possible and necessary, may be called *figurative* synthesis *(synthesis speciosa)*. This serves to distinguish it from the synthesis that would be thought, in the mere category, in regard to the manifold of an intuition as such; this latter synthesis is called combination of understanding *(synthesis intellectualis)*. Both these syntheses are *transcendental*, not just because they themselves proceed a priori, but because they also are the basis for the possibility of other a priori cognition.

However, when the figurative synthesis concerns merely the original synthetic unity of apperception, i.e., merely this transcendental unity thought in the categories, then it must be called the *transcendental synthesis of imagination*, to distinguish it from the merely intellectual combination. **Imagination** is the power of presenting an object in intuition even *without the object's being present*. Now, all our intuition is sensible; and hence the imagination, because of the subjective condition under which alone it can give to the concepts of understanding a corresponding intuition, belongs to *sensibility*. Yet the
B152 synthesis of imagination is an exercise of spontaneity, which is determinative, rather than merely determinable, as is sense; hence this synthesis can a priori determine sense in terms of its form in accordance with the unity of apperception. To this extent, therefore, the imagination is a power of determining sensibility a priori; and its synthesis of intuitions *in accordance with the categories* must be the transcendental synthesis of *imagination*. This synthesis is an action of the understanding upon sensibility, and is the understanding's first application (and at the same time the basis of all its other applications) to objects of the intuition that is possible for us. As figurative, this synthesis is distinct from the intellectual synthesis, which proceeds without any imagination but merely through understanding. Now insofar as the imagination is spontaneity, I sometimes also call it the *productive* imagination, thereby distinguishing it from the *reproductive* imagination. The synthesis of the reproductive imagination is subject solely to empirical laws, viz., to the laws of association. Therefore this synthesis contributes nothing to the explanation of the possibility of a priori cognition, and hence belongs not in transcendental philosophy but in psychology. [...]

B157

§ 25

By contrast, in the transcendental synthesis of the manifold of presentations as such, and hence in the synthetic original unity of apperception, I am not conscious of myself as I appear to myself, nor as

I am in myself, but am conscious only that I am. This *presentation* is a *thought*, not an *intuition*. Now *cognition* of ourselves requires not only the act of thought that brings the manifold of every possible intuition to the unity of apperception, but requires in addition a definite kind of intuition whereby this manifold is given. Hence although my own existence is not appearance (still less mere illusion), determination of my existence[12] can occur only in conformity with the form of inner sense and according to the particular way in which the manifold that I combine is given in inner intuition. Accordingly I have no *cognition* of myself as I am but merely cognition of how I appear to myself. Hence consciousness of oneself is far from being a cognition of oneself, regardless of all the categories, which make up the thought of an *object as such* through the combination of the manifold in one apperception. We saw that in order for me to cognize an object different from myself, I not only require the thinking (which I have in the category) of an object as such, but do also require an intuition whereby I determine that universal concept. In the same way, in order to cognize myself, too, I not only require the consciousness of myself or the fact that I think myself, but require also an intuition of the manifold in me whereby I determine this thought. And I exist as an intelligence. This intelligence is conscious solely of its power of combination. But as regards the manifold that it is to combine, this intelligence is subjected to a limiting condition (which it calls inner sense). As subjected to this condition, it can make that combination intuitable only in terms of time relations, which lie wholly outside the concepts of understanding, properly so called. And hence this intelligence can still cognize itself only as, in regard to an intuition

B158

B159

---

12. The *I think* expresses the act of determining my existence. Hence the existence [of myself] is already given through this *I think;* but there is not yet given through it the way in which I am to determine that existence, i.e., posit the manifold belonging to it. In order for that manifold to be given, self-intuition is required; and at the basis of this self-intuition lies a form given a priori, viz., time, which is sensible and belongs to the ability to receive the determinable. Now unless I have in addition a different self-intuition that gives, prior to the act of *determination*, the *determinative* in me (only of its spontaneity am I in fact conscious) just as *time* so gives the determinable, then I cannot determine my existence as that of a self-active being; instead I present only the spontaneity of my thought, i.e., of the [act of] determination, and my existence remains determinable always only sensibly, i.e., as the existence of an appearance. But it is on account of this spontaneity that I call myself an *intelligence*.

(one that cannot be intellectual and given by the understanding itself), it merely appears to itself; it cannot cognize itself as it would if its *intuition* were intellectual.

§ 26
TRANSCENDENTAL DEDUCTION OF THE UNIVERSALLY POSSIBLE USE IN EXPERIENCE OF THE PURE CONCEPTS OF UNDERSTANDING

In the *metaphysical deduction* we established the a priori origin of the categories as such through their complete concurrence with the universal logical functions of thought. But in the *transcendental deduction* we exhibited the possibility of them as a priori cognitions of objects of an intuition as such (§§ 20, 21). We must now explain how it is possible, through *categories,* to cognize a priori whatever objects *our senses may encounter*—to so cognize them as regards not the form of their intuition, but the laws of their combination—and hence, as it B160 were, to prescribe laws to nature, and even to make nature possible. For without this suitability of the categories, one would fail to see how everything that our senses may encounter would have to be subject to the laws that arise a priori from the understanding alone.

First of all, let me point out that by *synthesis of apprehension* I mean that combination of the manifold in an empirical intuition whereby perception, i.e., empirical consciousness of the intuition (as appearance), becomes possible.

We have a priori, in the presentations of space and time, *forms* of both outer and inner sensible intuition; and to these forms the synthesis of apprehension of the manifold of appearance must always conform, because that synthesis itself can take place only according to this form. But space and time are presented a priori not merely as *forms* of sensible intuition, but as themselves *intuitions* (containing a manifold), and hence are presented with the determination of the B161 *unity* of this manifold in them (see the Transcendental Aesthetic).[13]

---

13. Space, presented as *object* (as we are actually required to present it in geometry), contains more than the mere form of intuition; namely, it also contains *combination* of the manifold given according to the form of sensibility into an *intuitive* presentation—so that the *form of intuition* gives us merely a manifold, but *formal intuition* gives us unity of presentation. In the Transcendental Aesthetic I had merely included this unity with sensibility, wanting only to point out that it

Therefore even *unity of synthesis* of the manifold outside or within us, and hence also a *combination* to which everything that is to be presented determinately in space or time must conform, is already given a priori as condition of the synthesis of all *apprehension*—given along with (not in) these intuitions. This synthetic unity, however, can be none other than the unity of the combination, conforming to the categories but applied to our *sensible intuition*, of the manifold of a given *intuition as such* in an original consciousness. Consequently all synthesis, the synthesis through which even perception becomes possible, is subject to the categories; and since experience is cognition through connected perceptions, the categories are conditions of the possibility of experience and hence hold a priori also for all objects of experience.

Hence, e.g., when I turn the empirical intuition of a house into a   B162
perception by apprehending the intuition's manifold, then in this apprehension I use as a basis the *necessary unity* of space and of outer sensible intuition as such; and I draw, as it were, the house's shape in conformity with this synthetic unity of the manifold in space. But this same unity, if I abstract from the form of space, resides in the understanding, and is the category of the synthesis of the homogeneous in an intuition as such, i.e., the category of *magnitude*. Hence the synthesis of apprehension, i.e., perception, must conform throughout to that category.[14]

When (to take a different example) I perceive the freezing of water, then I apprehend two states (fluidity and solidity) as states that stand to each other in a relation of time. Since the appearance is   B163

---

precedes any concept. But in fact this unity presupposes a synthesis; this synthesis does not belong to the senses, but through it do all concepts of space and time first become possible. For through this unity (inasmuch as understanding determines sensibility) space or time are first *given* as intuitions, and hence the unity of this a priori intuition belongs to space and time, and not to the concept of understanding (see § 24).

14. In this way we prove that the synthesis of apprehension, which is empirical, must conform necessarily to the synthesis of apperception, which is intellectual and is contained wholly a priori in the category. The spontaneity that brings combination into the manifold of intuition is one and the same in the two cases: in apprehension it does so under the name of power of imagination; in apperception it does so under the name of understanding.

inner *intuition,* I lay time at its basis. But in time I necessarily present synthetic *unity* of the manifold; without this unity, that relation could not be given *determinately* (as regards time sequence) in an intuition. However, this synthetic unity, as a priori condition under which I combine the manifold of an *intuition as such,* is—if I abstract from the constant form of *my* inner intuition, i.e., from time—the category of *cause;* through this category, when I apply it to my sensibility, *everything that happens is, in terms of its relation, determined* by me *in time as such.* Therefore apprehension in such an event, and hence the event itself, is subject—as regards possible perception—to the concept of the *relation of effects and causes;* and thus it is in all other cases.

Categories are concepts that prescribe laws a priori to appearances, and hence to nature regarded as the sum of all appearances *(natura materialiter spectata).* And now this question arises: Since the categories are not derived from nature and do not conform to it as their model (for then they would be merely empirical), how are we to comprehend the fact that nature must conform to the categories, i.e., how can the categories determine a priori the combination of nature's manifold without gleaning that combination from nature? Here now is the solution of this puzzle.

B164   How it is that the laws of appearances in nature must agree with the understanding and its a priori form, i.e., with the understanding's power to combine the manifold as such, is not any stranger than how it is that appearances themselves must agree with the form of a priori sensible intuition. For just as appearances exist not in themselves but only relatively to the subject in whom the appearances inhere insofar as the subject has senses, so the laws exist not in the appearances but only relatively to that same being insofar as that being has understanding. Things in themselves would have their law-governedness necessarily, even apart from an understanding that cognizes them. But appearances are only presentations of things that exist uncognized as regards what they may be in themselves. As mere appearances, however, they are subject to no law of connection whatever except the one prescribed by the connecting power. Now what connects the manifold of sensible intuition is imagination; and imagination depends on understanding as regards the unity of its intellectual synthesis, and on sensibility as regards the manifoldness of apprehension. Now all possible perception depends on this synthesis of

apprehension; but it itself, this empirical synthesis, depends on transcendental synthesis and hence on the categories. Therefore all possible perceptions, and hence also everything whatever that can reach   B165
empirical consciousness, i.e., all appearances of nature, must in regard
to their combination be subject to the categories. Nature (regarded
merely as nature as such) depends (as *natura formaliter spectata*) on
the categories as the original basis of its necessary law-governedness.
But even the pure power of understanding does not suffice for pre-
scribing a priori to appearances, through mere categories, more laws
than those underlying a *nature as such* considered as law-governedness
of appearances in space and time. Particular laws, because they concern appearances that are determined empirically, are *not derivable
completely* from those laws, although the particular laws are one and
all subject to the categories. Experience must be added in order for us
to become acquainted with particular laws *at all;* but the a priori laws
alone give us information about experience as such and about what
can be cognized as an object of that experience.

§27
RESULT OF THIS DEDUCTION OF THE
CONCEPTS OF UNDERSTANDING

We cannot *think* an object except through categories; we cannot *cognize* an object thought by us except through intuitions corresponding to those concepts. Now all our intuitions are sensible, and this   B166
[sensible] cognition is empirical insofar as its object is given. Empirical cognition, however, is experience. *Consequently no cognition is
possible for us a priori except solely of objects of possible experience.*[15]
   But this cognition, which is limited to just objects of experience, is
not therefore all taken from experience. Rather, as far as pure intuitions

---

15. In order to keep my readers from being troubled prematurely by the worri-
some detrimental consequences of this proposition, let me just remind them
that in our *thinking* the categories are not limited by the conditions of our sensible intuition, but have an unbounded realm. Intuition is required only for *cognizing* what we think, i.e., only for determining the object. Thus if intuition is
lacking, the thought of the object can otherwise still have its true and useful consequences for the subject's *use of reason.* But because the use of reason is not always directed to the determination of the object and hence to cognition, but is
sometimes directed also to the determination of the subject and his volition, it
cannot yet be set forth here.

as well as pure concepts of understanding are concerned, they are elements of cognition that are found in us a priori. Now, there are only two ways in which one can conceive of a *necessary* agreement of experience with the concepts of its objects: either experience makes B167 these concepts possible, or these concepts make experience possible. The first alternative is not what happens as regards the categories (nor as regards pure sensible intuition). For they are a priori concepts and hence are independent of experience. (To assert that their origin is empirical would be to assert a kind of *generatio aequivoca*). There remains, consequently, only the second alternative (a system of *epigenesis*, as it were, of pure reason): viz., that the categories contain the bases, on the part of the understanding, of the possibility of all experience as such. But as to how the categories make experience possible, and as to what principles of the possibility of experience they provide us with when applied to appearances, more information will be given in the following chapter on the transcendental use of our power of judgment.

Someone might want to propose, in addition to the two sole ways mentioned above, a middle course between them: viz., that the categories are neither *self-thought* a priori first principles of our cognition, nor again are drawn from experience, but are subjective predispositions for thinking that are implanted in us [and given to us] simultaneously with our existence; and that they were so arranged by our originator that their use harmonizes exactly with the laws of nature governing the course of experience (this theory would be a kind of *preformation system* of pure reason). If such a middle course were B168 proposed, the following would decide against it (apart from the fact that with such a hypothesis one can see no end to how far the presupposition of predetermined predispositions to future judgments might be carried): viz., that the categories would in that case lack the *necessity* which belongs essentially to the concept of them. For, the concept of cause, e.g., which asserts the necessity of a result under a presupposed condition, would be false if it rested only on an arbitrary subjective necessity, implanted in us, to link certain empirical presentations according to such a rule of relation. I could then not say that the effect is connected with the cause in the object (i.e., connected with it necessarily), but could say only that I am so equipped that I cannot think this presentation otherwise than as thus connected. And this is just what the skeptic most longs [to hear]. For then all our insight, achieved through the supposed objective validity of our judgments, is nothing but sheer illusion; and there would also be no lack of people who would not concede this subjective necessity (which must be felt) in themselves. At the very least one could not quarrel with anyone about something that rests merely on the way in which his [self as] subject is organized.

Brief Sketch of This Deduction

This deduction is the exhibition of the pure concepts of understanding (and, with them, of all theoretical a priori cognition) as principles of the possibility of experience; the exhibition of these principles, however, as the *determination* of appearances in space and time *as such;* and the exhibition, finally, of this determination as arising from the *original* synthetic unity of apperception, this unity being the form of understanding as referred to space and time, the original forms of sensibility. [...]

B169

TRANSCENDENTAL ANALYTIC

BOOK II
ANALYTIC OF PRINCIPLES

[...] [T]his *transcendental doctrine of the power of judgment* will comprise two chapters. The *first* chapter deals with the sensible condition under which alone pure concepts of understanding can be used, i.e., with the schematism of pure understanding. The *second* chapter deals with the synthetic judgments that under these conditions emanate a priori from pure concepts of understanding and that lie a priori at the basis of all other cognitions; i.e., it deals with the principles of pure understanding.

TRANSCENDENTAL DOCTRINE OF THE POWER OF JUDGMENT
(OR ANALYTIC OF PRINCIPLES)

Chapter I
On the Schematism of the Pure Concepts of Understanding

Whenever an object is subsumed under a concept, the presentation of the object must be *homogeneous* with the concept; i.e., the concept must contain what is presented in the object that is to be subsumed under it. For this is precisely what we mean by the expression that an object is contained *under* a concept. Thus the empirical concept of a *plate* is homogeneous with the pure geometrical concept of a *circle*, inasmuch as the roundness thought in the concept of the plate can be intuited [also] in the circle.

Pure concepts of understanding, on the other hand, are quite heterogeneous from empirical intuitions (indeed, from sensible intuitions generally) and can never be encountered in any intuition. How, then, can an intuition be *subsumed* under a category, and hence how can a category be *applied* to appearances—since surely no one will say that a category (e.g., causality) can also be intuited through senses and is contained in appearances? Now this question, natural and important as it is, is in fact the cause that necessitates a transcendental doctrine of the power of judgment. The doctrine is needed, viz., in order to show how it is possible for *pure concepts of understanding* to be applied to appearances as such. In all the other sciences no such need arises. For there the concepts through which the object is thought in a universal way are not so distinct and heterogeneous from the concepts presenting the object *in concreto,* as it is given. And hence there is no need there to provide a special exposition concerning the application of the first kind of concept to the second kind.

A138/B177

Now clearly there must be something that is third, something that must be homogeneous with the category, on the one hand, and with the appearance, on the other hand, and that thus makes possible the application of the category to the appearance. This mediating presentation must be pure (i.e., without anything empirical), and yet must be both *intellectual,* on the one hand, and *sensible,* on the other hand. Such a presentation is the *transcendental schema.*

A concept of understanding contains pure synthetic unity of the manifold as such. Time, as the formal condition for the manifold of inner sense and hence for the connection of all presentations, contains an a priori manifold in pure intuition. Now, a transcendental time determination is homogeneous with the *category* (in which its unity consists) insofar as the time determination is *universal* and rests on an a priori rule. But it is homogeneous with *appearance,* on the other hand, insofar as every empirical presentation of the manifold contains *time.* Hence it will be possible for the category to be applied to appearances by means of the transcendental time determination, which, as the schema of the concepts of understanding, mediates the subsumption of appearances under the category.

A139/B178

In view of what has been shown in the deduction of the categories, I hope that no one will have doubts in deciding this question: whether these pure concepts of understanding have a merely empirical use [only] or also a transcendental one; i.e., whether, as conditions of a possible experience, they refer a priori solely to appearances; or whether they can be extended, as conditions for the possibility of things as such, to objects in themselves (without any restriction to our sensibility). For we saw in the deduction that concepts are quite

impossible, and cannot have any signification, unless an object is given for the concepts themselves or at least for the elements of which they consist; and that hence they cannot at all concern things in themselves (i.e., [things considered] without regard to whether
B179   and how they may be given to us). We saw, moreover, that the only way in which objects can be given to us is by modification of our sen-
A140   sibility; and, finally, that pure a priori concepts, besides containing the function of understanding implicit in the category, must also a priori contain formal conditions of sensibility (of inner sense, specif- ically), viz., conditions comprising the universal condition under which alone the category can be applied to any object. Let us call this formal and pure condition of sensibility, to which the concept of understanding is restricted in its use, the *schema* of this concept of un- derstanding; and let us call the understanding's procedure with these schemata the *schematism* of pure understanding.

A schema is, in itself, always only a product of the imagination. Yet, because here the imagination's synthesis aims not at an individ- ual intuition but at unity in the determination of sensibility, a schema must be distinguished from an image. Thus if I put five dots after one another, like this, ... , then this result is an image of the number five. Suppose, on the other hand, that I only think a number as such, which might then be five or a hundred. Then my thought is more the presentation of a method for presenting—in accordance with a certain concept—a multitude (e.g., a thousand) in an image, than this image itself. Indeed, in the case of a thousand I could hardly survey that image and compare it with the concept. Now, this
B180   presentation of a universal procedure of the imagination for provid- ing a concept with its image I call the schema for that concept.

In fact, it is schemata, not images of objects, that lie at the basis of
A141   our pure sensible concepts. No image whatever of a triangle would ever be adequate to the concept of a triangle as such. For it would never reach the concept's universality that makes the concept hold for all triangles (whether right-angled or oblique-angled, etc.), but would always be limited to only a part of this sphere. The schema of the triangle can never exist anywhere but in thoughts, and is a rule for the synthesis of imagination regarding pure shapes in space. Even less is an object of experience or an image thereof ever adequate to the empirical concept; rather, that concept always refers directly to the schema of imagination, this schema being a rule for determining our intuition in accordance with such and such a general concept.

The concept *dog* signifies a rule whereby my imagination can trace the shape of such a four-footed animal in a general way, i.e., without being limited to any single and particular shape offered to me by experience, or even to all possible images that I can exhibit *in concreto*. This schematism of our understanding, i.e., its schematism regarding appearances and their mere form, is a secret art residing in the depths of the human soul, an art whose true stratagems we shall hardly ever divine from nature and lay bare before ourselves. Only this much can we say: The *image* is [here] a product of the productive imagination's empirical ability. A *schema* of sensible concepts (such as the concepts of figures in space) is a product and, as it were, a monogram of the pure a priori imagination through which, and according to which, images become possible in the first place. But the images must always be connected with the concept only by means of the schema that they designate; in themselves the images are never completely congruent with the concept. A schema of a pure concept of understanding, on the other hand, is something that one cannot bring to any image whatsoever. Such a schema is, rather, only the pure synthesis conforming to a rule, expressed by the category, of unity according to concepts as such. It is a transcendental product of the imagination which concerns the determination of inner sense as such, according to conditions of that sense's form (viz., time), in regard to all presentations insofar as these are to cohere a priori, in conformity with the unity of apperception, in one concept.

B181

A142

Now, instead of letting ourselves be detained by a dry and tedious dissection of what is required for transcendental schemata of pure concepts of understanding as such, let us exhibit them, rather, according to the order of the categories and in connection with them.

The pure image of all magnitudes *(quanta)* for outer sense is space, whereas the pure image of the magnitudes of all sense objects as such is time. But the *pure schema of magnitude (quantitas)* taken as a [pure] concept of understanding is *number,* which is a presentation encompassing conjointly the successive addition of one item to another (homogeneous item). Therefore number is nothing other than the unity in the synthesis of the manifold of a homogeneous intuition as such, a unity that arises because I myself produce time in apprehending the intuition.

B182

A143

Reality, in the pure concept of understanding, is what corresponds to a sensation as such. Therefore reality is that whose very concept indicates a being [of something] (in time); and negation is that whose concept presents a not-being (in time). Hence the contrast of reality and negation is made by distinguishing the same time as either a filled or an empty time. Now, time is only the form of intuition, and hence only the form of objects as appearances; therefore what in these objects corresponds to sensation is the transcendental matter of all objects as things in their own right (i.e., their thinghood, reality). Now every sensation has a degree or magnitude whereby it can, in regard to the same presentation of an object, fill the same time—

B183 i.e., [form of] inner sense—more or fill it less, down to where the sensation ceases in nothingness (= 0 = *negatio*). Hence there is a relation and coherence, or rather a transition from reality to negation, which is responsible for every reality's being presented as a quantum. And the schema of a reality taken as the quantity of something insofar as it fills time is precisely this continuous and uniform production of that reality in time, where from a sensation having a certain degree we descend, in time, until the sensation vanishes, or ascend gradually from the sensation's negation to its [actual] magnitude.

A144   The schema of substance is permanence of the real in time; i.e., it is the presentation of the real as a substratum of empirical time determination as such, a substratum which therefore endures while all else varies. (Time is not in transition; rather, the existence of what is mutable is in transition in time. Hence to time, which itself is immutable and enduring, there corresponds in [the realm of] appearance what is immutable in existence, i.e., substance; and only by reference to substance can succession and simultaneity of appearances be determined in terms of time.)

    The schema of the cause and of the causality of a thing as such is the real upon which, whenever it is posited, something else always follows. Hence this schema consists in the manifold's succession insofar as this is subject to a rule.

    The schema of community (interaction), or [i.e.] of the reciprocal causality of substances in regard to their accidents, is the simultane-

B184 ity, according to a universal rule, of the determinations of the one substance with those of the other.

    The schema of possibility is the harmony of the synthesis of different presentations with the conditions of time as such. (Thus, e.g., what is opposite cannot be in a thing simultaneously, but can be in it only sequentially.) Hence this schema is the determination, at some time, of the presentation of a thing.

The schema of actuality is existence within a determinate time.   A145
The schema of necessity is the existence of an object at all time.

Now from all of this we see that the schema of each category contains, and is responsible for the presentation of, the following: the schema of magnitude, the production (synthesis) of time itself in the successive apprehension of an object; the schema of quality, the synthesis of sensation (perception) with the presentation of time—or, i.e., the filling of time; the schema of relation, the relation of perceptions among one another at all time (i.e., according to a rule of time determination); finally, the schema of modality and of its categories, time itself as the correlate of the determination of an object as to whether and how it belongs to time. Hence the schemata are nothing but a priori *time determinations* according to rules; and these rules, according to the order of the categories, deal with the *time series*, the   B185
time content, the *time order*, and finally *the time sum total* in regard to all possible objects.

Now, this shows that the schematism of understanding provided by the transcendental synthesis of imagination comes down to nothing other than the unity in inner sense of all the manifold of intuition, and thus comes down indirectly to the unity of apperception as a function corresponding to inner sense (a receptivity). The schemata   A146
of the pure concepts of understanding are, therefore, the true and sole conditions for providing these concepts with a reference to objects and hence with *signification*. And hence the categories have, in the end, no other use than a possible empirical one. For, by [being] bases of a unity that is a priori necessary (because of the necessary union of all consciousness in an original apperception), they serve merely to subject appearances to universal rules of synthesis, and thus to make them fit for thoroughgoing connection in one experience.

In the whole of all possible experience, however, lie all our cognitions; and the transcendental truth that precedes all empirical truth and makes it possible consists in the universal reference to this possible experience.

Yet it is obvious also that although the schemata of sensibility are what first realize the categories, they do nonetheless also restrict   B186
them, i.e., they limit them to conditions lying outside understanding (viz., in sensibility). Hence a schema is, properly speaking, only the phenomenon of an object, or the sensible concept of an object, in harmony with the category. (Numerus *est quantitas phaenomenon*,

sensatio *realitas phaenomenon*, constans et perdurabile rerum *substan-*
A147 *tia phaenomenon*, aeternitas *necessitas phaenomenon*, etc.) Now, it
seems that if we omit a restricting condition from a previously limited concept, then we amplify that concept. Thus it was supposed
that the categories in their pure signification—i.e., apart from all
conditions of sensibility—hold for things as such, *as they are*, instead
of the categories' having schemata that present these things only *as
they appear;* and hence it was supposed that the categories have a signification that is independent of all schemata and that extends much
farther than they do. The concepts of understanding do in fact retain
a signification, even after their separation from all sensible conditions. But this is only a logical signification, [where the concepts of
understanding signify] the mere unity of presentations. But these
concepts are then given no object, and hence also no signification
that could yield a concept of the object. Thus, e.g., [the concept of]
substance, if one omitted from it the sensible determination of permanence, would signify nothing more than something that can be
thought as a subject (i.e., thought without being thought as a predi-
B187 cate of something else). Now, this is a presentation that I cannot turn
into anything, because it does not at all indicate to me what determinations are possessed by the thing that is to count as such a primary
subject. Without schemata, therefore, the categories are only functions of the understanding for producing concepts, but they present
no object. This latter signification they get from sensibility, which
realizes the understanding while at the same time restricting it.

TRANSCENDENTAL DOCTRINE OF THE POWER OF JUDGMENT (OR ANALYTIC OF PRINCIPLES)

A148

Chapter II
System of All Principles of Pure Understanding

In the preceding chapter we examined the transcendental power of
judgment solely in terms of the universal conditions under which

alone it is entitled to use the pure concepts of understanding for making synthetic judgments. Our task now is to exhibit as systematically linked the judgments that the understanding, under this critical provision, actually brings about a priori. The natural and safe guidance for this task must doubtless be given to us by our table of categories. For precisely in the categories' reference to possible experience must all pure a priori cognition of understanding consist; and hence the categories' relation to sensibility as such will display, completely and in a system, all the transcendental principles for the use of understanding. B188

Now, first, a priori principles are so named not merely because they contain the bases of other judgments, but also because they themselves are not based on higher and more universal cognitions. Yet having this property does not always exempt such principles from requiring a proof. Such a proof could, to be sure, no longer be conducted objectively; [any a priori principle] lies, rather, at the basis of all cognition of its object. This does not, however, preclude the possibility of creating a proof that starts from the subjective sources underlying the possibility of cognizing an object as such. Nor, indeed, does it preclude that creation of such a proof is needed; for otherwise the proposition would still be under the greatest suspicion of being an assertion obtained merely surreptitiously. A149

Second, we shall limit ourselves to just those principles that refer to the categories. Hence the principles of the Transcendental Aesthetic, whereby space and time are the conditions of the possibility of all things as appearances, and likewise the restriction of those principles, viz., that they cannot be used in reference to things in themselves, do not belong within our allotted realm of inquiry. Mathematical principles, similarly, form no part of this system. For they are drawn only from intuition, not from the pure concept of understanding. Yet because they are nonetheless synthetic a priori judgments, their possibility also will necessarily be considered here. We must include their possibility here, not indeed in order to prove that they are correct and apodeictically certain—a proof that they do not require at all—but only in order to make comprehensible, and to deduce, the possibility of such evident a priori cognitions. [...] B189

System of All Principles of Pure Understanding

Section II
On the Supreme Principle of All Synthetic Judgments

Explaining the possibility of synthetic judgments is a problem with which general logic has nothing whatever to do; indeed, general logic need not even know the problem's name. But in a transcendental logic this explanation is the most important task of all—even the sole task, if we are talking about the possibility of synthetic judgments that are a priori, as well as about the conditions and the range of their validity. For after completing this task, transcendental logic is able to fulfill perfectly its purpose, viz., to determine the range and the bounds of pure understanding.

In an analytic judgment I keep to the given concept, in order to establish something about it. If the judgment is to be affirmative, then I ascribe to that concept only what was already thought in it; if the judgment is to be negative, then I exclude from the concept only its opposite. In synthetic judgments, however, I am to go outside the given concept, in order to consider, in relation with this concept, something quite different from what was thought in it. Hence this
relation is never a relation either of identity or of contradiction, so that by looking at the judgment taken by itself one cannot tell that it is true, or that it is erroneous.

If it is granted, then, that one must go outside a given concept in order to compare it synthetically with another concept, then something third is needed wherein alone the synthesis of two concepts can arise. But what, then, is this third something that is the medium of all synthetic judgments? There is only one sum total that contains all our presentations: viz., inner sense, and its a priori form, time. Moreover, the synthesis of presentations rests on imagination; but their synthetic unity (which is required for a judgment) rests on the unity of apperception. Hence the possibility of synthetic judgments will have to be sought therein; and since all three contain the sources for a priori presentations, the possibility of pure synthetic judgments will also have to be sought in them. Indeed, these judgments will even necessarily be founded on these three bases, if a cognition of objects is to come about that rests solely on the synthesis of presentations.

If a cognition is to have objective reality, i.e., if it is to refer to an object and have in that object its signification and meaning, then the object must be capable of being *given* in some way. For otherwise the concepts are empty; and though we have thought by means of them, we have in fact cognized nothing through this thinking, but have merely played with presentations. To be given an object—if this is not again to mean to be given it only indirectly, but is to mean, rather, to exhibit it directly in intuition—is nothing other than to refer the presentation of the object to experience (whether actual, or at least possible, experience). Even space and time, however pure these concepts are of anything empirical, and however certain it is that they are presented in the mind completely a priori, would yet be without objective validity, and without meaning and signification, if we did not show that their use with objects of experience is necessary. Indeed, the presentation of space and time is a mere schema that always refers to the reproductive imagination, this imagination summoning the objects of experience without which they would have no signification. And thus it is, without distinction, with all concepts whatsoever.

Hence the *possibility of experience* is what provides all our a priori cognitions with objective reality. Now experience rests on the synthetic unity of appearances, i.e., on a synthesis performed according to concepts of an object as such of appearances. Without such synthesis, experience would not even be cognition, but would be a rhapsody of perceptions. Such a rhapsody of perceptions would not fit together in any context conforming to rules of a thoroughly connected (possible) consciousness, and hence would also not fit together to agree with the transcendental and necessary unity of apperception. Hence at the basis of experience there lie, a priori, principles of its form. These principles are universal rules of unity in the synthesis of appearances; and the objective reality of these rules as necessary conditions can always be shown in experience—indeed, even in the possibility of experience. Without this reference, however, synthetic propositions are entirely impossible a priori. For they have then no third something, viz., no object in which the synthetic unity can establish the objective reality of their concepts.

Hence very much concerning space as such, or concerning the shapes traced in it by the productive imagination, is indeed cognized

B195

A156

B196
A157

by us a priori in synthetic judgments, so that for this cognition we actually require no experience at all. Yet to cognize all this would be nothing—but would be to deal with a mere chimera—if space did not have to be regarded as a condition of the appearances which amount to the material for outer experience. Hence those pure synthetic judgments refer—although only indirectly—to possible experience, or rather to the very possibility of experience, and on this reference alone do they base the objective validity of their synthesis.

Therefore experience, as empirical synthesis, is in [regard to] its possibility the only kind of cognition that provides reality to all other synthesis. By the same token, this latter synthesis, as a priori cognition, has truth (agreement with the object) only because it contains nothing more than what is necessary for synthetic unity of experience as such.

Hence the supreme principle of all synthetic judgments is this: Every object is subject to the conditions necessary for synthetic unity of the manifold of intuition in a possible experience.

Thus synthetic judgments are possible a priori if we refer the formal conditions of a priori intuition, the synthesis of imagination, and the necessary unity of this synthesis in a transcendental apperception to a possible experiential cognition as such, and if we then say that the conditions for the *possibility of experience* as such are simultaneously conditions for the *possibility of objects of experience* and hence have objective validity in a synthetic a priori judgment.

The System of the Principles of Pure Understanding

Section III

Systematic Presentation of All the Synthetic Principles of Pure Understanding

The fact that principles occur anywhere at all is attributable solely to pure understanding. For pure understanding not only is our power of rules regarding what happens, but is itself the source of principles, the source according to which everything (whatever we can encounter as an object) is necessarily subject to rules. For without rules there could never be for appearances any cognition of an object corresponding to them. Even natural laws, when considered as principles of understanding's empirical use, carry with them at the same time an expression of necessity, and hence at least the presumption of their being determined from bases that are valid a priori and prior to all experience. But all laws of nature, without distinction, fall under higher principles of understanding, inasmuch as they only apply these higher principles to particular cases of appearance. Hence these higher principles alone provide us with the concept that contains the condition and, as it were, the exponent for a rule as such; but experience provides us with the case that falls under the rule.

There can in fact be no danger, I suppose, that anyone will regard merely empirical principles as principles of pure understanding—or vice versa, for that matter. For this confusion can easily be prevented by attending to the necessity according to concepts that distinguishes the principles of pure understanding, and whose lack is easily perceived in every empirical proposition—no matter how generally such a proposition may hold. But there are pure a priori principles as well that I nonetheless do not wish to assign to pure understanding as belonging to it. For whereas understanding is our power of concepts, these principles are not drawn from pure concepts, but are drawn (even if by means of understanding) from pure intuitions. In mathematics there are such principles; but their application to experience, and hence their objective validity, still rests always on pure understanding—indeed, so does the possibility of such synthetic a priori cognition (i.e., the deduction of this possibility).   A160/ B199

Hence I shall not include among my principles the principles of mathematics themselves. But I shall indeed include the principles on which their possibility and objective validity is based a priori, and which must therefore be regarded as the principles [underlying] those mathematical principles. They do not emanate from intuition and proceed to concepts, but emanate from concepts and proceed to intuition.

When pure concepts of understanding are applied to possible experience, then the use of their synthesis is either *mathematical* or *dynamical*. For this application is concerned in part merely with the *intuition*, and in part with the *existence*, of an appearance as such. However, whereas the a priori conditions of intuition are thoroughly necessary in regard to a possible experience, those of the existence of the objects of a possible empirical intuition are in themselves only contingent. Hence the principles of the mathematical use will be unconditionally necessary, i.e., apodeictic. But as for those of the dynamical use, while they also carry with them the character of an a priori necessity, they do so only under the condition of there being

B200 empirical thought in an experience, and hence they do so only mediately and indirectly. They consequently lack (though without detriment to the certainty they have universally in reference to experience)

A161 that immediate evidence possessed by the former kind of principles. This, however, we shall be better able to judge at the conclusion of this system of principles.

The quite natural instruction for setting up the table of principles is provided to us by the table of categories. For these principles are nothing but the rules for the objective use of the categories. Accordingly, the following are all the principles of pure understanding.

1
Axioms
of intuition

2
Anticipations
of perception

3
Analogies
of experience

4
Postulates
of empirical thought as such

I have selected these names with care, in order not to leave unnoted the differences regarding the evidence and the employment of these

B201 principles. But we shall soon find that, in regard both to evidence and to a priori determination of appearances, the principles of the

A162 categories of *magnitude* and *quality* (if we attend solely to the form of these) do differ markedly from the remaining principles. For although both kinds of principles are capable of a complete certainty, in the former kind this certainty is intuitive but in the latter merely discursive. Hence I shall call the former kind the *mathematical* and the latter the *dynamical* principles. But we must note carefully that I do not have in mind here the principles of mathematics in the one case, any more than the principles of general (physical) dynamics in the other. I have in mind, rather, only the principles of pure understanding as related to inner sense (apart from any distinction of the

B202 presentations given in that sense). It is in fact through these latter

principles that the principles of mathematics and of general dynamics acquire, one and all, their possibility. Hence I name my principles
mathematical and dynamical more in view of their application than
for the sake of their content. I shall now proceed to examine them in
the same order as they are presented in the above table.

1. AXIOMS OF INTUITION

Their principle is: *All intuitions are extensive magnitudes.*

Proof

Appearances contain, as regards their form, an intuition in space and
time that underlies them, one and all, a priori. Hence they cannot be
apprehended, i.e., taken up into empirical consciousness, except
through the synthesis of the manifold whereby the presentations of a
determinate space or time are produced. I.e., appearances can be apprehended only through the assembly of what is homogeneous and   B203
the consciousness of the synthetic unity of this manifold (this manifold homogeneous). Now the consciousness of the synthetic unity of
the manifold homogeneous in intuition as such, insofar as through
this consciousness the presentation of an object first becomes possible, is the concept of a magnitude *(quantum)*. Therefore even the perception [itself] of an object as appearance is possible only through
the same synthetic unity (of the given sensible intuition's manifold)
whereby the unity of the assembly of the manifold homogeneous is
thought in the concept of a *magnitude*. I.e., appearances are, one and
all, magnitudes—specifically, *extensive magnitudes,* because as intuitions in space or time they must be presented through the same synthesis whereby space and time as such are determined.

Extensive is what I call a magnitude wherein the presentation of
the parts makes possible (and hence necessarily precedes) the presentation of the whole. I can present no line, no matter how small,   A163
without drawing it in thought, i.e., without producing from one
point onward all the parts little by little and thereby tracing this intuition in the first place. And the situation is the same with every time,
even the smallest. In any such time I think only the successive progression from one instant to the next, where through all the parts of
time and their addition a determinate time magnitude is finally produced. Since what is mere intuition in all appearances is either space
or time, every appearance is—as intuition—an extensive magnitude,   B204

inasmuch as it can be cognized only through successive synthesis (of part to part) in apprehension. Accordingly, all appearances are intuited already as aggregates (i.e., multitudes of previously given parts); precisely this is not the case with every kind of magnitudes, but is the case only with those that are presented and apprehended by us as magnitudes *extensively.*

This successive synthesis of the productive imagination in the generation of shapes is the basis of the mathematics of extension (i.e., geometry) with its axioms. These axioms express the conditions of sensible a priori intuition under which alone the schema of a pure concept of outer appearance can come about—e.g., the axioms that between two points only one straight line is possible; or that two straight lines enclose no space; etc. These are the axioms that, properly speaking, concern only magnitudes *(quanta)*, as such.

But as concerns magnitude *(quantitas)*, i.e., the answer to the
A164   question as to how large something is, there are for it no axioms in the proper meaning of the term, although a variety of such propositions are synthetic and directly certain *(indemonstrabilia).* For the propositions which assert that equals added to—or subtracted
B205   from—equals yield equals are analytic propositions, inasmuch as I am directly conscious of the identity of the one magnitude's production with the other magnitude's production. Axioms, however, are to be synthetic a priori propositions. The evident propositions of numerical relations, on the other hand, are indeed synthetic. Yet, unlike those of geometry, they are not universal; and precisely because of this, they also cannot be called axioms, but can be called only numerical formulas. The proposition that 7 + 5 = 12 is not an analytic proposition. For neither in the presentation of 7, nor in that of 5, nor in the presentation of the assembly of the two numbers do I think the number 12. (The fact that I ought to think the number 12 in *adding the two numbers* is not at issue here; for in an analytic proposition the question is only whether I actually think the predicate in the presentation of the subject.) But although the proposition 7 + 5 = 12 is synthetic, it is still only a singular proposition. For insofar as we here take account merely of the synthesis of the homogeneous (i.e., the units), the synthesis can here occur in only a single way, although the *use* made of these numbers afterwards is universal. [Geometry is different in this respect.] If I say that by means of three lines, two of which taken together are greater than the third, a
A165   triangle can be drawn, then I have here the mere function of the

productive imagination, which can make the lines be drawn greater or smaller, and can similarly make them meet at all kinds of angles chosen at will. By contrast, the number 7 is possible in only a single way, and so is the number 12, which is produced through the syn- B206 thesis of 7 with 5. Such propositions, therefore, must be called not axioms (for otherwise there would be infinitely many axioms), but numerical formulas.

This transcendental principle of the mathematics of appearances greatly expands our a priori cognition. For it alone is what makes pure mathematics in all its precision applicable to objects of experience. In the absence of the principle, this applicability might not be so self-evident, and has in fact been contested by many. For appearances are not things in themselves. Empirical intuition is possible only through pure intuition (of space and time). Hence what geometry says about pure intuition holds incontestably for empirical intuition also. And the subterfuges whereby objects of the senses need not conform to the rules of construction in space (e.g., the rule of the infinite divisibility of lines or angles) must be dropped. For by making them one denies objective validity to space, and thereby also to all mathematics, and one no longer knows why and how far mathe- A166 matics is applicable to appearances. The synthesis of spaces and times, which are the essential form of all intuition, is what also makes possible the apprehension of appearance, hence makes possible any outer experience, and consequently also makes possible all cognition of the objects of this experience. And thus what mathematics in its pure use proves for that synthesis holds necessarily also for this cognition. All objections against this are only the chicanery of a falsely B207 instructed reason: a reason that erroneously means to detach objects of the senses from the formal condition of our sensibility, and that despite their being mere appearances presents them as objects in themselves, given to the understanding. If that were the case, however, then there could be no synthetic a priori cognition of them at all, and hence also no such cognition through pure concepts of space; and the science that determines these concepts, viz., geometry, would itself not be possible.

2. Anticipations of Perception

Their principle is: *In all appearances the real that is an object of sensation has intensive magnitude,* i.e., a degree.

Proof

Perception is empirical consciousness, i.e., a consciousness in which there is sensation as well. Appearances, as objects of perception, are not pure (i.e., merely formal) intuitions, as space and time are (for these cannot in themselves be perceived at all). Hence appearances contain, in addition to [pure] intuition, the matter (through which something existent is presented in space or time) for some object as such. I.e., appearances contain also the real of sensation—sensation being merely subjective presentation, concerning which we can be-

B208 come conscious only of the fact that the subject is affected, and which we refer to an object as such. Now from empirical consciousness to pure consciousness, i.e., to the point where the real of that consciousness entirely vanishes and there remains a merely formal (a priori) consciousness of the manifold in space and time, a stepwise change is possible. Hence there is likewise possible a synthesis in the production of a sensation's magnitude, from the sensation's beginning, i.e., from pure intuition, $= 0$, up to this or that magnitude of the sensation. Now since sensation is in itself not at all an objective presentation, and since neither the intuition of space nor that of time is to be met with in it, sensation will indeed not have an extensive magnitude. Yet it will have a magnitude (viz., by virtue of the apprehension in sensation, in which the empirical consciousness can in a certain time increase from nothing, $= 0$, to the sensation's given measure). Therefore sensation will have an *intensive magnitude*. As corresponding to this intensive magnitude of sensation we must ascribe also to all objects of perception, insofar as perception contains sensation, an *intensive magnitude*, i.e., a degree of influence on sense.

All cognition whereby I can cognize and determine a priori what belongs to empirical cognition may be called an anticipation; and

A167 this is doubtless the signification in which Epicurus used the term πρόληψις. But there is something in appearances that is never cognized a priori and that hence amounts to the proper difference be-

B209 tween empirical and a priori cognition: viz., sensation (as the matter of perception); and hence it follows that what cannot at all be anticipated is, properly speaking, sensation. The pure determinations in space and time regarding both shape and magnitude, on the other hand, could be called anticipations of appearances; for they present a priori what may always be given a posteriori in experience. Suppose, however, that we do find something that is cognizable a priori in every sensation, as sensation as such (i.e., even though no particular sensation may be given); this something would, then, deserve to be called anticipation—in an exceptional meaning of the term. For it seems strange to say that we can anticipate experience in what concerns, of all things, its matter, which can be drawn only from experience. Yet such is actually the case here.

Apprehension merely by means of sensation (i.e., if I do not consider the succession of many sensations) fills only an instant. Hence [sensation], as something contained in appearance whose apprehension is not a successive synthesis proceeding from parts to the whole presentation, has no extensive magnitude; a lack of sensation at that same instant would present that instant as empty, and hence as = 0. A168 Now what in empirical intuition corresponds to sensation is reality *(realitas phaenomenon)*; what corresponds to the lack of sensation is negation, = 0. However, every sensation is capable of diminution, so B210 that it can decrease and thus gradually vanish. Hence between reality contained in appearance, on the one hand, and negation, on the other hand, there is a continuous coherence of many possible intermediate sensations, whose difference from one another is always smaller than the difference between the given sensation and zero, i.e., complete negation. In other words, the real contained in appearance has always a magnitude. But [this magnitude is not an extensive one], which is not to be met with in [such] apprehension; for apprehension by means of mere sensation occurs in an instant rather than through successive synthesis of many sensations, and hence does not proceed from the parts to the whole. Hence the real does indeed have a magnitude, but not an extensive one.

Now a magnitude that is apprehended only as unity, and in which multiplicity can be presented only by approaching [from the given magnitude] toward negation, = 0, I call an *intensive magnitude*. Hence any reality contained in appearance has intensive magnitude, i.e., a degree. And if this reality is considered as cause (whether of the sensation, or of other reality contained in appearance, e.g., a change), then the degree of the reality considered as cause is called a moment—e.g., the moment of gravity. It is called this because the degree desig- A169 nates only that magnitude whose apprehension is not successive but instantaneous. But here I touch on this only in passing, because for now I am not yet dealing with causality.

Therefore every sensation, and hence also every reality contained B211 in appearance, no matter how small either may be, has a degree, i.e., an intensive magnitude. This magnitude can always be lessened, and between reality and negation there is a continuous coherence of possible realities and of possible smaller perceptions. Every color, e.g., red color, has a degree that, no matter how small it may be, is never the smallest; and this is the situation throughout—with heat, with the moment of gravity, etc.

The property of magnitudes whereby no part in them is the smallest possible (i.e., no part is simple) is called their continuity. Space and time are *quanta continua*, because no part of them can be given without our enclosing it between boundaries (points or instants); and hence any part of them can be given only in such a way that this part itself is in turn a space or a time. Therefore space consists only of spaces, time only of times. Points and instants are only boundaries, i.e., mere positions limiting them. But positions always presuppose the intuitions that they are to delimit or determine; and neither space nor time can be assembled from mere positions if these are considered as components that could be given even prior to space or time. Such magnitudes may also be called *flowing* magnitudes, because the synthesis (of productive imagination) in their production is a progression in time, and the continuity especially of time is usually designated by the term flowing (flowing by).

A170

B212

Hence all appearances as such are continuous magnitudes—both in terms of their intuition, viz., as extensive magnitudes, and in terms of their mere perception (sensation, and hence reality), viz., as intensive magnitudes. If the synthesis of the manifold of appearance is interrupted, then this manifold is an aggregate of many appearances and is not, properly speaking, appearance as a quantum. Such an aggregate is not produced by merely continuing the productive synthesis of a certain kind, but is produced by repeating a synthesis that always ceases again. If I call 13 thalers a quantum of money, then I do so correctly insofar as I mean by this the [total] content of one mark of fine silver. For this mark is indeed a continuous magnitude, in which no part is the smallest but each part could constitute a coin that always contained material for still smaller coins. But if by that designation I mean 13 round thalers, as so many coins (whatever their silver content might be), then my calling this a quantum of thalers is inappropriate. I must call it, rather, an aggregate, i.e., a number of coins. But since with any number there must still be underlying unity, appearance as unity is a quantum, and as such is always a continuum.

A171

We saw that all appearances, considered extensively as well as intensively, are continuous magnitudes. If this is so, then the proposition that all change (a thing's transition from one state to another) is likewise continuous could be proved here easily and with mathematical self-evidence, were it not that the causality of a change as such lies wholly outside the bounds of a transcendental philosophy and presupposes empirical principles. For the understanding does not at all disclose to us a priori the possibility of a cause that changes the state of any things, i.e., determines them to enter the opposite of a certain given state. The understanding fails to do so not merely because it has no insight whatever into that possibility (indeed, we lack such insight in several a priori cognitions), but because changeability concerns only certain determinations of appearances, viz., those that experience alone can teach us, while only their cause is to be found in the unchangeable. Here, however, we have nothing available for our use except the pure basic concepts of all possible experience, among which there must be nothing empirical whatsoever. Hence we cannot, without violating the unity of the system, anticipate general natural science, which is built upon certain basic experiences.

Yet we have no lack of documentation for our principle's great influence in anticipating perceptions, and even in compensating for their lack insofar as the principle blocks all wrong inferences that might be drawn from that lack.

For we saw that all reality in perception has a degree between which and negation there is an infinite stepwise sequence of ever lesser degrees, and that every sense must likewise have a definite degree in the receptivity of sensations. But if this is so, then no perception and hence also no experience is possible that would prove, whether directly or indirectly (by whatever circuitous path in the inference), a complete lack in appearance of anything real. I.e., one can never obtain from experience a proof of empty space or of an empty time. For, first, the complete lack of the real in sensible intuition cannot itself be perceived. Second, this lack cannot be inferred from even a single appearance and from the difference in its reality, nor must it ever be assumed in order to explain that intuition. For suppose even that the whole intuition of a determinate space or time is real through and through, i.e., that no part of it is empty. Still, every reality has its degree, which can decrease to nothing (i.e., emptiness) by infinitely many steps, with the extensive magnitude of the appearance being unchanged. And hence there must be infinitely many different degrees with which space and time may be [wholly] filled; and it must be possible for the intensive magnitude in different appearances to be smaller or greater even with the extensive magnitude of the intuition being the same.

B215   Let us give an example of this. Natural scientists perceive (partly by the moment of gravity or weight, partly by the moment of resistance to other matter in motion) that the quantity of matter of various kinds differs greatly even with the volume being the same. Almost all natural scientists, when perceiving this, infer from it unanimously that in all kinds of matter this volume (i.e., extensive magnitude of the appearance) must—even if in varying measure—be empty. But to whom would it ever have occurred that these investigators of nature, who are for the most part mathematical and mechanical [in orientation], would base this inference of theirs solely on a metaphysical presupposition—which presuppositions, after all, they claim to avoid so very much? For they assume that the real in space (I do not want to call it impenetrability or weight here, because these are empirical concepts) is *everywhere uniform* and can differ only in extensive magnitude, i.e., in amount. This supposition, for which they could not have had a basis in experience and which is therefore merely metaphysical, I oppose with a transcendental proof. This

A174   proof, to be sure, is not meant to explain the difference in the filling of spaces. Yet it does completely annul the supposed necessity of that presupposition whereby the difference in question can be explained only by assuming empty spaces. And thus the proof has at least the merit of giving to the understanding the freedom to think this differ-

B216   ence in another way also—should explaining nature necessitate some other hypothesis to account for this difference. For we then see that although equal spaces may be filled completely by various kinds of matter, so that in none of them there is a point where no matter can be found to be present, yet everything real has, with its quality being the same, its degree (of resistance or weight); and this degree can—without any lessening of the extensive magnitude, or amount—be smaller *ad infinitum* before the real passes into emptiness and vanishes. Thus something that spreads and fills a space, as, e.g., heat, and likewise any other reality (contained in appearance), can decrease in its degree *ad infinitum* without leaving even the smallest part of this space in the least empty, and can nonetheless fill this space just as well with these smaller degrees as another appearance can with greater degrees. I do not by any means intend to assert here

that this is actually how kinds of matter differ in their specific gravity. Rather, I intend only to establish, from a principle of pure understanding, that the nature of our perceptions makes such a way of   A175
explaining possible, and that people are wrong when they assume
that the real [component] of appearance is the same in degree and
differs only in aggregation and the extensive magnitude thereof—
and when they assert this, allegedly, even a priori by means of a principle of understanding.

Nonetheless, something about this anticipation of perception is   B217
always striking to an investigator of nature who is accustomed to
transcendental deliberation and has thus become cautious. For the
anticipation arouses some concern about the claim that the understanding can anticipate a synthetic proposition such as this—i.e., a
synthetic proposition about the degree of everything real in appearances, and hence about the possibility of there being in sensation itself, if we abstract from its empirical quality, an intrinsic difference.
And hence there remains a question not unworthy of solution: viz.,
how the understanding can a priori make in this matter a synthetic
pronouncement about appearances, and how it can thus anticipate
appearances in what is strictly and merely empirical, i.e., in what
concerns sensation.

The *quality* of sensation (e.g., colors, taste, etc.) is always merely
empirical and cannot at all be presented a priori. But the real—as
opposed to negation, $= 0$ —that corresponds to sensation as such
presents only something whose concept itself contains a being [of
something], and signifies nothing but the synthesis in an empirical   A176
consciousness as such. For empirical consciousness can in inner
sense be raised from 0 to any higher degree, so that the same extensive magnitude of intuition (e.g., an illuminated surface) arouses as
great a sensation as does an aggregate of much else (that is less illuminated) taken together. We can, therefore, abstract entirely from   B218
the extensive magnitude of appearance, and can yet present in mere
sensation in one moment a synthesis of uniform ascent from 0 to the
given empirical consciousness. Hence although all sensations, as
such, are given only a posteriori, their property of having a degree
can be cognized a priori. It is remarkable that in magnitudes as such
we can cognize a priori only a single *quality*, viz., continuity, and that
in all quality (the real [component] of appearances) we can cognize a
priori nothing more than their having an intensive *quantity*, viz., the
fact that they have a degree; everything else is left to experience.

3. ANALOGIES OF EXPERIENCE

Their principle is: *Experience is possible only through the presentation of a necessary connection of perceptions.*

Proof

Experience is an empirical cognition, i.e., a cognition that determines an object through perceptions. Hence experience is a synthesis of perceptions that itself is not contained in perception but contains the synthetic unity of the manifold of perceptions in one B219 consciousness. This unity amounts to what is essential for a cognition of *objects* of the senses, i.e., for experience (rather than merely intuition or sensation of the senses). Now, in experience perceptions do indeed come together only contingently, so that no necessity in their connection is, or even can be, evident from the perceptions themselves. For apprehension is only a compilation of the manifold of empirical intuition; and we find in it no presentation of the necessity of the linked existence in space and time of the appearances that it compiles. Experience, on the other hand, is a cognition of objects through perceptions; and hence in experience the relation within the manifold's existence is to be presented not as the manifold is compiled in time, but as it objectively is in time. Time, however, cannot itself be perceived. Therefore determination of the existence of objects in time can come about only through the linking of perceptions in time as such, and hence only through concepts connecting them a priori. And since these concepts always carry with them necessity as well, experience is possible only through a presentation of the necessary connection of perceptions.

A177   The three modes of time are *permanence, succession,* and *simultaneity.* Hence there will be three rules governing all time relations of appearances, whereby every appearance's existence can be determined in regard to the unity of all time; and these rules will precede experience and make it possible in the first place.

B220   The general principle of all three analogies rests on the necessary *unity* of apperception in regard to all possible empirical consciousness (i.e., perception) *at every time;* and since this unity underlies [empirical consciousness] a priori, the principle rests on the synthetic unity of all appearances as regards their relation in time. For original apperception refers to inner sense (the sum of all presentations); specifically, it refers a priori to the form of inner sense, i.e., to

the relation in time of the manifold empirical consciousness. Now all this manifold is to be united, as regards its time relations, in original apperception—for so says this apperception's a priori transcendental unity, to which is subject whatever is to belong to my (i.e., to my one) cognition and hence is to be able to become an object for me. Hence this *synthetic unity* in the time relation of all perceptions, a unity   A178
which is determined a priori, is this law: that all empirical time determinations must be subject to rules of universal time determination. And the analogies of experience that we now want to deal with must be rules of this sort.

These principles have the peculiarity that they do not consider appearances and the synthesis of their empirical intuition, but consider merely [the appearances'] *existence* and their *relation* to one another in regard to that existence. Now the way in which something is apprehended in appearance can be determined a priori in such a   B221
manner that the rule of the appearance's synthesis can also give this a priori intuition, i.e., can produce the appearance from this intuition, in the case of every empirical example that comes to hand. The *existence* of appearances, however, cannot be cognized a priori; and even if we could in that just mentioned way contrive to infer some existent or other, we could still not cognize it determinately, i.e., we could not anticipate what distinguishes this existent's empirical intuition from [that of] others.

The previous two principles, which I called the mathematical principles because they justified applying mathematics to appearances, dealt with appearances in regard to their mere possibility; and they taught us how appearances could be produced, as regards both their intuition and the real in their perception, according to rules of a mathematical synthesis. Hence in both syntheses we can use numerical magnitudes and, with them, the determination of appearance as a magnitude. Thus, e.g., I can assemble the degree of sensations of sun-   A179
light from some 200,000 illuminations provided by the moon, and can determinately give that degree a priori, i.e., construct it. Those earlier two principles may therefore be called constitutive.

The situation must be quite different with those principles that are to bring a priori under rules the existence of appearances. For   B222
since existence cannot be constructed, the principles will deal only with the relation of existence, and will be able to yield none but merely *regulative* principles. Hence finding either axioms or anticipations is here out of the question. Thus if a perception is given to us

in a time relation to other (although indeterminate) perceptions, then we shall indeed not be able to say *what* is that other perception or *how great* a perception it is; rather, we shall be able to say how, as regards its existence, this other perception is necessarily linked with the former perception in this mode of time. Analogies signify something very different in philosophy from what they represent in mathematics. In mathematics they are formulas asserting the equality of two relations of magnitudes, and are always *constitutive;* so that if three members of the proportion are given, the fourth is thereby also given, i.e., it can be constructed. In philosophy, however, an analogy

A180   is the equality not of two *quantitative* but of two *qualitative* relations. Here I can from three given members cognize, and give a priori, only the *relation* to a fourth, but not *this* fourth *member* itself. But I do have a rule for seeking the fourth member in experience, and a mark for discovering it there. Hence an analogy of experience will be only a rule whereby unity of experience is to arise from perceptions (not a rule saying how perception itself, as empirical intuition as such, is to

B223   arise). And such an analogy will hold, as principle of objects (i.e., appearances), not *constitutively* but merely *regulatively*. But the same [restriction] will apply also to the postulates of empirical thought as such, which concern at once the synthesis of mere intuition (the form of appearance), the synthesis of perception (the matter of appearance), and that of experience (the relation of these perceptions). I.e., these postulates are only regulative principles. These principles do not indeed differ in certainty from the mathematical principles, which are constitutive; for this certainty is established a priori in both. But they do differ from the mathematical principles in [not having the latter's] kind of evidence, i.e., their intuitive character (and hence their ability to be demonstrated).

But what has been pointed out for all synthetic principles, and must be noted especially here, is this: these analogies have their sole signification and validity not as principles of understanding's transcendental use, but merely as principles of its empirical use, and

A181   hence can be proved only as principles of such use; and appearances must consequently be subsumed not under the categories taken absolutely, but only under their schemata. For if the objects to which these principles are to be referred were things in themselves, then cognizing anything about them synthetically a priori would be entirely impossible. But they are indeed nothing but appearances. And the complete cognition of appearances—which is, after all, what all a priori principles must ultimately always amount to—is merely our possible experience. Hence these principles can aim at nothing more B224 than being the conditions for the unity of empirical cognition in the synthesis of appearances. This unity, however, is thought solely in the schema of the pure concept of understanding. The function, unrestricted by any sensible condition, of the unity of the schema [as such], as the unity of a synthesis as such, is contained in the category. Hence these principles will entitle us to assemble appearances only by an analogy with the logical and universal unity of concepts. And hence in the principle itself we shall indeed make use of the category; but in employing the principle (i.e., in applying it to appearances) we shall put the category's schema, as the key to its use, in the category's place—or, rather, put the schema alongside the category as a restricting condition of it called a formula of the category.

A
First Analogy   A182

Principle of the Permanence of Substance

In all variation by appearances substance is permanent, and its quantum in nature is neither increased nor decreased.

Proof

All appearances are in time; and solely in time, as substrate (viz., as permanent form of inner intuition), can either *simultaneity* or *succes-* B225 *sion* be presented. Hence time, in which all variation by appearances is to be thought, endures and does not vary. For time is that in which, and as determinations of which, sequentiality or simultaneity can alone be presented. Now, time by itself cannot be perceived. Hence the substrate which presents time as such, and in which all variation or simultaneity can in apprehension be perceived through the appearances' relation to it, must be found in the objects of perception, i.e., in the appearances. But the substrate of everything real, i.e., of everything belonging to the existence of things, is *substance*. In substance alone, and as determination, can everything belonging to existence be thought. Hence the permanent in relation to which all time relations of appearances can alone be determined is substance [contained] in appearance, i.e., the real of appearance that as substrate of all variation remains always the same. Since, therefore, substance cannot vary in its existence, its quantum in nature can also be neither increased nor decreased.

Our *apprehension* of the manifold of appearance is always successive, and therefore is always varying. Hence through apprehension alone we can never determine whether this manifold considered as object of experience is simultaneous or sequential. We cannot determine this unless something underlying in experience is there *always*—i.e., something *enduring* and *permanent* of which all variation and simultaneity are only so many ways (modes of time) in which the permanent exists. Hence all time relations (for simultaneity and succession are the only relations in time) are possible only in the permanent. I.e., the permanent is the *substratum* of the empirical presentation of time itself; all time determinations are possible only in this substratum. Permanence expresses time as such as the constant correlate of all existence of appearances, of all variation and of all concomitance. For variation concerns not time itself, but only appearances in time (just as simultaneity is not a mode of time itself; for in time no parts are simultaneous, but all are sequential). If we wished to attribute to time itself a succession or sequentiality, then we would have to think yet another time wherein this succession would be possible. Solely through the permanent does sequential *existence* in different parts of the time series acquire a *magnitude,* called *duration.* For in mere succession by itself existence is always vanishing and starting, and never has the least magnitude. Without this permanent, therefore, there is no time relation. Now time cannot in itself be perceived. Therefore this permanent in appearances is the substratum of all time determinations. Hence it is also the condition for the possibility of all synthetic unity of perceptions, i.e., the possibility of experience; and all existence and all variation in time can only be regarded, by reference to this permanent, as a mode of the existence of what is enduring and permanent. Therefore in all appearances the permanent is the object itself, i.e., the (phenomenal) substance, whereas whatever varies or can vary belongs only to the way in which this substance or these substances exist, and hence to their determinations.

I find that in all ages not just philosophers but even the common understanding have presupposed this permanence as a substratum of all variation of appearances; and they probably always assume it, moreover, as indubitable. The only difference is that the philosopher expresses himself somewhat more determinately on this point than does the common understanding, by saying that in all changes in the world *substance* endures and only the *accidents* vary. Yet nowhere do I encounter so much as an attempt to prove this quite synthetic proposition. Indeed, only seldom is the proposition placed, as surely it deserves to be, at the top of the laws of nature that are pure and hold completely a priori. The mere proposition that substance is permanent is indeed tautological. For merely because of this permanence do we apply the category of substance to appearance, and people ought to have proved that in all appearances there is in fact something permanent wherein the mutable is nothing but a determination B228 of its existence. Such a proof, however, can never be conducted dogmatically, i.e., from concepts, because it concerns a synthetic a priori proposition; and people never thought of the fact that such propositions are valid only in reference to possible experience and hence can be proved only by a deduction of the possibility of experience. It is A185 no wonder, then, that although this proposition has been laid at the basis in all experience (because in empirical cognition one *feels* the need for it), yet it has never been proved.

A philosopher was asked, How much does smoke weigh? He replied: From the weight of the burnt wood subtract the weight of the ashes that remain, and you will have the weight of the smoke. He therefore presupposed as incontestable that *matter* (substance) does not pass away even in fire, but that its *form* only undergoes an alteration. Similarly the proposition that nothing arises from nothing was only another consequence inferred from the principle of permanence, or rather from the principle of the everlasting existence of the subject proper [contained] in appearance. For if the [component] in appearance that we wish to call substance is to be the substratum proper of all time determination, then all existence in past as well as future time must be determinable solely and exclusively by reference to it. Hence we can give the name substance to an appearance only because we presuppose the existence of substance at all time. This B229 existence at all time is not even well expressed by the word permanence, since permanence applies more to future time. On the other hand, the intrinsic necessity to be permanent is linked inseparably with the necessity always to have been, and therefore the expression A186 may be allowed to remain. *Gigni de nihilo nihil, in nihilum nil posse reverti* are two propositions that were connected by the ancients as unseparated and that are now sometimes separated. They are separated, through misunderstanding, because of a conception that they concern things in themselves and that the first proposition might therefore run counter to the world's depending (even in terms of its substance) on a supreme cause. But there is no need for such worry. For we are here talking only about appearances[, which are] in the realm of experience; and the unity of experience would never be possible if we were to let new things originate (in terms of substance). For there would then no longer be what alone can present the unity of time, viz., the identity of the substratum, by reference to which alone all variation has thoroughgoing unity. On the other hand, this permanence is nothing more than our way of presenting the existence of things (in appearance).

The determinations of a substance, which are nothing but particular ways for the substance to exist, are called *accidents*. They are always real, because they concern the existence of substance. (Negations are only determinations expressing the nonexistence of something in sub-
B230 stance.) If now we attribute a special existence to this real in substance (e.g., motion, as an accident of matter), then this existence is called inherence, as distinguished from the existence of substance, which is called subsistence. From this [attribution of a differentiated existence to the real in substance], however, arise many misinterpretations; and
A187 we speak more accurately and correctly if we characterize an accident only as the way in which the existence of a substance is determined positively. Yet by virtue of the conditions of our understanding's logical use we cannot avoid separating, as it were, what can vary in a substance's existence while the substance itself endures, and examining it in relation to what is properly permanent and radical. And hence this category has indeed been put under the heading of the relations, but more as the condition of relations than as itself containing a relation.

Now this permanence is also the basis for the following correction of the concept of *change*. Arising and passing away are not changes of what arises or passes away. Change is a way of existing that ensues upon another way of existing of the same object. Hence whatever does change *endures*, and only its *state* varies. This variation, therefore, concerns only the determinations, which can cease or, for that
B231 matter, start. Hence we can say, using an expression that seems somewhat paradoxical: only the permanent (i.e., substance) undergoes change; the mutable undergoes no change but only a *variation*, since some determinations cease and others start.
A188 Hence change can be perceived only in substances; and an arising or passing away taken absolutely, i.e., without its pertaining merely

to a determination of the permanent, cannot at all be a possible perception. For precisely this permanent makes possible the presentation of the transition from one state to another, and from not-being to being; and hence these can be cognized empirically only as varying determinations of what endures. Suppose that something absolutely begins to be. If you suppose this, then you must have a point of time in which it was not. But to what will you fasten this point of time, if not to what is already there? For an empty time that would precede is not an object of perception; but if you tie this arising to things that were beforehand and that continue up to the something that arises, then this something was only a determination of what, as the permanent, was beforehand. The case is the same with passing away also; for it presupposes the empirical presentation of a time where an appearance no longer is.

Substances ([contained] in appearance) are the substrates of all time determinations. If some substances arose and others passed away, this would itself annul the sole condition of the empirical unity of time; and appearances would then refer to two different times wherein existence would be flowing by concurrently—which is absurd. For there is *only one* time, wherein all different times must be posited not as simultaneous but as sequential. B232 A189

Permanence, accordingly, is a necessary condition under which alone appearances are determinable as things or objects in a possible experience. But as to what is the empirical criterion of this necessary permanence and, with it, of the substantiality of appearances, the opportunity to make the needed comments will be provided by what follows.

B
Second Analogy

Principle of Temporal Succession According to the Law of Causality

All changes occur according to the law of the connection of cause and effect.

Proof

(The previous principle has established that all appearances [forming part] of the temporal succession are one and all only *changes;* i.e., they are a successive being and not-being of the determinations of substance, which itself is permanent. The principle has established, therefore, that there is no such thing as the being of substance B233 itself as succeeding its not-being, or its not-being as succeeding its existence; in other words, there is no such thing as the arising or passing away of substance itself. The principle could also have been expressed thus: *All variation (succession) on the part of appearances is only change;* for an arising or passing away of substance would not be changes of it, because the concept of change presupposes the same subject as existing, and hence as being permanent, with two opposite determinations. After this preliminary reminder, there now follows the proof.)

I perceive that appearances succeed one another, i.e., that at one time there is a state of things whose opposite was there in the things' previous state. Hence I am in fact connecting two perceptions in time. Now connection is not the work of mere sense and intuition, but is here the product of a synthetic ability of our imagination which determines inner sense in regard to time relation. But imagination can link those two states in two ways, so that either the one or the other state precedes in time. For time cannot in itself be perceived, and what precedes or follows cannot be determined by reference to it in the object—empirically, as it were. I am, therefore, conscious only that my imagination places one state before and the other after, but B234 not that the one state precedes the other in the object. In other words, mere perception leaves indeterminate the *objective relation* of the appearances following one another. Now in order for this objective relation to be cognized as determinate, the relation between the two states must be thought as being such that it determines as necessary which of the states must be placed before and which after, rather than vice versa. But a concept carrying with it a necessity of synthetic unity can only be a pure concept of understanding, which therefore does not reside in perception. Here this concept is that of the *relation of cause and effect;* of these two, the cause is what determines the effect in time, and determines it as the consequence, rather than as something that [as occurring] merely in imagination might [instead] precede (or might not even be perceived at all). Therefore experience itself—i.e., empirical cognition of appearances—is possible only inasmuch as we subject the succession of appearances, and hence all change, to the law of causality. Hence appearances themselves, taken as objects of experience, are possible only in accordance with this law.

Apprehension of the manifold of appearances is always successive. The presentations of the parts succeed one another. Whether they also follow one another in the object is a second point for reflection which is not already contained in the first point. Now it is true that anything, even every presentation insofar as one is conscious of it, can be called an object. Yet what this word might signify in the case of appearances, not insofar as they (as presentations) are objects but insofar as they only designate an object, calls for deeper investigation. Insofar as appearances, taken only as presentations, are simultaneously objects of consciousness, they are not at all distinct from apprehension, i.e., from the taking up into the synthesis of imagination; and we must say, therefore, that the manifold of appearances is always produced in the mind successively. If appearances were things in themselves, then no human being could gather from the succession of presentations how their manifold is combined in the object. For we deal, after all, only with our presentations; how things may be in themselves (i.e., apart from taking account of presentations whereby they affect us), is entirely outside our sphere of cognition. Appearances, then, are indeed not things in themselves; but they are all that can be given to us for cognition. And now, whereas the presentation [as such] of the manifold in apprehension is always successive, I am to indicate what sort of combination in time belongs to the manifold in appearances themselves. Thus, e.g., the apprehension of the manifold in the appearance of a house standing before me is successive. Now the question is whether the manifold of this house itself is successive intrinsically as well; and this, to be sure, no one will grant. But once I raise my concepts of an object to the level of transcendental signification, the house is not at all a thing in itself, but is only an appearance, i.e., a presentation, whose transcendental object is unknown. What, then, do I mean by the question as to how the manifold may be combined in appearance itself (which, after all, is nothing in itself)? Here what lies in the successive apprehension is regarded as presentation; but the appearance that is given to me, despite being nothing more than a sum of these presentations, is regarded as their object, with which the concept that I obtain from the presentations of apprehension is to agree. We soon see that, since agreement of cognition with the object is truth, the question can only be inquiring after the formal conditions of empirical truth; and we see that appearance, as contrasted with the presentations of apprehension, can be presented as an object distinct from them only if it is subject to a rule that distinguishes it from any other

A190/ B235

B236

A191

apprehension and that makes necessary one kind of combination of the manifold. That [element] in the appearance which contains the condition of this necessary rule of apprehension is the object.

Let us now proceed to our problem. That something occurs, i.e., that something, or a state that was not there before, comes to be cannot be perceived empirically unless it is preceded by an appearance that does not contain this state. For an actuality succeeding an empty time, i.e., an arising not preceded by any state of things, cannot be apprehended any more than empty time itself. Hence any apprehension of an event is a perception succeeding another perception. But because, as I showed above by reference to the appearance of a house, this is so in all synthesis of apprehension, the apprehension of an event is not yet distinguished thereby from other apprehensions. Yet I also observe that if, in an appearance containing an occurrence, I call A the preceding state of the perception and B the succeeding state, then B can in apprehension only succeed A, and similarly perception A cannot succeed B but can only precede it. For example, I see a ship floating down the river. My perception of its position lower down in the course of the river succeeds the perception of its position higher up, and there is no possibility that in the apprehension of this appearance the ship should be perceived first lower down and afterwards higher up in the river. Hence the order in the perceptions' succession in apprehension is here determinate, and apprehension is tied to this order. In the previous example of a house my perceptions could, in apprehension, start from the house's top and end at the bottom, but they could also start from below and end above; and they could likewise apprehend the manifold of the empirical intuition by proceeding either to the right or to the left. Hence in the series of these perceptions there was no determinate order making necessary the point in apprehension where I must begin in order to combine the manifold empirically. In the perception of what occurs, however, this rule is always to be found, and through it the order of the perceptions succeeding one another (in the apprehension of this appearance) is made *necessary*.

In our case, therefore, I shall have to derive the *subjective succession* of apprehension from the *objective succession* of appearances; for otherwise the subjective succession is entirely indeterminate and fails to distinguish any one appearance from some other appearance. The subjective succession by itself, being entirely arbitrary, proves nothing about the connection of the manifold in the object. Hence the objective succession will consist in the order of the manifold of appearance whereby the apprehension of the one item (viz., what occurs) succeeds the apprehension of the other (viz., what precedes) *according to a rule.* This alone can entitle me to say of the appearance itself, and not merely of my apprehension, that a succession is to be found in it—which means the same as that I cannot perform the apprehension except in precisely this succession.

In accordance with such a rule, therefore, what precedes an event as such must contain the condition for a rule whereby this event always and necessarily follows. But I cannot go, conversely, from the event backward and determine (through apprehension) what precedes. For no appearance goes back from the succeeding point of time to the previous one, although it does refer *to some previous one.* The progression from a given time to the determinate following time, on the other hand, is necessary. Hence because it is, after all, something that follows, I must necessarily refer it to something else as such that precedes it and that it succeeds according to a rule, i.e., necessarily. Thus the event, as the conditioned, directs us reliably to some condition, while this condition determines the event.

Suppose that an event is not preceded by anything that it must succeed according to a rule. Then all succession of perception would be determined solely in apprehension, i.e., merely subjectively; but this would not at all determine objectively which item in fact precedes in perception and which follows. We would in that way have only a play of presentations that would not refer to any object whatever; i.e., our perception would not at all distinguish one appearance from all others in terms of time relation. For the succession in apprehending is in that case everywhere the same, and hence there is in appearance nothing determining this succession so that a certain succession is, as objective, made necessary by it. Hence I shall in that case not say that two states succeed each other in appearance. Rather, I shall say only that one apprehension succeeds the other; and this is merely something *subjective* and determines no object, and hence cannot count as cognition of any object (not even of an object in [the realm of] appearance).

Hence when we experience that something occurs, then in doing so we always presuppose that it is preceded by something or other that it succeeds according to a rule. Otherwise I would not say of the object that it succeeds; for the mere succession in my apprehension, if it is not determined by a rule by reference to something preceding

B239
A194

B240
A195

it, justifies no [assumption of a] succession in the object. Hence it is always on account of a rule that I make my subjective synthesis (of apprehension) objective, viz., a rule according to which appearances in their succession, i.e., as they occur, are determined by the previous state. And the experience itself of something that occurs is possible solely and exclusively under this presupposition.

It is true that this seems to contradict all the remarks that people have always made about the course taken by our understanding. According to those remarks, it is only by perceiving and comparing the agreeing successions of events that follow upon preceding appearances that we are first led to discover a rule whereby certain events always succeed certain appearances, and only thereby are we first prompted to frame the concept of cause. This concept would, on such a basis, be merely empirical. And the rule whereby everything that occurs has a cause, as this concept provides it, would be just as contingent as the experience itself. The rule's universality and necessity would then be attributed to it only fictitiously and would have no true universal validity, because they would be based not on anything a priori, but only on induction. But the case with this rule is the same as that with other pure a priori presentations (e.g., space and time): we can extract them as clear concepts from experience solely because we have put them into experience and hence have brought experience about through them in the first place. To be sure, this presentation of a rule determining the series of events, as a concept of cause, can have logical clarity only once we have made use of it in experience. Yet [our] taking account of this presentation, [viz.,] as a condition of the synthetic unity in time of appearances, was nonetheless the basis of the experience itself, and hence the experience was preceded a priori by this condition.

Hence we must show, in the example [of an event], that even in experience we never attribute succession (in the case of an event—where something occurs that was not there before) to the object and we never distinguish this succession from the subjective one in our apprehension, except when there lies at the basis a rule that compels us to observe this order of perceptions rather than some other order; indeed, we must show that this compulsion is what in fact makes the presentation of a succession in the object possible in the first place.

We have within us presentations of which we can also become conscious. But no matter how far this consciousness may extend and how accurate and punctilious it may be, they still remain forever only

B241
A196

B242

A197

presentations, i.e., inner determinations of our mind in this or that time relation. How is it, then, that we posit an object for these presentations; or how is it that in addition to the subjective reality that they have as modifications [of the mind], we also attribute to them who knows what sort of objective reality? Their objective signification cannot consist in the reference to another presentation (of what one would want to call object). For otherwise the question returns: how does this other presentation, in turn, go beyond itself and acquire objective signification in addition to the subjective one that it possesses by being a determination of the mental state? Suppose that we inquire what new character is given to our presentations by the *reference to an object*, and what is the dignity that they thereby obtain. We then find that this reference does nothing beyond making necessary the presentations' being combined in a certain way and being subjected to a rule; and we find, conversely, that only through the   B243
necessity of a certain order in the time relation of our presentations is objective signification conferred on them.

In the synthesis of appearances the manifold of presentations is al-   A198
ways successive. Now, through this succession no object whatever is presented; for through this succession, which is common to all apprehensions, nothing is distinguished from anything else. But once I perceive, or assume in advance, that there is in this succession a reference to the preceding state, upon which the presentation follows according to a rule, then something presents itself as an event, or as something that occurs. I.e., I then cognize an object that I must posit in a certain determinate position in time—a position that in view of the preceding state cannot be assigned to it differently. Hence when I perceive that something occurs, then this presentation contains, first, [the presupposition] that something precedes; for precisely by reference to this preceding something does the appearance acquire its time relation, viz., its existing after a preceding time in which it was not. But, second, it can obtain its determinate time position in this relation only inasmuch as in the preceding state something is presupposed that it succeeds always, i.e., succeeds according to a rule. And from this results, first, that I cannot reverse the series, taking what occurs and putting it ahead of what it succeeds; and, second, that if the state that precedes is posited, then this specific event suc-   B244
ceeds unfailingly and necessarily. Thus it is that among our presentations there comes to be an order in which what is present directs us   A199
(insofar as it has come to be) to some preceding state as a correlate of

the happening that is given. And although this correlate is still indeterminate, it does refer determinatively to this happening as its consequence and in the time series connects it with itself necessarily.

Suppose, then, that it is a necessary law of our sensibility, and
hence a *formal condition* of all perceptions, that the previous time
necessarily determines the following one (inasmuch as I cannot arrive at the following time except through the preceding one). If this
is so, then it is also an indispensable *law of empirical presentation* of
the time series that the appearances of past time determine every existent in the following time; and that these existents, as events, do not
take place except insofar as their existence is determined in time—
i.e., fixed in time according to a rule—by those appearances of past
time. For *only in appearances can we cognize empirically this continuity
in the coherence of times.*

Understanding is required for all experience and for its possibility.
And the first thing that understanding does for these is not that of
making the presentation of objects distinct, but that of making the
presentation of an object possible at all. Now, this is done through
the understanding's transferring the time order to the appearances
and to their existence, by allotting to each appearance, as consequence,
a position in time determined a priori with regard to the preceding
appearances; without this position in time the appearance would not
agree with time itself, which a priori determines for all its parts their
position. Now this determination of an appearance's position cannot
be taken from the relation of appearances toward absolute time (for
absolute time is not an object of perception). Rather, conversely, the
appearances must themselves determine for one another their positions in time, and must make these positions necessary in the time
order; i.e., what follows or occurs must succeed what was contained
in the previous state and must do so according to a universal rule.
This results in a series of appearances that, by means of the understanding, produces and makes necessary in the series of possible perceptions the same order and steady coherence that is found a priori
in the form of inner intuition (i.e., in time), in which all [such] perceptions would have to have their position.

Hence that something occurs is a perception belonging to a possible experience. This experience becomes actual when I view the appearance as determined as regards its position in time, and hence
view it as an object that in the coherence of perceptions can always
be found according to a rule. This rule, however, for determining

B245

A200

B246

something in regard to temporal succession, is that the condition under which an event always (i.e., necessarily) follows is to be found in what precedes the event. Hence the principle of sufficient basis is the basis of possible experience, i.e., of objective cognition of appearances with regard to their relation in time sequence. A201

The basis for proving this proposition, however, rests solely on the following moments. All empirical cognition involves the synthesis of the manifold by the imagination. This synthesis is always successive, i.e., in it the presentations always succeed one another. In the imagination itself, however, the sequence is not at all determined as regards order (i.e., as to what must precede and what must follow), and the series of the presentations following one another can be taken as proceeding backward just as well as forward. But if this synthesis is a synthesis of apprehension (of the manifold of a given appearance), then the order is determined in the object, or—to speak more accurately—there is in this apprehension an order of successive synthesis that determines an object; and according to this order something must necessarily precede, and when this something is posited then the other event must necessarily follow. Hence if my perception is to contain the cognition of an event, i.e., of something's actually occurring, then it must be an empirical judgment in which we think of the consequence as determined, i.e., as presupposing in terms of time another appearance that it succeeds necessarily, or according to a rule. Otherwise, if I posited what precedes and the event did not succeed it necessarily, then I would have to regard this event as only a subjective play of my imaginings; and if I still presented by it something objective, then I would have to call it a mere dream. Therefore the relation of appearances (as possible perceptions) whereby what follows (occurs) is with regard to its existence determined in time, necessarily and according to a rule, by something preceding it—in other words, the relation of cause to effect—is the condition of the objective validity of our empirical judgments as regards the series of perceptions, and hence is the condition of these judgments' empirical truth and therefore of experience. The principle of the causal relation in the succession of appearances holds, therefore, also for all objects of experience ([insofar as they are] under the conditions of succession), because it is itself the basis of the possibility of such experience.

B247

A202

Here, however, emerges a perplexity that must still be removed. The principle of the causal connection among appearances is, in our

formulation, limited to their [occurring in] sequence. Yet in using
the principle we find that it fits also the case of their concomitance,
B248 and that cause and effect can be simultaneous. E.g., there is heat in
the room which is not found in the open air. I look around for the
cause, and discover a heated stove. Now this stove, as cause, is simultaneous with its effect, the room's heat. Hence here there is between
cause and effect no sequence in terms of time. They are, rather, si-
A203 multaneous; and yet the law of cause and effect does hold. The ma-
jority of efficient causes in nature are simultaneous with their effects,
and the temporal succession of the effects is due only to the fact that
the cause cannot accomplish its entire effect in one instant. But at
the instant when the effect first arises, it is always simultaneous with
the causality of its cause. For if the cause had ceased to be an instant
before, then the effect would not have arisen at all. It must be noted
carefully, here, that what we are considering is the *order* of time, not
the *lapse* of time; the relation remains even if no time has elapsed.
The time between the causality of the cause and the cause's direct effect may be *vanishingly brief,* but yet the relation of the cause to the
effect always remains determinable in terms of time. If I consider as
cause a [lead] ball that lies on a stuffed cushion and makes an indentation in it, then this cause is simultaneous with the effect. But I
nonetheless distinguish the two by the time relation of their dynamical connection. For if I lay the ball on the cushion, then the previous
B249 smooth shape of the cushion is succeeded by the indentation; but if
the cushion has an indentation (no matter from where), then this is
not succeeded by a lead ball.

Hence temporal succession is indeed an effect's sole empirical cri-
A204 terion in reference to the causality of the cause preceding it. The
[totally filled] tumbler is the cause of the water's rising above the
horizontal plane [at the top] of the tumbler, although the two appearances are simultaneous. For as soon as water is scooped from a larger
vessel with [an empty] tumbler, there ensues this: the horizontal
level that the water had in the larger vessel changes to a concave level
in the [partially filled] tumbler.

This causality leads to the concept of action; action leads to the
concept of force and thereby to the concept of substance. Since my
critical project deals solely with the sources of synthetic a priori cognition and I do not want to mingle with it dissections [of concepts],
which concern merely the elucidation (rather than the expansion) of
concepts, I leave the detailed exposition of these concepts to a future

system of pure reason—although such an analysis can also be found in abundance in the textbooks of this kind that are already familiar. What I must, however, touch upon is the empirical criterion of a substance insofar as it seems to manifest itself not through the permanence of appearance but better and more easily through action.

Where there is action and hence activity and force, there is also   B250
substance, and in substance alone must be sought the seat of that fertile source of appearances. That is nicely said; but if we are to explain what we mean by substance and want to avoid the fallacy of circular reasoning, then the answer is not so easy. How, from action on some-   A205
thing, are we to infer at once *the agent's permanence*—this permanence being, after all, so essential and peculiar a characteristic of substance ([as] *phaenomenon*)? Yet according to our previous remarks, solving the question is not so difficult after all, even though the question would be quite insoluble according to the usual way (of proceeding with one's concepts, viz., merely analytically). Action already means the relation of the causality's subject to the effect. Now any effect consists in what occurs, and hence in the mutable that designates time in terms of succession. Therefore the ultimate subject of the mutable is the *permanent* as the substratum of everything that varies, i.e., substance. For according to the principle of causality actions are always the first basis of all variation by appearances; hence actions cannot reside in a subject that itself varies, since otherwise other actions and another subject determining that variation would be required. By virtue of this does action prove, as a sufficient em-   B251
pirical criterion, the substantiality of a subject, without my needing first of all to search for the subject's permanence by perceptions that I have compared. Nor could proving this substantiality along this path of comparison be accomplished as comprehensively as is required by the magnitude and strict universality of the concept of substance. For, that the first subject of the causality of all arising and   A206
passing away cannot itself arise and pass away (in the realm of appearances) is a safe inference that issues in empirical necessity and permanence in existence, and hence in the concept of a substance as appearance.

When something occurs then the mere arising, even if we take no account of what arises, is in itself already an object of inquiry. The transition itself from a state's not-being to this state, even supposing that this state contained no quality in [the realm] of appearance, already calls for inquiry. This arising, as was shown in the First

Analogy, concerns not substance (for substance does not arise) but its state. Hence arising is only change, and not origination from nothing. For if this origination from nothing is regarded as effect of an extraneous cause, then it is called creation; and creation cannot be admitted as an event among appearances, because its very possibility would already annul the unity of experience. If, on the other hand, I B252 regard all things not as phenomena but as things in themselves and as objects merely of understanding, then despite their being substances they can still be regarded as being dependent, in terms of their existence, on an extraneous cause. That alternative, however, would then entail quite different significations of the words, and would not fit appearances, as possible objects of experience.

Now, we do not a priori have the least concept as to how anything A207 can be changed at all, i.e., how it is possible that one state occurring at one point of time can be succeeded by an opposite state occurring at another point of time. This [concept of how change is possible] requires knowledge of actual forces—e.g., knowledge of the motive forces, or, which is the same, of certain successive appearances (as motions) indicating such forces—and such knowledge can be given only empirically. But we can nonetheless examine a priori, according to the law of causality and the conditions of time, the form of every change, i.e., the condition under which alone, as an arising of a different state, change can take place (no matter what may be its content, i.e., the state being changed); and hence we can so examine the succession itself of the states (i.e., the occurrence).[16]

B253   When a substance passes from one state, a, to another, b, then the point of time of the second state is different from the point of time of the first, and follows it. In the same way, too, the second state as reality (in [the realm of] appearance) differs from the first, in which this A208 reality was not, as b differs from zero; i.e., even if state b were to differ from state a only in magnitude, the change is [still] an arising of $b - a$, which in the previous state was not and in regard to which that state $= 0$.

The question, therefore, is how a thing passes from one state, $= a$, to another, $= b$. Between two instants there is always a time, and be-

16. It should be noted carefully that I am talking not about the change of certain relations as such, but about change of a state. Thus if a body moves uniformly then it does not change its state (of motion) at all; but it does change its state if its motion increases or decreases.

tween two states at those instants there is always a difference that has a magnitude (for all parts of appearances are always magnitudes in turn). Hence any transition from one state to another occurs in a time that is contained between two instants, the first instant determining the state that the thing leaves and the second instant determining the state that it enters. Both instants, therefore, are bounds of the time of a change and hence bounds of the intermediate state between the two states, and as such belong also to the entire change. Now every change has a cause that manifests its causality in the entire time wherein the change takes place. Hence this cause produces   B254
its change not suddenly (i.e., all at once, or in one instant), but in a time; so that, as the time increases from its initial instant *(a)* up to its completion (in *b*), the reality's magnitude *(b − a)* is also produced through all the smaller degrees contained between the first degree and the last. Hence all change is possible only through a continuous action of the causality; this action, insofar as it is uniform, is called a moment. Change does not consist of these moments, but is produced   A209
by them as their effect.

This, then, is the law of the continuity of all change. The basis of this law is this fact: that neither time nor, for that matter, appearance in time consists of parts that are the smallest; and that nonetheless, as a thing changes, its state passes through all these parts, as elements, to the thing's second state. *No difference* of the real in [the realm of] appearance is *the smallest*, just as no difference in the magnitude of times is the smallest. And thus the reality's new state grows, starting from the first state, in which it was not, through all the infinite degrees of this reality; and the differences of the degrees from one another are all smaller than the difference between 0 and *a*.

What benefit this principle may have for the investigation of nature is of no concern to us here. But how is such a principle, which thus seems to expand our cognition of nature, possible completely a priori? This question very much requires our examination, even though what the principle says is [so] obviously actual and correct   B255
that we might believe ourselves to be exempted from the question as to how the principle was possible. For there is such a variety of unfounded claims about our cognition's expansion by pure reason, that we must adopt as a universal principle [the resolve] to be throughout distrustful on that account, and not to believe or assume anything of   A210
the sort, even upon the clearest dogmatic proof, without documentation that can provide a well-founded deduction.

All increase of empirical cognition and any progress of perception—no matter what the objects may be, whether appearances or pure intuitions—is nothing but an expansion of the determination of inner sense, i.e., a progression in time. This progression in time determines everything and is in itself determined through nothing further. I.e., the progression's parts are given only in time and through the synthesis of time; they are not given prior to the synthesis. Because of this, every transition in perception to something that follows in time is a determination of time through the production of this perception; and since time is always and in all its parts a magnitude, every such transition is the production of a perception as a magnitude that goes through all degrees, none of which is the smallest, from zero onward up to the perception's determinate degree. From this, then, is evident the possibility of cognizing a priori a law governing changes as regards their form. For we only anticipate our own apprehension, whose formal condition, since it resides in ourselves prior to all given appearance, must indeed be capable of being cognized a priori.

B256

We have seen that time contains the sensible a priori condition for the possibility of a continuous progression of what exists to what follows. In the same way the understanding, by means of the unity of apperception, is the a priori condition for the possibility of a continuous determination, through the series of causes and effects, of all positions for appearances in this time—the causes entailing unfailingly the existence of the effects, and thereby making the empirical cognition of time relations valid for every time (i.e., universally) and hence valid objectively.

A211

C
THIRD ANALOGY

PRINCIPLE OF SIMULTANEITY ACCORDING TO THE LAW OF
INTERACTION OR COMMUNITY

All substances, insofar as they can be perceived in space as simultaneous, are in thoroughgoing interaction.

B257   Proof

Things are *simultaneous* if their perceptions can in empirical intuition succeed one another *reciprocally* (which cannot occur in the temporal succession of appearances, as was shown under the second principle). Thus I can carry on my perception either first with the moon and thereafter with the earth, or, vice versa, first with the earth and then with the moon. And because the perceptions of these objects can succeed each other reciprocally, I say that the objects exist simultaneously. Now simultaneity is the existence of the manifold in the same time. However, time itself cannot be perceived; and hence from the fact that things are placed in the same time we cannot glean that their perceptions can follow one another reciprocally. Hence the synthesis of imagination in apprehension would indicate for each of these perceptions only that it is there in the subject when the other is not, and vice versa. But it would not indicate that the objects are simultaneous; i.e., that if the one is there then the other is also there in the same time, and that this simultaneity of the objects is necessary in order that the perceptions can succeed one another reciprocally. Hence for things existing outside one another simultaneously we require a concept of understanding of the reciprocal succession of their determinations, in order to say that the reciprocal succession of the perceptions has its basis in the object and in order thus to present the simultaneity as objective. But the relation of substances wherein the one substance contains determinations whose basis is contained in the other substance is the relation of influence; and if this latter thing reciprocally contains the basis of the determinations in the for- B258 mer thing, then the relation is that of community or interaction. Therefore the simultaneity of substances in space cannot be cognized in experience except under the presupposition that they interact with one another. Hence this interaction is also the condition for the possibility of the things themselves as objects of experience.

Things are simultaneous insofar as they exist in one and the same time. But whereby do we cognize that they are in one and the same time? They are so when the order in the synthesis of this manifold's apprehension is indifferent, i.e., when that synthesis can go either from A through B, C, D, to E, or vice versa from E to A. For if the synthesis is sequential in time (in the order starting from A and ending in E), then starting the apprehension in perception from E and proceeding backwards to A is impossible, since A belongs to past time and hence can no longer be an object of apprehension.

Now suppose that in a manifoldness of substances taken as appear- A212 ances each of them were completely isolated, i.e., that no substance effected influences in another and reciprocally received influences B259 from it. I say that in that case their *simultaneity* would not be an object of a possible perception, and that the existence of one substance could not by any path of empirical synthesis lead to the existence of another. For if you bear in mind that the substances would be separated by a completely empty space, then although the perception proceeding in time from one substance to the other would determine this other substance's existence by means of a perception that follows, yet it could not distinguish whether objectively the appearance succeeds the first or is, rather, simultaneous with it.

Hence there must be something else, besides mere existence, whereby A determines for B—and also, vice versa, B in turn for A—their positions in time. For only under this condition can those substances be presented empirically as *existing simultaneously*. Now only what is the cause of something else, or of its determinations, determines for that something its position in time. Therefore every substance (since it can be a consequence only in regard to its determinations) must contain within itself the causality of certain determinations in the other substance and simultaneously must contain within itself the effects of the other substance's causality—i.e., they must stand (directly or indirectly) in dynamical community—if their simultaneity is to be cognized in any possible experience. However, something is necessary in regard to objects of experience if without that something the experience of these objects would itself be impossible. Hence for all substances in [the realm of] appearance, insofar as they are simultaneous, it is necessary that they stand in thoroughgoing community of interaction.

The word community is ambiguous in our language; it can mean the same as *communio* or as *commercium*. We here employ it in the latter sense, as meaning a dynamic community, without which even locational community *(communio spatii)* could never be cognized empirically. We can easily tell by our experiences: that only the continuous influences in all positions of space can lead our sense from one object to another; that the light playing between our eye and the celestial bodies can bring about an indirect community between us and them and can thereby prove their simultaneity; that we cannot empirically change place (and perceive this change) unless matter everywhere makes possible the perception of our position; and that only by means of matter's reciprocal influence can matter establish its simultaneity and thereby establish (although only indirectly) the coexistence of objects, down to the most remote ones.

A213

B260

Without community every perception (of appearance in space) A214
would be severed from any other; the chain of empirical presentations—i.e., experience—would begin entirely anew with each new
object, and the previous chain could not in the least cohere with it or B261
stand to it in a time relation. By this I do not in any way wish to dis-
prove empty space. For there may be such space wherever perceptions
cannot reach at all and where there occurs, therefore, no empirical
cognition of simultaneity. But such space is then no object whatever
for all our possible experience.

The following may serve as elucidation. In our mind all appearances, as contained in a possible experience, must stand in community
(communio) of apperception; and insofar as objects are to be presented
as connected inasmuch as they exist simultaneously, they must reciprocally determine each other's position in one time and thereby make
up a whole. If this subjective community is to rest on an objective
basis, or be referred to appearances as substances, then the perception of the one appearance, as basis, must make possible the perception of the other, and thus also vice versa. Only then will the
succession, which is always there in perceptions as apprehensions,
not be attributed to the objects, but these objects can, rather, be presented as existing simultaneously. This, however, is a reciprocal influence, i.e., a real community *(commercium)* of substances; without A215
this community the empirical relation of simultaneity could not
occur in experience. Through this *commercium* appearances, insofar
as they stand outside one another and yet in connection, make up a B262
composite *(compositum reale)*, and such composites become possible
in various ways. Hence the three dynamical relations from which all
other relations arise are those of inherence, consequence, and composition.

These, then, are the three analogies of experience. They are nothing but principles for the determination of the existence of appearances in time, according to all three modes of time: viz., according to
the relation to time itself as a magnitude (the magnitude of existence,
i.e., duration); according to the relation in time as a series (i.e., as sequential); and, finally, also according to the relation in time as a sum
of all existence (i.e., as simultaneous). This unity of time determination is dynamical through and through. I.e., time is not regarded as
that wherein experience directly determines for each existent its position; for such determination is impossible, because absolute time is

not an object of perception to which appearances could be held up. Rather, the rule of understanding through which alone the existence of appearances can acquire synthetic unity in terms of time relations is what determines for each appearance its position in time, hence doing so a priori and validly for all and every time.

A216
B263   By nature (in the empirical meaning of the term) we mean the coherence of appearances as regards their existence according to necessary rules, i.e., according to laws. There are, then, certain laws— which are, moreover, a priori—that make a nature possible in the first place. Empirical laws can occur and can be found only by means of experience; and this, moreover, in consequence of those original laws through which experience itself becomes possible in the first place. Hence our analogies in fact exhibit the unity of nature, in the coherence of all appearances, under certain indices; these indices express nothing but the relation of time (insofar as time comprises all existence) to the unity of apperception—a unity that can occur only in synthesis according to rules. Hence together the analogies say that all appearances reside, and must reside, in one nature; for without this a priori unity no unity of experience, and hence also no determination of objects in experience, would be possible. [...]

B274   Refutation of Idealism [Second Edition]

Idealism (I mean *material* idealism) is the theory that declares the existence of objects in space outside us either to be merely doubtful and *unprovable*, or to be *false* and *impossible*. The *first* is the *problematic* idealism of *Descartes;* it declares only one empirical assertion *(assertio)* to be indubitable, viz.: *I am.* The *second* is the *dogmatic* idealism of Berkeley; it declares space, with all the things to which space attaches as inseparable condition, to be something that is in itself impossible, and hence also declares the things in space to be mere imaginings. Dogmatic idealism is unavoidable if one regards space as a property that is to belong to things in themselves; for then space, with everything that space serves as condition, is a nonentity. However, the basis for this idealism has already been removed by us in the

B275   Transcendental Aesthetic. Problematic idealism, which asserts nothing about this but only alleges that we are unable to prove by direct experience an existence apart from our own, is reasonable and is in accordance with a thorough philosophical way of thinking—viz., in permitting no decisive judgment before a sufficient proof has been found. The proof it demands must, therefore, establish that regarding external things we have not merely *imagination* but also *experience*. And establishing this surely cannot be done unless one can prove that even our *inner* experience, indubitable for Descartes, is possible only on the presupposition of *outer* experience.

Theorem

The mere, but empirically determined, consciousness of my own existence proves the existence of objects in space outside me.

Proof

I am conscious of my existence as determined in time. All time determination presupposes something *permanent* in perception. But this permanent something cannot be something within me, precisely because my existence can be determined in time only by this permanent something.[17] Therefore perception of this permanent something is possible only through a *thing* outside me and not through mere *presentation* of a thing outside me. Hence determination of my existence in time is possible only through the existence of actual things that I perceive outside me. Now consciousness of my existence in time is necessarily linked with consciousness of the possibility of this time determination; therefore it is necessarily linked also with the existence of things outside me, as condition of the time determination. I.e., the consciousness of my own existence is simultaneously a direct consciousness of the existence of other things outside me.

Comment 1. In the preceding proof one becomes aware that the game that idealism played is being turned around and against it—and more rightly so. Idealism assumed that the only direct experience is inner experience and that from it we only *infer* external things; but we infer them only unreliably, as happens whenever we infer *determinate* causes from given effects, because the cause of the

B276

B277

17. [In a footnote to the second edition preface, Kant indicates that this sentence should be replaced with the following: "But this permanent something cannot be an intuition within me. For all bases determining my existence that can be encountered within me are presentations; and, being presentations, they themselves require something permanent distinct from them, by reference to which their variation, and hence my existence in the time in which they vary, can be determined."]

presentations that we ascribe—perhaps falsely—to external things may also reside in ourselves. Yet here we have proved that outer experience is in fact direct,[18] and that only by means of it can there be inner experience—i.e., not indeed consciousness of our own existence, but yet determination of that existence in time. To be sure, the presentation *I am,* which expresses the consciousness that can accompany all thinking, is what directly includes the existence of a subject; but it is not yet a *cognition* of that subject, and hence is also no empirical cognition—i.e., experience—of it. For such experience involves, besides the thought of something existent, also intuition, and here specifically inner intuition, in regard to which—viz., time—the subject must be determined; and this determination definitely requires external objects. Thus, consequently, inner experience is itself only indirect and is possible only through outer experience.

Comment 2. Now, all experiential use that we make of our cognitive power in determining time agrees completely with this view. Not only can we perceive any time determination solely through the variation in external relations (i.e., through motion) by reference to the permanent in space (e.g., the sun's motion with respect to the earth's objects); but except merely for *matter* we do not even have anything permanent on which, as intuition, we could base the concept of a substance. And even this permanence is not drawn from outer experience, but is presupposed a priori as necessary condition of all time determination, and hence presupposed also as determination of inner sense, with regard to our own existence, through the existence of external things. The consciousness that I have of myself in the presentation *I* is not an intuition at all, but is a merely *intellectual* presentation of a thinking subject's self-activity. Hence this *I* also does not have the least predicate of intuition that, *as permanent,* could serve as correlate for the time determination in inner sense—

B278

18. In the preceding theorem, the *direct* consciousness of the existence of external things is not presupposed but proved, whether or not we have insight into the possibility of this consciousness. The question concerning that possibility would be whether we have only an inner sense, and no outer sense but merely outer imagination. Clearly, however, in order for us even to imagine something—i.e., exhibit it to sense in intuition—as external, we must already have an outer sense, and must thereby immediately distinguish the mere receptivity of an outer intuition from the spontaneity that characterizes all imagining. For if even outer sense were merely imagined, this would annul our very power of intuition which is to be determined by the imagination.

as, say, *impenetrability* is such a predicate of *empirical* intuition in matter.

Comment 3. It does not follow, from the fact that the existence of external objects is required for the possibility of a determinate consciousness of ourselves, that every intuitive presentation of external things implies also these things' existence; for the presentation may very well be (as it is in dreams as well as in madness) the mere effect of the imagination. Yet it is this effect merely through the reproduction of former outer perceptions; and these, as has been shown, are possible only through the actuality of external objects. What was here to be proved is only that inner experience as such is possible B279 only through outer experience as such. Whether this or that supposed experience is not perhaps a mere imagining must be ascertained by reference to its particular determinations and by holding it up to the criteria of all actual experience. [...]

TRANSCENDENTAL LOGIC

DIVISION II
TRANSCENDENTAL DIALECTIC

INTRODUCTION

I
ON TRANSCENDENTAL ILLUSION

Above we called dialectic as such a *logic of illusion*. This does not
mean that it is a doctrine of *probability*. For probability is truth, but
truth cognized through insufficient bases; and although cognition of
such truth is therefore deficient, yet it is not on that account deceptive, and hence must not be separated from the analytic part of logic.

Still less may *appearance* and *illusion* be regarded as being the same.
For truth and illusion are not in the object insofar as it is intuited,
but are in the judgment made about the object insofar as it is
thought. Hence although it is correct to say that the senses do not
err, this is so not because they always judge correctly but because
they do not judge at all. Thus both truth and error, and hence also illusion as the process of mistakenly leading to error, are to be found
only in the judgment, i.e., only in the relation of the object to our
understanding. In a cognition that accords throughout with the laws
of understanding there is no error. There is also no error in a presentation of the senses (because it contains no judgment at all). But no
force of nature can deviate from its own laws by itself. Thus neither
the understanding on its own (i.e., apart from the influence of another cause), nor the senses by themselves would err. The understanding would not err, because, if it acts merely in accordance with
its laws, then the effect (the judgment) must necessarily agree with
these laws; but the formal [element] of all truth consists in the agreement with the laws of the understanding. And in the senses there is
no judgment at all, neither a true nor a false one. Now because we
have no other sources of cognition besides these two, it follows that
error comes about only by sensibility's unnoticed influence on understanding. Through this influence it comes about that the subjec-

tive bases of the judgment meld with the objective ones and make   B351
them deviate from their [proper] determination—just as a body in
motion would indeed by itself always keep to a straight line in the
same direction, but is deflected into curvilinear motion if influenced
at the same time by another force acting in another direction. Hence   A295
in order to distinguish the action peculiar to understanding from the
force that mingles with it, we shall need to regard an erroneous judgment as the diagonal between two forces determining the judgment
in two different directions that—as it were—enclose an angle, and to
resolve this composite action into the simple ones of understanding
and of sensibility. In the case of pure a priori judgments we must do
this by transcendental deliberation, whereby (as has already been
shown) every presentation is assigned its place in the cognitive power
appropriate to it, and whereby the influence of sensibility on understanding is therefore also distinguished.

It is not our task here to deal with empirical (e.g., optical) illusion,
which occurs in the empirical use of otherwise correct rules of under-   B352
standing, and through which our power of judgment is misled by the
influence of imagination. Here we have to do, rather, solely with *transcendental illusion,* which influences principles whose use is not even
designed for experience; if it were, then we would, after all, at least have
a touchstone of their correctness. Rather, transcendental illusion carries
us, even despite all the warnings issued by critique, entirely beyond
the empirical use of the categories and puts us off with the deception
of there being an expansion of *pure understanding.* Let us call the principles whose application keeps altogether within the limits of possible   A296
experience *immanent* principles, and those that are to fly beyond these
limits *transcendent principles.* But by transcendent principles I do not
mean the *transcendental* use or misuse of the categories, which is a
mere mistake made by the power of judgment when, not being duly
curbed by critique, it does not pay enough attention to the boundaries
of the territory on which alone our pure understanding is permitted to
engage in its play. Rather, I mean by them actual principles requiring
us to tear down all those boundary posts and to claim an entirely new
territory that recognizes no demarcation at all. Hence *transcendental*
and *transcendent* are not the same. The principles of pure understanding that we have put forth above are to be of empirical and not of tran-   B353
scendental use, i.e., use extending beyond the boundary of experience.
But a principle that removes these limits—indeed, even commands us
to step beyond them—is called *transcendent.* If our critique can

manage to uncover the illusion in these claimed principles, then the principles of merely empirical use may be called, in contrast to the transcendent ones, immanent principles of pure understanding.

Logical illusion (the illusion of fallacious inferences), which consists in the mere imitation of the form of reason, arises solely from a lack of attentiveness in regard to the logical rule. Hence as soon as our attentiveness is sharpened in regard to the case before us, the illusion entirely vanishes. Transcendental illusion, on the other hand, does not cease even when we have already uncovered it and have, through transcendental critique, had distinct insight into its nullity. (An example is the illusion in the proposition that the world must have a beginning in terms of time.) The cause of this is that in our reason (regarded subjectively as a human cognitive power) there lie basic rules and maxims of its use that have entirely the look of objective principles; and through this it comes about that the subjective necessity of a certain connection of our concepts for the benefit of understanding is regarded as an objective necessity of the determination of things in themselves. This is an *illusion* that we cannot at all avoid any more than we can avoid the illusion that the sea seems to us higher in the center than at the shore because we see the center through higher light rays than the shore; or—better yet—any more than even the astronomer can prevent the moon from seeming larger to him as it rises, although he is not deceived by this illusion.

Hence the transcendental dialectic will settle for uncovering the illusion of transcendent judgments, and for simultaneously keeping it from deceiving us. But that the illusion should even vanish as well (as does logical illusion) and cease to be an illusion—this the transcendental dialectic can never accomplish. For here we are dealing with a *natural* and unavoidable *illusion* that itself rests on subjective principles and foists them on us as objective ones, whereas a logical dialectic in resolving fallacious inferences deals only with a mistake in the compliance with principles, or with an artificial illusion created in imitating such inferences. Hence there is a natural and unavoidable dialectic of pure reason. This dialectic is not one in which a bungler might become entangled on his own through lack of knowledge, or one that some sophist has devised artificially in order to confuse reasonable people. It is, rather, a dialectic that attaches to human reason unpreventably and that, even after we have uncovered this deception, still will not stop hoodwinking and thrusting reason incessantly into momentary aberrations that always need to be removed.

A297

B354

A298

B355

INTRODUCTION

II
ON PURE REASON AS THE SEAT OF TRANSCENDENTAL ILLUSION

C. On the Pure Use of Reason

A305/
B362

Can one isolate reason? And is it then still on its own a source of concepts and judgments which arise solely from it and through which it refers to objects? Or is it then a merely subsidiary power to provide given cognitions with a certain form, a form which is called logical and through which the cognitions of understanding are only subordinated to one another, and lower rules subordinated to other and higher rules (whose condition comprises in its sphere the condition of the lower rules), to whatever extent this can be accomplished by comparing them? This is the question with which we are now dealing only provisionally. Manifoldness of rules and unity of principles is indeed a demand of reason. Reason makes this demand in order to bring the understanding into thoroughgoing coherence with itself, just as the understanding brings the manifold of intuition under A306 concepts and thereby brings the intuition into connection. But such a principle prescribes no law to objects, and does not contain the basis for the possibility of cognizing and determining them as objects at all. It is, rather, merely a subjective law for the management of understanding's supplies, [instructing understanding] to reduce the universal use of its concepts—by comparing them—to their small- B363 est possible number. This [instruction] does not entitle us to demand from objects themselves such accordance as would promote the convenience and the broadening of our understanding, and to provide that maxim with objective validity as well. In a word, the question is: Does reason in itself, i.e., pure reason, a priori contain synthetic principles and rules; and in what may these principles consist?

Reason's formal and logical procedure in syllogisms already gives us sufficient guidance concerning the basis on which will rest reason's transcendental principle as used in synthetic cognition through pure reason.

First, an inference of reason does not deal with intuitions in order to bring them under rules (as does understanding with its categories), but deals with concepts and judgments. Hence even if pure

131

A307

reason deals with objects, it still has no direct reference to them and their intuition, but refers directly only to understanding and its judgments; understanding and its judgments are what initially turn to the senses and their intuition in order to determine the object of these. Hence unity of reason is not unity of a possible experience—which is the unity of understanding—but the former unity is essentially different from the latter unity. The principle that everything that occurs has a cause is not at all a principle cognized and prescribed by reason. It makes possible the unity of experience and borrows nothing from reason; reason could not, without this reference to possible experience and hence from mere concepts, have commanded such synthetic unity.

B364

Second, reason in its logical use seeks the universal condition of its judgment (i.e., of the conclusion), and a syllogism is itself nothing but a judgment made by means of subsuming its condition under a universal rule (major premise). Now this rule is in turn exposed to the same attempt by reason, and thus the condition of the condition must, as long as doing so is feasible, be sought (by means of a prosyllogism); and hence we readily see that the principle peculiar to reason as such (in its logical use) is: to find, for understanding's conditioned cognition, the unconditioned whereby the cognition's unity is completed.

But this logical maxim can become a principle of *pure reason* only by our assuming that, if the conditioned is given, then the entire series of conditions subordinated to one another—a series that is hence itself unconditioned—is also given (i.e., contained in the object and its connection).

A308

Such a principle of pure reason, however, is plainly *synthetic;* for although the conditioned does refer analytically to some condition, it does not so refer to the unconditioned. Moreover, from this principle there must arise various synthetic propositions of which pure understanding knows nothing; for pure understanding has to do only with objects of a possible experience, and the cognition and synthesis of such objects is always conditioned. But the unconditioned, if such there actually is, may be examined specially according to all those determinations that distinguish it from everything conditioned, and must thereby provide material for many synthetic a priori propositions.

B365

The principles arising from this supreme principle of reason will, however, be *transcendent* in regard to all appearances; i.e., no empirical use adequate to this principle can ever be made of it. It will, therefore, be entirely different from all principles of understanding (whose use is wholly *immanent*, because they have as their subject only the possibility of experience). Our task in the transcendental dialectic, then, will be to answer the following questions. Does that principle—i.e., that the series of conditions (in the synthesis of appearances, or, for that matter, in that of the thinking of things as such) extends up to the unconditioned—have, or does it not have, its objective correctness; and what inferences issue from it for the empirical use of understanding? Or is there, rather, no such objectively valid proposition of reason at all, but a merely logical precept to seek, in ascending to ever higher conditions, to approach their completeness and thereby to bring into our cognition the highest unity of reason that is possible for us? In other words: Has this need of reason been regarded, by a misunderstanding, as a transcendental principle of pure reason that rashly postulates such unlimited completeness in the series of conditions found in the objects themselves? But, in that case, what misunderstandings and delusions may be creeping also into syllogisms, whose major premise has been taken from pure reason (and is perhaps more a petition than a postulate), and which ascend from experience upward to its conditions? These questions, then, will be at issue in the transcendental dialectic. Let us now unfold this dialectic from its sources, which are deeply hidden in human reason. [...]

A309

B366

Transcendental Dialectic

Book II
On the Dialectical Inferences
of Pure Reason

Chapter I
On the Paralogisms of Pure Reason
[Second Edition]

B406   [...] The proposition *I think* (taken problematically) contains, then, the form of any of understanding's judgments as such, and accompanies all categories as their vehicle. Clearly, therefore, the inferences from this proposition can contain merely a transcendental use of understanding. Such use allows no experience to be mixed in, and hence regarding its progress we can—by what we have shown above—frame even in advance none but an unfavorable conception. Let us, therefore, trace this use, with a critical eye, through all the predicaments of pure psychology. For the sake of brevity, however, let us allow their examination to proceed in an uninterrupted continuity.

First of all, the following general remark may make us more keenly attentive to this kind of inference. I do not cognize any object by merely thinking, but I can cognize any object only by determining a given intuition with respect to the unity of consciousness in which all thought consists. Hence I do not cognize myself by being conscious of myself as thinking, but I cognize myself when I am conscious of the intuition of myself as determined with regard to the

B407   function of thought. All the *modes* of self-consciousness in thought as such are, therefore, not yet understanding's concepts of objects (categories), but are mere functions that do not allow thought to cognize any object at all, and hence also do not allow it to cognize myself as an object. The *object* is not the consciousness of the *determining* self, but only that of the *determinable* self, i.e., of my inner intuition (insofar as its manifold can be combined in accordance with the universal condition of the unity of apperception in thought).

1. Now in all judgments I am always the *determining* subject of the relation that makes up the judgment. But that I, who think, must be considered in such thought always as a *subject* and as something that cannot be regarded as merely attaching to thought like a predicate—this is an apodeictic and even identical proposition. But this proposition does not mean that I am, as an *object*, a *being subsisting* by myself or [i.e.] *substance*. This latter claim goes very far, and hence it also requires data that are in no way found in thought, and perhaps (insofar as I consider the thinking [self] merely as thinking) requires more than I shall ever find (in thought) at all.

2. That the *I* of apperception, and hence in all thought, is a *singular* that cannot be resolved into a plurality of subjects and therefore designates a logically simple subject—this lies already in the concept of thought and hence is an analytic proposition. But this does not mean that the thinking *I* is a simple *substance;* that would be a synthetic proposition. The concept of substance always refers to intuitions that, in me, cannot be other than sensible and hence lie entirely outside the realm of understanding and its thought; yet here we are in fact talking only about this thought when we say that the *I* in thought is simple. Indeed, it would be miraculous if what otherwise requires so much effort for distinguishing what is substance in what intuition displays—but even more for distinguishing (as with the parts of matter) whether this substance can also be simple—were here in the poorest of all presentations given to me thus straightforwardly, as if through a revelation, as it were. B408

3. The proposition of the identity of myself in all the manifold whereof I am conscious is likewise a proposition that lies in the concepts themselves and hence is analytic. But this identity of the subject, of which I can become conscious in all presentations of this subject, does not concern the subject's intuition whereby it is given as object. Hence this identity also cannot mean identity of the person, by which we understand the consciousness of the subject's own substance as a thinking being in all variation of its states. Proving this identity could not be accomplished by merely analyzing the proposition *I think*, but would require various synthetic judgments based on the given intuition. B409

4. I distinguish my own existence, as that of a thinking being, from other things outside me (which include my body)—this is likewise an analytic proposition. For *other* things are things that I think as *distinct* from me. But from this I do not in any way know whether this

consciousness of myself is at all possible without things outside me whereby presentations are given to me, and hence whether I can exist as merely a thinking being (i.e., without being human).

Hence analyzing the consciousness of myself in thought as such does not yield the slightest gain as regards the cognition of myself as object. The logical exposition of thought as such is wrongly considered to be a metaphysical determination of the object.

It would be for our entire critique a great stumbling-block—indeed, even the only one—if there were a possibility of proving a priori that all thinking beings are in themselves simple substances; and that, being such, they therefore (as a consequence from the same basis of proof) inseparably carry with them personality and are conscious of their existence as one that is set apart from all matter. For in this way B410   we would, after all, have taken a step beyond the world of sense; we would have entered the realm of *noumena*—and now let no one deny us the right to expand further into this realm, to settle in it, and to take possession in it according as each of us is favored by his lucky star. For the proposition, Any thinking being is, as such, a simple substance, is a synthetic a priori proposition. For, first, it goes beyond the concept on which it is based and adds to thinking being as such its *way of existing;* and, second, it adds to that concept a predicate (that of simplicity) that cannot be given in any experience whatever. Hence it would then seem that synthetic a priori propositions are feasible and admissible not merely, as we have asserted, in reference to objects of possible experience—viz., as principles of the possibility of this experience itself—but that they can apply also to things as such and in themselves. And this is a conclusion that would put an end to this entire critique and would dictate that we leave everything as it was. Once we step closer to the matter, however, we see that the danger here is not so great.

In the procedure of rational psychology a paralogism prevails, which is exhibited by the following syllogism:

What cannot be thought otherwise than as subject also does not exist otherwise than as subject, and therefore is substance.

B411   *Now a thinking being, considered merely as such, cannot be thought otherwise than as subject.*

Therefore it also exists only as a subject, i.e., as substance.

In the major premise one talks about a being that can be thought in general, in every respect, and hence also as it may be given in intuition. But in the minor premise one talks about it insofar as it considers itself, as subject, only relatively to thought and the unity of consciousness, but not simultaneously in reference to the intuition whereby it is given as object for such thought. Therefore, one is inferring the conclusion *per sophisma figurae dictionis*, and hence by a fallacious inference.[19]

That resolving a famous argument into a paralogism in this way is entirely correct is distinctly evident when one consults the general comment on the systematic presentation of the principles and the section on the *noumena*.[20] There we proved that the concept of a thing that can exist by itself as subject but not as mere predicate does not yet carry with it, on that account, any objective reality; i.e., we proved that—since we have no insight into the possibility of such a way of existing—we cannot know whether an object belongs to this concept at all, and consequently proved that this concept yields absolutely no cognition. Hence if this concept is to indicate, under the name of substance, an object that can be given, and the concept is to become a cognition, then we must lay at its basis a permanent intuition; for intuition—i.e., that whereby alone the object is given—is the indispensable condition of a concept's having objective reality. In inner intuition, however, we have nothing permanent at all, for the *I* is only the consciousness of my thinking. Hence if one remains with mere thinking, then one also lacks the necessary condition for applying the concept of substance—i.e., the concept of a self-subsistent subject—to oneself as a thinking being. And the simplicity of the substance, which is linked with this concept, then drops out entirely along with that concept's reality, and is transformed into nothing

B412

B413

19. Thought is taken in two entirely different meanings in the two premises. In the major premise it is taken as it applies to an object as such (and hence also to an object as it may be given in intuition). But in the minor premise it is taken only as it consists in the reference to self-consciousness; hence here one thinks of no object whatsoever, but represents only the reference to oneself as subject (as the form of thought). In the first premise one talks about things that cannot be thought otherwise than as subjects. In the second premise, however, one talks (by abstracting from any object) not about *things* but about *thought*, in which the *I* always serves as the subject of consciousness. Hence in the conclusion it cannot follow that I cannot exist otherwise than as subject, but merely that in thinking my existence I can use myself only as the judgment's subject. And this is an identical proposition that reveals absolutely nothing concerning the way in which I exist.

20. [These sections have not been included in this abridgment.]

more than a logical qualitative unity of self-consciousness in thought as such—no matter whether the subject is composite or not. [...]

TRANSCENDENTAL DIALECTIC

BOOK II
ON THE DIALECTICAL INFERENCES OF PURE REASON

Chapter II
The Antinomy of Pure Reason

We have shown in the introduction to this part of our work that all transcendental illusion of pure reason rests on dialectical inferences whose schema is provided by logic, viz., in the three formal kinds of syllogisms as such—roughly as the categories find their logical schema in the four functions of all judgments. The *first kind* of these subtly reasoning inferences dealt with the unconditioned unity of the *subjective* conditions of all presentations as such (of the subject or soul); it corresponds to **categorical** syllogisms, whose major premise, as principle, states the reference of a predicate to a *subject*. Thus the *second* kind of dialectical argument will, by analogy with **hypothetical** syllogisms, take as its content the unconditioned unity of the objective conditions in [the realm of] appearance—just as the *third kind* of dialectical inferences, which will come up in the following [third] chapter, has as its topic the unconditioned unity of the objective conditions for the possibility of objects as such.

It is noteworthy, however, that the transcendental paralogisms brought about a merely one-sided illusion regarding the idea of the subject of our thought, and that not the slightest illusion of plausibility arising from concepts of reason can be found for the assertion of the opposite. The advantage is entirely on the side of pneumatism, although this view cannot deny having the built-in defect that, despite all the illusion of plausibility in its favor, in the critique's ordeal by fire it dissolves entirely into smoke.

A406

B433

The outcome is quite different when we apply reason to the *objective synthesis* of appearances. Here, although reason means to validate A407
its principle of unconditioned unity with much illusion of plausibility, it soon becomes entangled in such contradictions that it is compelled, in regard to cosmology, to renounce its demand for such unity.

For here a new phenomenon of human reason manifests itself, viz., an entirely natural antithetic: i.e., an antithetic for [the discov- B434
ery of] which no one needs to ponder or artfully lay snares, but into which reason falls on its own and, moreover, inevitably. And although this antithetic protects reason from the slumber—produced by a merely one-sided illusion—of an imaginary conviction, yet it also tempts reason either to submit to a skeptical hopelessness, or to adopt a dogmatic defiance and rigidly stand up for certain assertions without granting a hearing or doing justice to the bases supporting the opposite. Both [the slumber of imaginary conviction and this skepticism or dogmatism] are the death of a sound philosophy, although the slumber might at least still be called pure reason's *euthanasia.*

Before we unveil the instances of discord and disarray to which this conflict of laws (antinomy) of pure reason gives rise, let us offer certain points that may elucidate and justify the method employed by A408
us in treating our topic. All transcendental ideas insofar as they concern absolute totality in the synthesis of appearances I call world concepts, partly because of precisely this unconditioned totality—on which rests also the concept, which itself is only an idea, of the world whole—and partly because they deal with the synthesis of appearances only, and hence with empirical synthesis. By contrast, absolute B435
totality in the synthesis of the conditions of all possible things as such will give rise to an ideal of pure reason; this ideal, although it has reference to a world concept, is yet entirely distinct from it. Hence just as the paralogisms of pure reason laid the basis for a dialectical psychology, so will the antinomy of pure reason put before us the transcendental principles of a supposed pure (rational) cosmology. The antinomy will do so not in order to find this cosmology valid and adopt it, but—as is, indeed, already indicated by the very name, conflict of reason—in order to exhibit it in its beguiling but deceptive illusion, as an idea that cannot be reconciled with appearances.

The Antinomy of Pure Reason

Section I
System of Cosmological Ideas

Now in order for us to be able to enumerate these ideas with systematic precision according to a principle, we must note two points.
A409 *First,* pure and transcendental concepts can arise only from the understanding. Reason does not in fact produce any concept, but at most *frees* the *concept of understanding* of the inevitable limitations of a possible experience; and thus reason tries to expand the concept beyond the bounds of the empirical, but yet in connection with the
B436 empirical. Reason does this by demanding, for a given conditioned, absolute totality on the side of the conditions (under which the understanding subjects all appearances to synthetic unity). It thereby turns the category into a transcendental idea, in order that, by continuing empirical synthesis up to the unconditioned (which is never found in experience but only in the idea), reason may provide this synthesis with absolute completeness. Reason demands this totality according to the principle that *if the conditioned is given, then the entire sum of conditions and hence the absolutely unconditioned* (through which alone the conditioned was possible) *is also given.* Hence, *first,* transcendental ideas will in fact be nothing but categories expanded up to the unconditioned, and they can be put in a table arranged according to the [four] headings of the categories. However, *second,* not all categories will be suitable for this, but only those categories in which the synthesis makes up a *series*—a series, moreover, of condi-
A410 tions for a conditioned that are subordinated to (not coordinated with) one another. Absolute totality is demanded by reason only insofar as this totality concerns the ascending series of conditions for a given conditioned, and hence not when we are talking about the descending line of consequences, nor yet when we are talking about the aggregate of coordinated conditions for these consequences. For as
B437 regards the given conditioned, conditions are already presupposed and must be regarded as given with it. Consequences, on the other hand, do not make their conditions possible, but rather presuppose them; hence in proceeding to the consequences (or [i.e.] in descending from the given condition to the conditioned) we do not have to

worry whether or not the series ceases, and the question concerning the totality of this series is, indeed, no presupposition of reason at all. [...]

The Antinomy of Pure Reason

A420/
B448

Section II
Antithetic of Pure Reason

If thetic is the term for any sum of dogmatic doctrines, then by anti-thetic I mean not dogmatic assertions of the opposite, but the conflict of seemingly dogmatic cognitions *(thesis cum antithesi)* without attribution to one of them of a superior claim to approval over the other. Thus the antithetic does not deal at all with one-sided assertions, but considers universal cognitions of reason only in regard to their conflict with one another and to the causes of this conflict. The transcendental antithetic is an inquiry concerning the antinomy of pure reason, its causes, and its result. When we apply our reason not merely—for the sake of using the principles of understanding—to objects of experience, but venture to extend our reason beyond the bounds of experience, then there arise *subtly reasoning* doctrines. These doctrines neither may hope to be confirmed in experience, nor need they fear being refuted in it; and each of them not only is in itself without contradiction, but even encounters conditions of its necessity in the nature of reason—except that, unfortunately, the counterproposition has on its side equally valid and necessary bases for its assertion.

A421

B449

The questions, then, that naturally arise in such a dialectic of pure reason are the following. (1) What are, in fact, the propositions in which pure reason is unfailingly subject to an antinomy? (2) To what causes is this antinomy due? (3) Despite this contradiction, does a path to certainty yet remain open to reason, and in what way?

Accordingly, a dialectical doctrine of pure reason must have this twofold feature distinguishing it from all sophistical propositions: First, it must concern not a chosen question that one is raising only for this or that arbitrary aim, but a question that any human reason must in its progress necessarily come upon. And second, such a doctrine, with its counterproposition, must carry with it not a merely

A422

B450   artificial illusion that immediately vanishes once we have insight into it, but a natural and unavoidable illusion that still continues to delude us—although not to deceive us—even when we are no longer tricked by it, and that hence can be rendered innocuous, but never obliterated.

Such a dialectical doctrine will refer not to the unity of understanding in experiential concepts, but to the unity of reason in mere ideas. But as synthesis according to rules this unity is still to be congruent, first, with the understanding, and yet as absolute unity of this synthesis it is to be congruent simultaneously with reason. Hence if this unity is adequate to reason then its conditions will be too great for the understanding, and if the unity is commensurate with the understanding then its conditions will be too small for reason. And from this there must arise a conflict that cannot be avoided, no matter how one goes about doing so.

These subtly reasoning assertions thus reveal a dialectical combat arena. There any party permitted to make the attack keeps the upper

A423   hand, and the party compelled to proceed merely defensively is certain to be defeated. Vigorous knights, by the same token, whether they pledge themselves to the good or to the evil cause, are sure to carry off the wreath of victory—provided they take care to have the prerogative of making the last attack and are not obliged to withstand a new onslaught by the opponent. We can indeed readily conceive

B451   that this contest arena has all along been entered often enough and that many victories have been won by both sides, but that for the last and decisive victory care has always been taken—by forbidding the opponent to take up arms thenceforth—that solely the champion of the good cause would prevail in the arena. We, however, as impartial arbiters of combat, must set aside entirely whether the cause for which the contestants are fighting is the good or the evil one, and must let them decide their cause between themselves. Perhaps, after having more exhausted than harmed each other, they will become aware on their own of the nullity of their contest, and will part as good friends.

This method of watching—or, rather, of occasioning on one's own—a contest of assertions, not in order finally to decide in favor of

A424   one or the other party, but in order to inquire whether the contest's object is not perhaps a mere deception for which each party grasps in vain and from which it cannot gain anything even if not resisted at all—this procedure, I say, may be called the *skeptical method*. It is entirely distinct from *skepticism,* a principle of technical and scientific ignorance—a principle that undermines the foundations of all cognition in order, if possible, to leave cognition without any reliability and security whatsoever. For the skeptical method aims at certainty. It B452 does so by seeking to discover the point of misunderstanding in such a dispute—a dispute that on both sides is meant sincerely and is conducted with understanding—in order that, as wise legislators do, it may from the perplexity of judges in lawsuits obtain information for itself about what is deficient and not precisely determined in its laws. [...]

The Antinomy of Pure Reason
Section II
Antithetic of Pure Reason

FIRST CONFLICT OF TRANSCENDENTAL IDEAS

THESIS	ANTITHESIS
The world has a beginning in time and is also enclosed within bounds as regards space.	The world has no beginning and no bounds in space, but is infinite as regards both time and space.
PROOF	PROOF
For assume that the world has no beginning as regards time. In that case, up to every given point in time an eternity has elapsed and hence an infinite series of successive states of things in the world has gone by. However, the infinity of a series consists precisely in the fact that it can never be completed by successive synthesis. Therefore an infinite bygone world series is impossible, and hence	For suppose that it has a beginning. In that case, since the beginning is an existence preceded by a time in which the thing is not, a time must have preceded wherein the world was not, i.e., an empty time. In an empty time, however, no arising of any thing is possible; for no part of such a time has, in preference to another part, any distinguishing condition of existence rather

THESIS PROOF

ANTITHESIS PROOF

a beginning of the world is a necessary condition of the world's existence—which was the first point to be proved.

As regards the *second* point in the thesis, assume again the opposite. In that case the world will be an infinite given whole of things existing simultaneously. Now in the case of a *quantum* that is not given within certain limits of any intuition, we can think of this quantum's magnitude in no other way than through the synthesis of its parts, and can think of the totality of such a quantum only through the completed synthesis, or through repeated addition of unit to unit. Accordingly, in order for the world—which occupies all spaces—to be thought as a whole, the successive synthesis of the parts of an infinite world would have to be regarded as completed, i.e., in the enumeration of all coexisting things an infinite time would have to be regarded as having elapsed—which is impossible. Accordingly, an infinite aggregate of actual things cannot be regarded as a given whole, and hence also not as given *simultaneously*.

than nonexistence (whether one assumes that the world arises of itself or through another cause). Hence although many a series of things can begin in the world, the world itself cannot have a beginning and hence is infinite with regard to past time.

As concerns the second point in the antithesis, assume, first of all, the opposite: viz., that the world is, as regards space, finite and bounded. In that case the world is located in an empty space that is not bounded. Hence we would find here not only a relation of things *in space* but also a relation of things *to space*. Now the world is an absolute whole, outside of which there is to be found no object of intuition, and hence no correlate of the world to which the world stands in relation; therefore the relation of the world to empty space would be a relation of it to *no object*. But such a relation—and hence also the bounding of the world by empty space—is nothing. Therefore the world is, as regards space, not bounded at all; i.e., it is infinite with regard to extension.[21]

A428/ B456

A429/ B457

21. Space is merely the form of outer intuition (i.e., it is merely formal intuition), but not an actual object that can be intuited externally. Space, as prior to

THESIS PROOF	ANTITHESIS PROOF

Consequently, a world is, as regards extension in space, not *infinite* but is enclosed in its bounds—which was the second point to be proved.

Comment on the First Antinomy

I. On the Thesis	II. On the Antithesis

In these mutually conflicting arguments I have not sought to use deceptions in order perhaps to conduct (as we say) a lawyer's proof—which employs the opponent's carelessness to its own advantage and gladly accepts his appeal to a misunderstood law in order to build its own illegitimate claims on that law's refutation. Each of these proofs is drawn from the nature of the case, and the advantage obtainable from the fallacious inferences of the

The proof for the infinity of the given world series and the infinity of the world sum-total rests on this: that in the opposite case an empty time and similarly an empty space would have to make up the boundary of the world. Now, I am not unaware that philosophers seek subterfuges against this implication, by claiming that a boundary of the world as regards both time and space is indeed entirely possible without one's needing to assume an

---

all things that determine (occupy or bound) it—or that, rather, give us an *empirical intuition* conforming to its form—is called absolute space; absolute space is nothing but the mere possibility of outer appearances insofar as they either exist in themselves or can still be added to given appearances. Hence empirical intuition is not composed of appearances and space (i.e., perception and empty intuition). The one is not the other's correlate in synthesis, but is only linked with the other in one and the same empirical intuition, viz., as its matter and form. If we try to posit one of these two items outside the other (viz., space outside all appearances), then there arise from this all sorts of empty determinations of outer intuition that yet are not possible perceptions: e.g., the distinction between the world's motion or rest in infinite empty space—a determination of the relation of the two to each other that can never be perceived and that, by the same token, is therefore the predicate of a mere thought-entity.

I. ON THE THESIS

II. ON THE ANTITHESIS

dogmatists from both parties has been put aside.

I could also seemingly have proved the thesis by starting, in accordance with the custom of the dogmatists, from a defective concept of the infinity of a given magnitude. A magnitude [so I could have argued] is *infinite* if beyond it (i.e., beyond what multitude of a given unit it contains) no greater one is possible. Now no magnitude is the greatest, because one or more units can always still be added. Therefore an infinite given magnitude, and hence also an infinite world (infinite as regards both the bygone series and extension), is impossible; therefore the world is bounded in both respects. Thus could I have conducted my proof. However, this concept of the infinity of a given magnitude does not agree with what is meant by an infinite whole. For we do not represent through this concept *how great* this whole is, and hence the concept of this whole is also not the concept of a *maximum*. Rather, through this concept we think only the whole's rela-

absolute time prior to the beginning of the world, or an absolute space spread out outside of the actual world—both of which are impossible. With the latter part of this opinion of the philosophers from the Leibnizian school I am entirely satisfied. Space is merely the form of outer intuition, but not an actual object that can be intuited externally, and not a correlate of appearances but the form of appearances themselves. Hence space cannot occur absolutely (by itself) as something determinative in the existence of things, since it is no object at all but only the form of possible objects. Hence things considered as appearances do indeed determine space; i.e., they bring about the fact that among all its possible predicates (of magnitude and relation) certain ones belong to actuality. But space considered as something self-subsistent cannot conversely determine the actuality of things as regards magnitude or shape, because it is nothing actual in itself. Hence a space (whether full or empty)[22] can indeed be

A432/
B460

---

22. It will readily be discerned that I mean by this the following: *empty space insofar as it is bounded by appearances*—hence empty space *within the world*—at least does not contradict transcendental principles, and thus may, as far as they

I. On the Thesis

II. On the Antithesis

tion to an arbitrarily assumed unit, in regard to which this whole is greater than any number. Now according as the unit is assumed greater or smaller, the infinite whole would be greater or smaller. Only infinity, since it consists merely in the relation to these given units, would always remain the same; but through this concept, of course, the absolute magnitude of the whole would not be cognized—nor, indeed, is cognizing this magnitude at issue here.

The true (transcendental) concept of infinity is this: that the successive synthesis of unit[s] in measuring by means of a quantum can never be completed.[23] From this it follows quite surely that an eternity of actual successive states up to a given point in time (the present one) cannot have gone by, and that the world must therefore have a beginning.

In regard to the second part of the thesis the difficulty concerning an infinite and yet elapsed series does, indeed, go away; for the manifold of a

bounded by appearances, but appearances cannot be bounded by an empty space outside them. The same holds also for time. But all of this being granted, the fact is nonetheless indisputable that these two non-entities—empty space outside, and empty time prior to, the world—must assuredly be assumed if one assumes a boundary of the world, whether in regard to space or time.

For as concerns the above implication—whereby we say that if the world has bounds (as regards time and space) then the infinite void must determine the existence of actual things as regards their magnitude—the escape by which philosophers seek to evade this implication consists, although covertly, only in this: that instead of thinking of a *world of sense* one thinks of who knows what kind of intelligible world; instead of the first beginning (an existence preceded by a time of nonexistence) one thinks an existence as such that *presupposes no other condition* in the world; and instead of the

A433/
B461

are concerned, be granted (although its possibility may not therefore immediately be asserted).

23. The quantum thereby contains a multitude (of [a] given unit) that is greater than any number—which is the mathematical concept of the infinite.

I. ON THE THESIS

world that is infinite as regards extension is given *simultaneously*. Consider, however, the totality of such a multitude: since we cannot appeal to bounds that by themselves make up this totality in intuition, we must, in order to think this totality, account for our concept. However, this concept cannot in such a case proceed from the whole to the determinate multitude of parts, but must establish the possibility of a whole through the successive synthesis of the parts. Now because this synthesis would have to make up a series that can never be completed, one cannot think a totality of such a synthesis, and hence also not by means of it. For the concept of totality itself is in this case the representation of a completed synthesis of the parts; but this completion, and hence also the concept of it, is impossible.

II. ON THE ANTITHESIS

boundary of extension one thinks *limits* of the world whole; and thus one gets away from time and space. But we are here talking only about the *mundus phaenomenon* and its magnitude, and in the case of this world we can by no means abstract from the mentioned conditions of sensibility without annulling the essence of that world. The world of sense, if it is bounded, lies necessarily in the infinite void. If one wants to leave out the void, and hence space as such, as an *a priori* condition for the possibility of appearances, then the entire world of sense drops out. In our problem, this world alone is given to us. The *mundus intelligibilis* is nothing but the universal concept of a world as such. In this concept one abstracts from all conditions of the intuition of the world, and therefore in regard to this concept no synthetic proposition whatever is possible either affirmatively or negatively.

Section II
Antithetic of Pure Reason

Sᴇᴄᴏɴᴅ Cᴏɴꜰʟɪᴄᴛ ᴏꜰ Tʀᴀɴꜱᴄᴇɴᴅᴇɴᴛᴀʟ Iᴅᴇᴀꜱ

Tʜᴇꜱɪꜱ	Aɴᴛɪᴛʜᴇꜱɪꜱ
Every composite substance in the world consists of simple parts, and nothing at all exists but the simple or what is composed of it.	No composite thing in the world consists of simple parts, and there exists in the world nothing simple at all.

Pʀᴏᴏꜰ	Pʀᴏᴏꜰ
For suppose that composite substances did not consist of simple parts. In that case, if all composition were annulled in thought, then there would remain no composite part and (since on this supposition there are no simple parts) also no simple part; hence there would remain nothing at all, and consequently no substance would have been given. Therefore, either one cannot possibly annul in thought all composition, or after its annulment there must remain something that subsists without any composition, i.e., the simple. In the first case, however, the composite would again not consist of substances; (for with substances composition is only a contingent relation of substances—a relation without which substances, as by themselves permanent	Suppose that a composite thing (as substance) consists of simple parts. Now all external relation and hence also all composition from substances is possible only in space; hence however many parts the composite consists of, the space that it occupies must also consist of as many parts. Now space consists not of simple parts but of spaces. Hence every part of the composite must occupy a space. However, the absolutely first parts of anything composite are simple. Therefore the simple occupies a space. Now anything real that occupies a space comprises a manifold [of elements] outside one another and hence is composite; as a real composite, moreover, it is composed not from accidents (for these cannot without substance be

149

A436/
B464

beings, must still subsist). Now since this case contradicts the presupposition, there remains only the second case: viz., that the substantive composite in the world consists of simple parts.

From this it follows directly that the things in the world are, one and all, simple beings; that composition is merely an external state of them; and that although we can never put elementary substances completely out of this state of combination and isolate them, yet reason must think them as the first subjects of all composition, and hence must think them, prior to any composition, as simple beings.

outside one another) but, hence, from substances; therefore the simple would be a substantive composite—which is self-contradictory.

The second proposition of the antithesis—that nothing simple whatsoever exists in the world—is to mean no more here than this: the existence of the absolutely simple cannot be established from any experience or perception, whether outer or inner; and the absolutely simple is, therefore, a mere idea the objective reality of which can never be established in any possible experience, and which is hence without any application and object in the exposition of appearances. For let us assume that an object of experience could be found for this transcendental idea; then the empirical intuition of some object would have to be cognized as one containing absolutely no manifold [of elements] outside one another and combined into unity. Now from our not being conscious of such a manifold we cannot validly infer that such a manifold is entirely impossible in any intuition of an object; yet this impossibility is assuredly needed for absolute simplicity. Thus it follows that this sim-

A437/
B465

ANTITHESIS PROOF

plicity cannot be inferred from any perception whatsoever. Since, therefore, nothing can ever be given as an absolutely simple object in any possible experience, but since the world of sense must be regarded as the sum of all possible experiences, nothing simple is given in it at all.

This second proposition of the antithesis goes much further than the first. The first proposition banishes the simple only from the intuition of the composite; the second, by contrast, removes the simple from all of nature—which is also the reason why we were able to prove this proposition not from the concept of a given object of outer intuition (of the composite), but only from the concept's relation to a possible experience as such.

A438/
B466

Comment on the Second Antinomy

A439/
B467

I. ON THE THESIS

In talking about a whole that necessarily consists of simple parts I mean only a substantial whole—this being the composite proper, i.e., the contingent unity of the manifold that, *given separately* (at least in thought), is put into a

II. ON THE ANTITHESIS

Against this proposition— whose basis of proof is merely mathematical—concerning an infinite division of matter, objections have been advanced by the *monadists*. These objections already arouse suspicion by the fact that the monadists refuse

I. On the Thesis

reciprocal linkage and thereby makes up a unity. Space should properly be called not a *compositum* but a *totum*, because its parts are possible only in the whole, not the whole through the parts. At most space could be called a *compositum ideale*, rather than *reale*. But this is mere subtlety. Space is not a composite made up from substances (not even from real accidents). Hence if I annul all composition in it, then nothing must remain, not even a point; for a point is possible only as the boundary of a space (hence of a composite). Therefore, space and time do not consist of simple parts. If something belongs only to the state of a substance, then—even if it has a magnitude (e.g., change)—it also does not consist of the simple; i.e., a certain degree of change does not come about by an accretion of many simple changes. Our inference from the composite to the simple holds only for self-subsistent things. But accidents of the state are not self-subsistent. Hence one can easily ruin the proof for the necessity of the simple, as the components of any substantive composite, and thereby ruin one's case as such: viz., if one extends the proof

II. On the Antithesis

to accept the clearest mathematical proofs as being insights into the character of space— insofar as space is in fact the formal condition for the possibility of all matter—but they regard such proofs only as inferences from abstract but chosen concepts that could not be referred to actual things. The monadists downgrade these proofs as if, indeed, it were so much as possible to think up a different kind of intuition from the one that is given in the original intuition of space, and as if the a priori determinations of this space did not pertain simultaneously to whatever is possible only through the fact that it occupies this space. If we listened to them, then besides the mathematical point— which, although simple, is not a part but merely the limit of a space—we would have to think also physical points; these, although likewise simple, have the advantage that, as parts of space, they occupy it by their mere aggregation. Now, I shall not repeat here the common and clear refutations of this absurdity—since, indeed, the attempt by means of merely discursive concepts to subtly reason away the self-evidence of mathematics is entirely

I. ON THE THESIS

too far and tries to make it hold, without making a distinction, for anything composite—as has actually already happened repeatedly.

I am, besides, talking here only about the simple insofar as it is necessarily given in the composite—inasmuch as the composite can be resolved into the simple as its components. The proper meaning of the term *monad* (according to Leibniz's use) should presumably apply only to the simple that is given *directly* as simple substance (e.g., in self-consciousness), rather than given as element of the composite, which might better be called an *atomus*. And since it is only with regard to the composite that I wish to prove simple substances, as elements of the composite, I could call the thesis of the second antinomy transcendental *atomism*. However, inasmuch as this term has long since already been used to designate a particular way of explaining bodily appearances *(moleculae)* and hence presupposes empirical concepts, the thesis may be called the dialectical principle of *monadology*.

A442/
B470

II. ON THE ANTITHESIS

futile. I shall note only that if philosophy here plays tricks with mathematics, then this happens only because philosophy forgets that in this question the concern is only with *appearances* and their conditions. Here, however, it is not enough that for the *understanding's concept* of the composite we find the concept of the simple. Rather, for the *intuition* of the composite (the intuition of matter) we must find the intuition of the simple; and this, according to laws of sensibility and hence also for objects of the senses, is entirely impossible. Hence for a whole composed from substances that is thought merely through the pure understanding it may indeed hold that we must, prior to any composition of this whole, have the simple; yet this does not hold for the *totum substantiale phaenomenon* [whole of phenomenal substances], which, as empirical intuition in space, carries with it the necessary property that no part of it is simple—because no part of space is simple. The monadists, however, have been acute enough to try to evade this difficulty: viz., by presupposing not space as a condition for the possibility of objects of outer

A441/
B469

II. ON THE ANTITHESIS

intuition (bodies), but instead these objects and the dynamical relation of substances as such as the condition for the possibility of space. Now, we have a concept of bodies only as appearances; as appearances, however, they necessarily presuppose space as the condition for the possibility of all outer appearances. Hence this subterfuge of the monadists is futile—and it has, indeed, been sufficiently cut down above, in the Transcendental Aesthetic. If bodies were things in themselves, [on the other hand] then the proof of the monadists would indeed hold.

The second dialectical assertion has the peculiarity of having against it a [special] dogmatic assertion that, among all subtly reasoning assertions, is the only one that undertakes to prove manifestly, in an object of experience, the actuality of what above we ascribed merely to transcendental ideas: viz., the absolute simplicity of substance. I mean the assertion that the object of inner sense, the *I* that thinks, is an absolutely simple substance. Now without here entering into this issue (since it has been examined more elaborately above), I shall note only this: that when

A443/ B471

II. ON THE ANTITHESIS

we think something merely as an object without adding any synthetic determinations of its intuition (and this is, in fact, what we do through the entirely bare representation *I*), then of course we cannot perceive in such a representation anything manifold and any composition. Moreover, since the predicates through which I think this object are merely intuitions of inner sense, there also cannot occur in it anything that would prove a manifold [of elements] outside one another and hence prove real composition. Thus what prompts the mentioned assertion is only that our self-consciousness is such that, because the subject that thinks is simultaneously its own object, this subject cannot divide itself (although it can divide the determinations inhering in it); for in regard to itself any object is an absolute unity. Nonetheless, if this subject were to be contemplated *externally* as an object of intuition, then presumably it would in appearance manifest in itself composition. That, however, is how it must always be contemplated if we want to know whether or not there is in it a manifold [of elements] *outside* one another.

Section II
Antithetic of Pure Reason

THIRD CONFLICT OF TRANSCENDENTAL IDEAS

THESIS	ANTITHESIS
The causality according to laws of nature is not the only causality, from which the appearances of the world can thus one and all be derived. In order to explain these appearances, it is necessary to assume also a causality through freedom.	There is no freedom, but everything in the world occurs solely according to laws of nature.

PROOF	PROOF
Assume that there is no other causality than the one according to laws of nature. In that case, everything that *occurs* presupposes a previous state upon which it unfailingly follows according to a rule. The previous state, however, must itself be something that has occurred (has come to be in the time wherein previously it was not); for if it had always been, then its consequence also would always have been and would not now first of all have arisen. Hence the cause's causality, through which something occurs, is itself something which has *occurred* and which, according to the laws of nature, again presupposes a previous state and its causality,	Suppose there is, in the transcendental meaning of the term, a *freedom* as a special kind of causality according to which the events of the world could happen: viz., a power of absolutely beginning a state, and hence also of absolutely beginning a series of consequences thereof. In that case, not only will a series begin absolutely through this spontaneity, but the determination of this spontaneity itself to produce the series—i.e., the causality—will begin absolutely, so that nothing precedes by which this occurring action is determined according to constant laws. However, any beginning to act presupposes a state of the not yet acting cause; and a dynam-

THESIS PROOF

ANTITHESIS PROOF

but this state similarly presupposes a still earlier one, etc. Hence if everything occurs according to mere laws of nature, then there is always only a subsidiary but never a first beginning, and hence there then is on the side of the causes originating from one another no completeness of the series at all. The law of nature, however, consists precisely in this: that nothing occurs without a cause sufficiently determined a priori. Hence the proposition, in its unlimited universality, whereby any causality is possible only according to natural laws contradicts itself; and hence this causality cannot be assumed as being the only one.

Accordingly, we must assume a causality through which something occurs without its cause's being determined still further, according to necessary laws, by another, preceding cause. I.e., we must assume an *absolute spontaneity* of causes whereby they can begin *on their own* a series of appearances that runs according to natural laws—hence transcendental freedom—without which even in the course of nature the sequence of appearances on the side of the causes is never complete.

ically first beginning of action presupposes a state that has no connection of causality at all with the preceding state of the same cause, i.e., in no way results from that preceding state. Therefore, transcendental freedom runs counter to the causal law; and hence a linkage of successive states of efficient causes according to which no unity of experience is possible—and which, therefore, is also not encountered in any experience—is an empty thought-entity.

We have, therefore, nothing but *nature* as the place wherein we must seek the coherence and order of events in the world. Freedom (independence) from the laws of nature is indeed a *liberation* from *constraint*, but also from the *guidance* of all rules. For one cannot say that instead of the laws of nature, laws of freedom enter into the causality of the course of nature, because if freedom were determined according to laws then it would not be freedom but would itself be nothing but nature. Hence nature and freedom differ as do law-governedness and lawlessness. Nature does indeed burden the understanding with the difficulty of seeking the origin of events ever

ANTITHESIS PROOF

higher up in the series of causes, because the causality in them is always conditioned; but for compensation it promises us thoroughgoing and law-governed unity of experience. The deception of freedom, on the other hand, does indeed promise to the investigating understanding a point of rest in the chain of causes, by leading it to an unconditioned causality that on its own starts to act; but, being blind itself, it disrupts the guidance of rules that alone makes possible an experience having thoroughgoing coherence.

A448/
B476

Comment on the Third Antinomy

A449/
B477

I. ON THE THESIS

The transcendental idea of freedom does not, indeed, amount to the entire content—which is in large part empirical—of the psychological concept of that name; rather, the transcendental idea's content is only the absolute spontaneity of action, as the proper basis for the action's imputability. But this idea is nonetheless the stumbling-block proper for philosophy, which finds insurmountable difficulties in granting such a kind of

II. ON THE ANTITHESIS

The defender of the omnipotence of nature (transcendental *physiocracy*) would, in opposing the doctrine of freedom, maintain his proposition against this doctrine's subtly reasoning inferences in the following manner. *If you do not assume in the world something mathematically first as regards time, then you also do not need to seek something dynamically first as regards causality*. Who told you to think up an absolutely first state of the world and hence an

I. ON THE THESIS

II. ON THE ANTITHESIS

unconditioned causality. Hence what in the question about the freedom of the will has all along put speculative reason in a great quandary is—properly speaking—only *transcendental,* and concerns merely this: whether we must assume a power of beginning *spontaneously* a series of successive things or states. Being able to answer the question as to how such a power is possible is not equally necessary. For in the causality according to natural laws we must likewise settle for cognizing a priori that such a causality must be presupposed, even though we do not comprehend in any way the possibility whereby through a certain [thing's] existence the existence of another is posited, and must thus keep solely to experience. Now, to be sure, we have in fact established this necessity of a first beginning, issuing from freedom, only insofar as this is required for making comprehensible an origin of the world, whereas all subsequent states can be taken to be a succession according to mere natural laws. Yet, having once proved thereby (although not gained insight into) the power of beginning entirely spontaneously a series in time,

A450/
B478

absolute beginning of the gradually passing series of appearances, and to set bounds to limitless nature in order to provide your imagination with a resting-point? Since the substances in the world have always been—or since at least the unity of experience makes such a presupposition necessary— there is no difficulty in also assuming that the variation by the states of these substances, i.e., a series of their changes, has likewise always been, and that we therefore need not seek a first beginning, whether mathematical or dynamical.

The possibility of such an infinite origination, without a first member in regard to which everything else is merely subsequent, cannot be made comprehensible. But if you want therefore to dismiss this puzzle of nature, then you will find yourselves compelled to reject many basic synthetic characteristics (basic forces) that you are just as little able to comprehend, and even the possibility of a change as such must then become objectionable to you. For if you did not find through experience that change is actual, then you would never be able to excogitate a priori how such an

A451/
B479

I. ON THE THESIS

we are now also permitted to let different series begin spontaneously, even in the midst of the course of the world, as regards [not time but] causality, and to attribute to their substances a power of acting from freedom. Here we must not let ourselves be detained, however, by a misunderstanding: viz., that because a successive series in the world can have only a comparatively first beginning, since a state of things in the world does always precede it, perhaps no absolutely first beginning of any series is possible during the course of the world. For we are here talking about an absolutely first beginning not as regards time but as regards causality. If (for example) I now get up from my chair completely freely and without the influence of natural causes, which is determinative necessarily, then in this event—along with its natural consequences *ad infinitum*—a new series begins absolutely, although as regards time this event is only the continuation of a preceding series. For this decision and act of mine do not lie at all in the succession of mere natural effects, and are not a mere continuation of them. Rather, as regards this

II. ON THE ANTITHESIS

unceasing sequence of being and not-being is possible.

However, even if a transcendental power of freedom is perhaps conceded in order to begin the changes of the world, yet this power would at any rate have to be solely outside the world (although to assume, outside of the sum of all possible intuitions, a further object that cannot be given in any possible perception always remains bold presumption). But to attribute such a faculty to substances in the world itself cannot be permitted on any account. For then the coherence—which is called nature—of appearances determining one another necessarily according to universal laws, would for the most part vanish, and along with it so would the mark of empirical truth which distinguishes experience from a dream. For alongside such a lawless power of freedom, nature can scarcely be thought any more, because the laws of nature are altered incessantly by the influences of freedom, and the play of appearances—which according to mere nature would be regular and uniform—is thereby rendered confused and incoherent.

I. On the Thesis

happening of my decision and act, the determinative natural causes entirely cease above them; and although this happening follows upon the determinative natural causes, it does not result from them, and hence must be called—not, indeed, as regards time, but yet with regard to causality—an absolutely first beginning of a series of appearances.

Reason's requirement to appeal, in the series of natural causes, to a first beginning issuing from freedom is confirmed with great clarity by the fact that (except for the Epicurean School) all the philosophers of antiquity found themselves constrained, in order to explain the world's motions, to assume a *prime mover*, i.e., a freely acting cause that first and on its own began this series of states. For they did not undertake to make a first beginning comprehensible from mere nature. [...]

The Antinomy of Pure Reason

Section VII
Critical Decision of the Cosmological Dispute That Reason Has with Itself

The entire antinomy of pure reason rests on this dialectical argument: If the conditioned is given, then the entire series of all its conditions is also given; now objects of the senses are given to us as conditioned; consequently, etc. Now through this syllogism, whose major premise seems so natural and evident, as many cosmological ideas are introduced as there are different conditions (in the synthesis of appearances), insofar as these conditions make up a series. The cosmological ideas postulate the absolute totality of these series, and precisely thereby put reason inevitably in conflict with itself. But before we uncover what is deceptive in this subtly reasoning argument,
B526 we must enable ourselves to do so, by correcting and making determinate certain concepts occurring in it.

First, the following proposition is clear and indubitably certain:
A498 that if the conditioned is given, then precisely thereby a regression in the series of all conditions for this conditioned is assigned to us. For the very concept of the conditioned implies that through this concept something is referred to a condition; and if this condition is in turn conditioned, then that something is referred to a more remote condition, and thus is referred through all the members of the series. The above proposition, therefore, is analytic and rises above any fear from a transcendental critique. It is a logical postulate of reason, viz., to pursue and as far as possible extend, by means of understanding, that connection of a concept with its conditions which attaches to the very concept itself.

Furthermore, if both the conditioned and its condition are things in themselves, and if the conditioned has been given, then not merely is the regression to the condition *assigned*, but this condition is thereby actually already given with the conditioned. And since this holds for all members of the series, the complete series of conditions—and hence also the unconditioned—is given, or, rather, presupposed, simultaneously through the fact that the conditioned, which was possible only through that series, is given. Here the synthesis of the conditioned with its condition is a synthesis of the mere understanding, which presents things *as they are* without considering whether and how we can reach a cognition of them. Appearances, on the other hand, are mere presentations, and as such are not given at all unless I reach cognition of them (i.e., unless I reach the appearances themselves, for they are nothing but empirical cognitions). Hence if I deal with appearances then I cannot say, in the same meaning of the term, that if the conditioned is given then all conditions for it (as appearances) are also given, and hence I can in no way infer the absolute totality of the series of these conditions. For *appearances* themselves are, in apprehension, nothing but an empirical synthesis (in space and time) and hence are given only *in this synthesis*. Now it does not follow at all that if the conditioned is given (in appearance), then the synthesis amounting to its empirical condition is thereby also given with it and presupposed; rather, this synthesis first occurs in the regression, and never without it. What we can indeed say in such a case, however, is that a *regression* to the conditions, i.e., that a continued empirical synthesis on this side is dictated or *assigned* to us, and that there can be no lack of conditions given through this regression.

This shows that the major premise of the cosmological syllogism takes the conditioned in the transcendental meaning of a pure category, but the minor premise takes it in the empirical meaning of a concept of understanding applied to mere appearances. Therefore, we find in this syllogism the dialectical deception called *sophisma figurae dictionis*. This deception, however, is not contrived, but is a quite natural delusion of common reason. For by this delusion, if something is given as conditioned, then (in the major premise) we presuppose the conditions and their series—*uninspected,* as it were. For to do this is nothing other than [to satisfy] the logical demand to assume complete premises for a given conclusion; and here no time order is to be found in the connection of the conditioned with its condition, but they are presupposed in themselves, as given *simultaneously.* Furthermore, it is equally natural (in the minor premise) to regard appearances as things in themselves and likewise as objects given to mere understanding—as was done in the major premise, where I abstracted from all conditions of intuition under which alone objects can be given. In this [natural treatment of the premises] we have, however, overlooked a noteworthy distinction between the concepts. The synthesis of the conditioned with its condition—and the entire series of conditions—carried with

B527
A499

B528

A500

it (in the major premise) nothing about limitation by time, and no concept of succession. On the other hand, the empirical synthesis—and the series of conditions in appearance—(which in the minor premise is subsumed [under the major]) is necessarily given successively and only in time, i.e., sequentially. Hence here I was not able to presuppose, as I was there, the absolute *totality* of the synthesis and

B529 of the series presented through this synthesis. For there all the members of the series are given in themselves (without time condition), but here they are possible only through the successive regression,

A501 which is given only by actually being carried out.

After having been convicted of such a slip in the argument that they jointly laid at the basis (of their cosmological assertions), both disputing parties may rightly be dismissed, as parties whose demand is based on no well-founded title. But although they did not know how to build their conclusions on sturdy bases of proof, their quarrel is not yet ended thereby in the respect that both or either of them has been shown to be wrong in the asserted matter itself (the conclusion). After all, nothing seems clearer than that if one of two persons asserts that the world has a beginning and the other asserts that the world has no beginning but has been there from eternity, then surely one must be right. Yet if that is so, then, because the clarity is the same on both sides, there is no possibility of ever ascertaining which side is in the right, and the dispute continues as before even though at the tribunal of reason the parties have been ordered to silence. Thus no remedy remains for ending the dispute thoroughly and to the satisfaction of both parties, except finally to show that—since, after all, they can so nicely refute each other—they are disputing

A502/ about nothing, and that a certain transcendental illusion has painted
B530 for them an actuality where none is to be found. Let us now enter upon this path on which a dispute that defies a verdict can be settled.

The *Eleatic philosopher Zeno*, a subtle dialectician, was severely rebuked as a mischievous sophist already by *Plato* because—to show his artistry—he sought to prove a proposition by plausible arguments and soon after to overturn the same proposition again by other arguments equally strong. Zeno asserted that God (this God presumably was for him nothing but the world) is neither finite nor infinite, neither in motion nor at rest, neither similar nor dissimilar to any other thing. To those who judged Zeno on this procedure he seemed to want entirely to deny two propositions contradicting each other—which is absurd. I believe, however, that he cannot rightly be

charged with this. The first of these propositions I shall soon examine more closely. As for the others, if by the word *God* Zeno meant
the universe, then he did indeed have to say that this universe neither
is permanently present in its location (at rest) nor changes its location (moves), because all locations are only in the universe and hence
the universe itself is in no location. Likewise, if the universe comprises all that exists, then it is to that extent also neither similar nor
dissimilar to any *other thing*, because there is apart from it *no other*   A503/
thing to which it could be compared. If two judgments that are op-   B531
posed to each other presuppose an inadmissible condition, then despite the conflict between them (which, however, is not a contradiction proper) both of them drop out, because the condition drops out
under which alone each of these propositions was to hold.

    If someone were to say that any body either smells good or smells
not good, then there is a third alternative, viz., that the body does not
smell (emit an odor) at all; and thus both of the conflicting propositions can be false. If I say that any body either is good-smelling or is
not good-smelling *(vel suaveolens vel non suaveolens)*, then the two
judgments are opposed to each other contradictorily and only the
first one is false, while its contradictory opposite—viz., that some
bodies are not good-smelling—comprises also those bodies *that do
not smell at all*. In the previous opposition *(per disparata)*, the contingent condition of the concept of bodies (smell) still *remained* in the
conflicting judgment and therefore was not also annulled by it;
hence this latter judgment was not the contradictory opposite of the
former judgment.

    Accordingly, if I say that, as regards space, either the world is infi-
nite or it is not infinite *(non est infinitus)*, then if the first proposition
is false, its contradictory opposite, that the world is not infinite, must
be true. By this [negative proposition] I would only annul an infinite
world, without positing another world, viz., the finite one. But if I   A504/
said that the world is either infinite or finite (noninfinite), then both   B532
of these propositions can be false. For I then regard the world as in
itself determined in terms of magnitude, because in the counterproposition I do not merely annul the infinity, and with it perhaps
the entire separate existence of the world; rather, I add a determination to the world taken as a thing that is actual in itself, and this may
likewise be false, viz., if the world were *not* given *as a thing in itself at
all* and hence also not in terms of its magnitude—neither as infinite
nor as finite. Permit me to call this sort of opposition *dialectical* but

that of contradiction *analytical opposition.* Thus of two dialectically opposed judgments both can be false, because one judgment not merely contradicts the other but says something more than is required for contradiction.

If one regards the two propositions, that the world is infinite in magnitude and that the world is finite in magnitude, as opposed to each other contradictorily, then one assumes that the world (the entire series of appearances) is a thing in itself. For [in either proposition] the world remains, whether I annul in the series of its appearances the infinite or the finite regression. But if I remove this presupposition—or [i.e.] this transcendental illusion—and deny that the world is a thing in itself, then the contradictory conflict of the two assertions is transformed into a merely dialectical one; and because the world does not exist in itself at all (i.e., independently of the regressive series of my presentations), it exists neither as *a whole that is infinite in itself* nor as *a whole that is finite in itself.* The world is to be met with only in the empirical regression of the series of appearances, and not at all by itself. If, therefore, this series is always conditioned, then it is never given wholly; and hence the world is not an unconditioned whole, and thus also does not exist as such a whole—neither with infinite nor with finite magnitude.

What has been said here about the first cosmological idea, viz., that of the absolute totality of magnitude in [the realm of] appearance, holds also for all the other cosmological ideas. The series of conditions is to be met with only in the regressive series itself, but not [as existing] in itself in appearance considered as a thing of its own given prior to all regression. Hence I shall also have to say that the multitude of parts in a given appearance is in itself neither finite nor infinite. For appearance is nothing that exists in itself, and the parts are first given by, and in, the regression of the decomposing synthesis, a regression that is never given in absolute *entirety*—neither as finite nor as infinite. The same holds for the series of causes superordinated to one another, or the series of the conditioned existence up to the unconditionally necessary existence. Here again this series can never be regarded as being in itself, as to its totality, either finite or infinite. For as a series of subordinated presentations it consists only in the dynamical regression; prior to this regression, however, and as a series of things in themselves that subsists by itself, it cannot exist at all.

A505/ B533

A506/ B534

Thus the antinomy of pure reason [that takes place] with pure reason's cosmological ideas is removed: viz., by showing that it is merely dialectical, and is a conflict due to an illusion that arises because the idea of absolute totality, which holds only as a condition of things in themselves, has been applied to appearances, which exist only in our presentation and—if they make up a series—in the successive regression, but otherwise do not exist at all. However, conversely, we can also draw from this antinomy a true benefit that, although not a dogmatic one, is yet a critical and doctrinal benefit: viz., we can by this antinomy prove indirectly the transcendental ideality of appearances—in case, perhaps, someone were not satisfied with the direct proof provided in the Transcendental Aesthetic. This indirect proof would consist in the following dilemma. If the world is a whole existing in itself, then it is either finite or infinite. Now, both of these alternatives are false (according to the proofs, adduced above, of the thesis and antithesis, respectively). Hence it is also false that the world (the sum of all appearances) is a whole existing in itself. From this it follows, then, that appearances as such are nothing apart from our presentations—which is precisely what we meant by their transcendental ideality.

A507/
B535

This comment is important. It shows that the above proofs of the fourfold antinomy were not deceptions but were well-founded. They were well-founded, viz., on the presupposition that appearances, or a world of sense comprising them all, are things in themselves. The conflict of the propositions drawn from these proofs reveals, however, that there is a falsehood in the presupposition, and thereby leads us to discover the true character of things as objects of the senses. Hence the dialectic by no means promotes skepticism. But it does promote the skeptical method, which can display the dialectic as an example of the method's great benefit: viz., when we let the arguments of reason come forward against each other in their greatest freedom; for although these arguments ultimately do not supply what we were searching for, yet they will always supply something beneficial and useful for correcting our judgments.

The Antinomy of Pure Reason

A508/
B536

Section VIII
Pure Reason's Regulative Principle
Regarding the Cosmological Ideas

Since through the cosmological principle of totality no maximum of
the series of conditions in a world of sense considered as a thing in
itself is *given*, but such a maximum can merely be *assigned* to us in
the regression of the series, this principle of pure reason, with its
meaning corrected in this manner, still retains all its validity—although not as an *axiom* for thinking the totality as actual in the object. The principle retains its validity, rather, as a *problem* for the understanding, and hence for the subject: viz., to perform and
continue, in accordance with the completeness in the idea, the regression in the series of conditions for a given conditioned. For in
sensibility, i.e., in space and time, any condition that we can reach in
the exposition of given appearances is in turn conditioned, because
these appearances are not objects in themselves—in which the absolutely unconditioned might, perhaps, occur. These appearances
are, rather, merely empirical presentations; and these must always
find their condition, which determines them as regards space or
time, in intuition. Hence the cosmological principle of reason is, in
A509/   fact, only a *rule* that commands us to perform, in the series of condi-
B537   tions of given appearances, a regression that is never permitted to
stop at anything absolutely unconditioned. It is, therefore, not a
principle for the possibility of experience and of the empirical cognition of objects of the senses, and hence it is not a principle of understanding; for every experience is enclosed (in accordance with the
given intuition) within its bounds. Nor is this cosmological principle
a *constitutive* principle of reason for expanding the concept of the
world of sense beyond all possible experience. Rather, it is a principle
of the greatest possible continuation and expansion of experience,
whereby no empirical boundary must count as absolute. Thus it is a
principle of reason that, *as rule*, postulates what is to be done by us in
the regression, and *does not anticipate* what is given in itself in the *object* prior to all regression. I therefore call this cosmological principle
a *regulative* principle of reason. By contrast, the principle of the ab-

168

solute totality of the series of conditions considered as given in the objects (the appearances) in themselves would be a constitutive cosmological principle. The nullity of this latter principle I wanted to indicate precisely by this distinction, and wanted thereby to prevent what otherwise inevitably occurs: our attributing (by transcendental subreption) objective reality to an idea that serves merely as a rule.

Now in order properly to define the meaning of this rule of pure reason, we must note, first of all, that this rule cannot tell us *what the object is*, but only *how the empirical regression is to be performed* in order for us to arrive at the complete concept of the object. For if the rule told us what the object is, then it would be a constitutive principle, and obtaining such a principle from pure reason is impossible. By this rule, therefore, we can in no way intend to mean that the series of conditions for a given conditioned is in itself finite or infinite. For then we would by a mere idea of absolute totality—a totality that is provided only in the idea itself—think an object that cannot be given in any experience; for we would confer on a series of appearances an objective reality independent of the empirical synthesis. Hence the rational idea will prescribe a rule only to the regressive synthesis in the series of conditions; according to that rule this synthesis proceeds from the conditioned, by means of all the conditions subordinated to one another, to the unconditioned—although this unconditioned is never reached, for the absolutely unconditioned is not found in experience at all.

Now to this end we must first accurately define the synthesis of a series insofar as this synthesis is never complete. For this aim, people usually employ two expressions that are intended to distinguish something in this synthesis, yet they do so without quite being able to indicate the basis of this distinction. The mathematicians speak solely of a *progressus in infinitum*. In its place, the investigators of concepts (philosophers) want to accept only the expression of a *progressus in indefinitum*. Without lingering upon an examination of the perplexity that has commended to them this distinction of two progressions, and upon the distinction's good or fruitless use, I want to try to define these two concepts accurately in reference to my aim.

Of a straight line we may rightly say that it can be extended to infinity, and here the distinction of an infinite and an indeterminably long progression *(progressus indefinitum)* would be an empty subtlety. To be sure, if one says, Continue drawing a line, then it is indeed more correct to add *in indefinitum* than to say *in infinitum*. For the first means no more than, Extend the line as far as *you want;* but the second means, *You shall* never stop extending it (which, of course, is not the aim here). Nevertheless, if only what *can* be done is at issue, then the first expression is quite correct; for you can go on augmenting the line to infinity. And so is it also in all cases where one speaks not of the *regressus* but only of the *progressus,* i.e., of the progression from the condition to the conditioned; in the series of appearances this possible progression proceeds to infinity. From a pair of parents you can progress without end in the descending line of procreation, and you can quite readily think that the line actually progresses thus in the world. For here reason never requires absolute totality of the series, because it does not presuppose such totality of the series as a condition and as *given (datum),* but presupposes it only as something conditioned that is only alleged and givable *(dabile)* and is added to without end.

A512/
B540

But the situation is quite different with the problem concerning regression: How far does the regression extend that ascends in a series from the given conditioned to the conditions? Can I say that it is a **regression to infinity,** or only that it is a regression extending *indeterminably far (in indefinitum)*? Hence can I from the now living human beings ascend, in the series of their progenitors, to infinity? Or can I say only that, no matter how far I have gone back, I have never encountered an empirical basis for regarding the series as limited somewhere, and thus for each of the forefathers I am entitled and also obligated to go on locating—although indeed not presupposing—his ancestor also?

In answer to these questions I say this: (a) If the whole has been given in empirical intuition, then the regression in the series of the whole's internal conditions proceeds to infinity. (b) If [the regression is not one of decomposition,] however, i.e., if only a member of the series is given and the regression is first of all to proceed from this member to absolute totality, then there takes place only a regression to an undetermined distance *(in indefinitum)*. Hence the division of some matter given between its bounds (i.e., a body) must be said to proceed to infinity. For this matter is given as a whole, and consequently with all its possible parts, in empirical intuition. But the condition of this whole is its part, and the condition of this part is the part of the part, etc.; and in this regression of decomposition an unconditioned (indivisible) member of this series of conditions is never encountered. Therefore, not only is there nowhere an empiri-

A513/
B541

cal basis for stopping in the division, but the further members of the division that is to be continued are themselves empirically given prior to this continuing division; i.e., the division proceeds to infinity. By contrast, the series of progenitors for a given human being is not given in its absolute totality in any possible experience. But the regression still proceeds from each member of this [series of] procreation to a higher member, so that no empirical boundary is to be encountered that would exhibit a member as absolutely unconditioned. Nevertheless, since even the members that might provide the condition for such [exhibition of a member as absolutely unconditioned] do not already lie, prior to the regression, in the empirical intuition of the whole, the regression proceeds not to infinity (in dividing the given) but to an indeterminable distance in locating further members for the given ones, and these further members are always given in turn only as conditioned.

In neither of the two cases, the *regressus in infinitum* and the *regressus in indefinitum,* is the series of conditions regarded as being given as infinite in the object. These conditions are not things that are given in themselves, but only appearances, which are given as conditions of one another only in the regression itself. Hence the question no longer is how large this series of conditions is in itself, i.e., whether it is finite or infinite; for the series is nothing in itself. The question is, rather, how we are to perform the empirical regression, and how far we are to continue it. And here there is indeed a notable difference regarding the rule for this advance. If the whole (a) has been given empirically, then it is *possible* to go back *to infinity* in the series of the whole's internal conditions. However, if the whole (b) is not given but is first to be given through empirical regression, then I can say only that it is *to infinity possible* to proceed to still higher conditions of the series. In the first case I was able to say that always more members are there, and are empirically given, than I reach through the regression (of decomposition). But in the second case I am able to say only that I can always proceed still further in the regression, because no member is empirically given as absolutely unconditioned, and thus any member always still admits a higher member as possible, and hence admits as necessary the inquiry about it. In the first case it was necessary to *encounter* further members; in the second, however, it is necessary always to *inquire* about further members, because no experience bounds anything absolutely. For either you have no perception that bounds your empirical regression absolutely; and then you must not regard your regression as completed. Or you do have such a perception that bounds your series; and then this perception cannot be a part of the series that you have traversed (because what *bounds* must be distinguished from *what is bounded* by it); and thus you must continue your regression still further to this condition also, and so on.

The following section will put these remarks in their proper light by applying them.

The Antinomy of Pure Reason

Section IX

On the Empirical Use of the Regulative Principle of Reason in Regard to All Cosmological Ideas

There is, as we have shown repeatedly, no transcendental use of pure concepts either of understanding or of reason. The absolute totality of the series of conditions in the world of sense is based solely on a transcendental use of reason that demands this unconditioned completeness from what it presupposes as being a thing in itself. The world of sense, however, does not contain such completeness. Therefore, the issue can never again be the absolute magnitude of the series that occur in the world of sense, i.e., whether they may be bounded or *in themselves unbounded*. Rather, the issue can only be how far, in tracing experience back to its conditions, we are to go back in the empirical regression in order that—in accordance with the rule of reason—we may stop at no other answer to reason's questions than one that is commensurate with the object.

A516/
B544

Hence what alone remains to us is the *validity of the principle of reason* taken only as a rule of the *continuation* and magnitude of a possible experience—the principle's invalidity as a constitutive principle of appearances [taken as things] in themselves having been established sufficiently. Moreover, if we can beyond doubt display that validity of the principle taken as such a rule, reason's dispute with itself is wholly ended. For not only have we, through this critical solution, annulled the illusion that put reason at variance with itself; but, in its place, we are disclosing the sense in which reason agrees with itself and the misinterpretation of which alone prompted the dispute, and are thus transforming what would otherwise be only a *dialectical* principle into a *doctrinal* one. Indeed, if this principle can be verified in its subjective signification, whereby it is to determine understanding's greatest possible use in experience commensurately with the objects of experience, then this is to achieve just as much as if, like an axiom, the principle determined objects in themselves a priori (which is impossible from pure reason). For even such a priori determination could have, in regard to objects of experience, no greater influence on the expansion and correction of our cognition than would actively manifest itself in the most extensive experiential use of our understanding.

A517/
B545

I
Solution of the Cosmological Idea of the Totality of Composition of Appearances of a World Whole

Here, as with the remaining cosmological questions, the basis of the regulative principle of reason is this proposition: that in empirical regression we can encounter *no experience of an absolute boundary,* and hence no experience of any condition as one that is *absolutely unconditioned empirically.* The basis of this, however, is that such an experience would have to contain a bounding of appearances by nothing, or [i.e.] the void, [as something] that the continued regression could come upon by means of a perception—which is impossible.

Now this proposition, which says as much as that in empirical regression I always arrive only at a condition that must itself be regarded in turn as empirically conditioned, contains this rule *in terminis:* that however far I may have got with this inquiry in the ascending series, I must always inquire about a still higher member of the series, whether or not I become acquainted with this member through experience.

A518/
B546

Now nothing further is needed for the solution of the first cosmological problem than to establish also whether, in the regression to the unconditioned magnitude of the world whole (as regards time and space), this never bounded ascending can be called (a) a *regression to infinity* or (b) only an *indeterminably continued regression (in indefinitum).*

The mere general presentation of the series of all past states of the world, as well as that of the series of all things that are simultaneous in cosmic space, is itself nothing but a possible empirical regression that I think, although still indeterminately; and only through this possible regression can there arise the concept of such a series of conditions for the given perception.[24] Now, I have the world whole always only in concept, and by no means (as a whole) in intuition. Hence I cannot from that whole's magnitude infer the magnitude of the regression and determine the regression's magnitude in accordance with that of the world; rather, I must frame a concept of the world's magnitude in the first place through the magnitude of the empirical regression. But of this regression I never know anything more than that from any given member of the series of conditions I must always proceed empirically to a still higher (more remote) member. Therefore, the magnitude of the whole of appearances is not thereby determined absolutely at all. Hence we also cannot say that this regression proceeds to infinity. For saying this would anticipate the members not yet reached by the regression, and would present their multitude as so great that it could not be reached by any empirical synthesis, and consequently would *determine* (although only negatively) the world's magnitude prior to the regression— which is impossible. For prior to the regression this [world] is not (as regards its totality) given to me at all; nor, therefore, is its magnitude. Accordingly, we cannot say anything at all about the world's magnitude in itself, not even that there occurs in the world a regression *in infinitum*, but we must merely search for the concept of the world's magnitude according to the rule that determines the empirical regression in the world. This rule, however, says no more than that however far we may have got in the series of empirical conditions, we are not to assume an absolute boundary anywhere, but are to subordinate every appearance, as conditioned, to another as its condition, and hence are to proceed onward to this condition; and this is the regression *in indefinitum*, which, because it determines no magnitude

A519/B547

A520/B548

---

24. Hence, by the same token, this world series cannot be either larger or smaller than the possible empirical regression on which alone its concept rests. And since this regression cannot give to us any determinate infinite, but just as little anything determinately finite (absolutely bounded), we clearly cannot assume the world's magnitude either as finite or as infinite, because the regression (through which this magnitude is presented) permits neither of the two.

in the object, can be distinguished distinctly enough from the regression *in infinitum*.

Therefore, I cannot say that the world is *infinite* as regards past time or as regards space; for such a concept of magnitude as a given infinity is empirical, and hence is also absolutely impossible in regard to the world taken as an object of the senses. Nor shall I say that the regression from a given perception onward to all that bounds it in a series, both in space and in past time, proceeds *to infinity;* for saying this presupposes the world's magnitude to be infinite. Nor shall I say that this regression is *finite;* for an absolute boundary is likewise empirically impossible. I shall, therefore, be unable to say anything about the whole object of experience (the world of sense), but shall be able to say something only about the rule according to which experience is to be engaged in, and continued, commensurately with its object.

Hence the first and negative answer to the cosmological question concerning the world's magnitude is this: the world has no first beginning as regards time and no outermost boundary as regards space.

For in the opposite case the world would be bounded by empty time, on the one hand, and by empty space, on the other. Now since the world as appearance cannot in itself be bounded in either of the two ways, because appearance is not a thing in itself, there would have to be possible a perception of bounding by absolutely empty time or space through which these world ends would be given in a possible experience. Such an experience, however, being completely empty of content, is impossible. Therefore, an absolute boundary of the world is impossible empirically, and hence also absolutely. [A521/B549]

From this, then, there follows simultaneously the *affirmative* answer: the regression in the series of the world's appearances, as a determination of the world's magnitude, proceeds *in indefinitum*. This is equivalent to saying: the world of sense has no absolute magnitude; rather, the empirical regression (through which alone the world can be given on the side of its conditions) has its rule, viz., that from any member in the series, as a conditioned member, we are always to advance (whether by our own experience, or the guide of history, or the chain of effects and their causes) to a still more remote member, and are not to refrain anywhere from expanding the possible use of our understanding—this expansion being, indeed, reason's proper and sole task with its principles. [A522/B550]

This rule does not prescribe a determinate empirical regression that continues ceaselessly in a certain kind of appearances. E.g., it

does not prescribe that from a living human being we must always ascend in a series of progenitors without expecting a first pair; or that
in the series of cosmic bodies we must always ascend without admit-
ting an outermost sun. Rather, the rule commands only the advance
from appearances to appearances, even if these were not to yield any
actual perception (if, viz., the perception is for our consciousness too
weak in degree to become experience); for these appearances do
nonetheless belong to possible experience.

Any beginning is in time, and any boundary of what is extended is
in space. Space and time, however, are only in the world of sense.
Hence only appearances *in the world* are conditionally bounded, but
the world itself is bounded neither in a conditioned nor in an unconditioned way.

Precisely on this account, and because the world can never *be given
wholly* and even the series of conditions for a given conditioned can-
A523/ not, as world series, *be given wholly*, the concept of the world's
B551 magnitude is given only through the regression, and not prior to it in
a collective intuition. This regression, however, always consists only
in the [continued] *determining* of the magnitude. Therefore, it yields
no *determinate* concept, and hence also no concept of a magnitude
that would with respect to a certain [unit of] measure be infinite.
The regression, therefore, does not proceed to infinity (as given, as it
were), but proceeds to an undetermined distance, in order to yield a
magnitude (of experience) which first becomes actual through this
regression.

II
SOLUTION OF THE COSMOLOGICAL IDEA
OF THE TOTALITY OF DIVISION OF A
WHOLE GIVEN IN INTUITION

If I divide a whole that is given in intuition, then I proceed from
something conditioned to the conditions of its possibility. The division of the parts *(subdivisio* or *decompositio)* is a regression in the series of these conditions. The absolute totality of this series would be
given only if the regression could reach *simple* parts. But if all the
parts of a continuously progressing decomposition are always in turn
divisible, then the division—i.e., the regression from the condi-
A524/ tioned to its conditions—proceeds *in infinitum*. For the conditions
B552 (the parts) are contained in the conditioned itself; and since the con-

ditioned is wholly given in an intuition that is enclosed between its bounds, the conditions are one and all given with it also. Hence the regression must not be called merely a regression *in indefinitum*, as we were permitted to call the previous cosmological idea only. In the previous case [also] I was to proceed from the conditioned to its conditions; but there the conditions were given outside the conditioned, and hence they were not given through the conditioned and simultaneously with it, but were first added in the empirical regression. Despite this, however, we are by no means permitted to say of such a whole which is divisible to infinity that *it consists of infinitely many parts*. For although the intuition of the whole contains all the parts, it yet does *not* contain the *whole division;* this division consists only in the progressing decomposition, or [i.e.] in the regression itself that first makes the series actual. Now since this regression is infinite, all the members (parts) that it reaches are indeed contained in the given whole taken as an *aggregate;* but not contained therein is the whole *series of the division,* which is infinite successively and never *whole* and hence can exhibit no infinite multitude of parts and no gathering together of such a multitude in a whole.

This general notice can quite readily be applied, first, to space. Any space intuited within its bounds is a *whole* such that its parts are, in any decomposition, always in turn spaces; and hence any such space is divisible to infinity.

From this the second application of the notice follows quite naturally: viz., to an outer appearance enclosed within bounds (a body). The divisibility of such an appearance is based on the divisibility of space, for space amounts to the possibility of a body as an extended whole. Hence a body is divisible to infinity, yet without therefore consisting of infinitely many parts.

A525/
B553

It seems, to be sure, that because a body must be presented in space as being a substance, it will be different from space as regards the law of the divisibility of space. For we may surely admit at least this difference: Decomposition can never remove all composition in space; for all space, which otherwise has nothing independent about it, would then cease to be (which is impossible). On the other hand, the claim that if all composition in matter were annulled in thought then nothing at all would remain seems not to be reconcilable with the concept of a substance; for a substance properly ought to be the subject of all composition, and would have to remain in its elements even if the connection of these elements in space, whereby they amount to a body, were annulled. However, what would indeed be thought [thus] concerning a thing in itself, through a pure concept of understanding, is not the case with what is called substance in [the realm of] appearance. This substance is not an absolute subject; it is, rather, a permanent image belonging to sensibility and is nothing but intuition, in which nothing unconditioned whatsoever is to be met with.

But although this rule of advance to infinity does without any doubt have its place in the subdivision of an appearance as a mere occupying of space, yet the rule cannot hold if we want to extend it also to the multitude of parts that—in the given whole—are already separated in a certain way so as to make up [an appearance as] a *quantum discretum*. To assume that in every structured (organized) whole each part is structured in turn, and that thus in dissecting the parts to infinity one always encounters new artful[ly structured] parts—in a word, that the whole is structured to infinity: this assumption is quite unthinkable, even though the alternative assumption that the parts of matter could to infinity become structured in their decomposition is indeed thinkable. For the infinity of the division of a given appearance in space is based solely on the fact that what is given through this appearance is merely [its] divisibility, i.e., merely a multitude of parts that in itself is absolutely indeterminate, whereas the parts themselves are given and determined only through the subdivision—in short, the fact that the whole is not in itself already divided. Hence in this whole the division can determine a multitude of parts that will go as far as one wants to advance in the regression of division. In the case of an organic body structured to infinity, on the other hand, the whole is—precisely through this concept of an organic body—already presented as divided, and one [conceives that one] encounters in it, prior to any regression of division, a multitude of parts that is in itself determinate but also infinite—and thereby one contradicts oneself. For this infinite involution is regarded as a series never to be completed (i.e., as infinite), and yet also—when gathered together—as nonetheless completed. Infinite division characterizes only appearance as *quantum continuum,* and is inseparable from the occupation of space; for precisely in this occupation lies the basis of infinite divisibility. But as soon as something is assumed as *quantum discretum,* then the multitude of units in it is determinate and hence, by the same token, is always equal to some number. Therefore, only experience can establish how far the organization in a structured body may go; and even if [actual] experience were certain to reach no inorganic part, yet such parts must lie at least in possible experience. But how far the transcendental division of an appearance as such extends is not a matter of experience at all, but is governed by a principle of reason whereby the empirical regression in the decomposition of what is extended is, in accordance with the nature of this appearance, never to be regarded as absolutely completed.

Concluding Comment on the Solution of the Mathematical-Transcendental Ideas, and Advance Notice on the Solution of the Dynamical-Transcendental Ideas

A528/
B556

We presented the antinomy of pure reason, through all the transcendental ideas, in a table. We also indicated the basis of this conflict and the only remedy for removing it, which consisted in declaring both the opposed assertions to be false. In doing all this, we everywhere presented the conditions as belonging to their conditioned according to relations of space and time, which is the usual presupposition of the common human understanding; and so this conflict was indeed based entirely on that presupposition. In this respect all the dialectical presentations of totality in the series of conditions for a given conditioned were indeed throughout of the same *kind*. There was always a series, and in it the condition and the conditioned were connected as members of this series and were thereby *homogeneous*. And thus the regression always had to be thought as uncompleted; or, if it was to be thought as completed, then a member that was in itself conditioned must falsely be assumed to be a first member and hence to be unconditioned. Therefore, although in all cases the object, i.e., the conditioned, was not considered merely according to its magnitude, yet the series of conditions for this object was considered merely in this way. And thus the difficulty, which could be removed by no settlement but only by entirely severing the knot, consisted in reason's making the series either *too long* or *too short* for the understanding, so that the understanding could never match reason's idea.

A529/
B557

In all this we did, however, overlook an essential difference obtaining among the objects—i.e., the concepts of understanding—that reason endeavors to raise to ideas; for according to our table of categories provided above, two of the categories signify a *mathematical* but the other two a *dynamical* synthesis of appearances. Up to this point we could, indeed, quite readily afford to overlook this difference. For just as in the general presentation of all the transcendental ideas we always remained subject to conditions *in* [the realm of] *appearance,* so in the two mathematical-transcendental ideas we also had no other *object* than the one in [the realm of] appearance. Now, however, we proceed to *dynamical* concepts of understanding insofar as these are to fit the idea of reason; and here this distinction becomes important, and opens up for us an entirely new outlook concerning the contest in which reason is embroiled. For previously this contest was *dismissed* as built, on both sides, on false presuppositions. But now, in the dynamical antinomy, perhaps there occurs a presupposition that can coexist with reason's pretension; and from this point of view, and with the judge compensating for the lack of legal bases that were mistaken [as being such] on both sides, the contest can be *settled* to the satisfaction of both parties—which could not be done with the dispute in the mathematical antinomy.

The series of conditions are indeed homogeneous insofar as we take account only of their *extent:* i.e., of whether they are commensurate with the idea, or whether the ideas are too large or too small for those series. However, the concept of understanding that underlies these ideas may contain either only a *synthesis of the homogeneous* (this homogeneous is presupposed with any magnitude, in both the composition and division thereof), or a *synthesis of the heterogeneous;* this heterogeneous can at least be admitted in the dynamical synthesis, i.e., the synthesis of both the causal linkage and the linkage of the necessary with the contingent.

Hence in the case of the mathematical connection of series of appearances none but a *sensible* condition can come in, i.e., a condition that is itself a part of the series. The dynamical series of sensible conditions, on the other hand, does also admit of a heterogeneous condition that is not part of the series but, *as merely intelligible,* lies outside the series. Thus reason is satisfied; for the unconditioned is put prior to appearances, and yet the series of appearances, as always conditioned, is not thereby confused and—contrary to the principles of understanding—cut off.

Now because the dynamical ideas admit of a condition of appearances that lies outside the series of these, i.e., a condition that is not itself appearance, something occurs here that is entirely different from the result of the mathematical antinomy. For the mathematical antinomy caused the result that both dialectical counterassertions had to be declared false. By contrast, in the dynamical series the thoroughly conditioned—which is inseparable from these series as appearances—can be connected with the condition which, although empirically unconditioned, is also *nonsensible*. As so connected, this thoroughly conditioned can satisfy the *understanding*, on the one hand, and *reason*, on the other.[25] Thus the dialectical arguments that in one way or another sought unconditioned totality in mere appearances drop out; and hence the propositions of reason—in their signification as corrected in this way—can, by contrast, *both* be *true*. This can never take place with the cosmological ideas that concern merely a mathematically unconditioned unity; for in their case we encounter no condition of the series of appearances that is not itself appearance and as such likewise a member of the series.

A532/
B560

III
SOLUTION OF THE COSMOLOGICAL IDEA OF TOTALITY IN THE DERIVATION OF WORLD EVENTS FROM THEIR CAUSES

Only two kinds of causality can be conceived in regard to what occurs, viz., either a causality according to *nature* or one from *freedom*. The causality according to nature is the connection, in the world of sense, of one state with a previous state upon which the state follows according to a rule. Now the *causality* of appearances rests on conditions of time; and the previous state, if it had always been there, would not have produced an effect that first arises in time. Therefore, the causality of the cause of what occurs or comes about has likewise *come about*, and—according to the principle of understanding—itself requires a cause in turn.

By freedom, on the other hand, in the cosmological sense of the term, I mean the power to begin a state *on one's own*. Thus the causality of freedom is not in turn subject, according to the law of nature, to another cause that determines it as regards time. Freedom, in this meaning of the term, is a pure transcendental idea. This idea, first,

A533/
B561

---

25. For, the understanding does not permit among *appearances* any condition that would itself be empirically unconditioned. But if for some conditioned one could conceive an *intelligible* condition—which thus would not likewise belong, as a member, in the series of appearances—but without thereby in the least interrupting the series of empirical conditions, then such a condition could be admitted as *empirically unconditioned*, and yet the empirical continuous regression would not thereby be impaired anywhere.

contains nothing borrowed from experience. Moreover, second, the object of this idea cannot be given determinately in any experience, because there is a universal law of the very possibility of all experience whereby whatever occurs must have a cause, and whereby, therefore, also the cause's causality which *itself has occurred* or come about must in turn have a cause. And thus the entire realm of experience, however far it may extend, is transformed into a sum of what is mere nature. But since in this way no absolute totality of conditions in the causal relation can be obtained, reason creates for itself the idea of a spontaneity that can, on its own, start to act—without, i.e., needing to be preceded by another cause by means of which it is determined to action in turn, according to the law of causal connection.

Extremely noteworthy is the fact that this *transcendental idea of freedom* is the basis of the practical concept of freedom, and that transcendental freedom is what in practical freedom amounts to the proper moment of the difficulties that have all along surrounded the question of practical freedom's possibility. *Freedom in the practical meaning* of the term is the independence of our power of choice from coercion by impulses of sensibility. For a power of choice is *sensible* insofar as it is *pathologically affected* (i.e., affected by motivating causes of sensibility); it is called animal power of choice *(arbitrium brutum)* if it can be *pathologically necessitated*. The human power of choice, although an *arbitrium sensitivum,* is an *arbitrium* not *brutum* but *liberum;* for its action is not made necessary by sensibility, but the human being has a power to determine himself on his own, independently of coercion by sensible impulses.

We readily see that if all causality in the world of sense were merely nature, then every event would be determined by another event in time and according to necessary laws; and hence, since appearances insofar as they determine the power of choice would have to make every action necessary as their natural result, the annulment of transcendental freedom would simultaneously eliminate all practical freedom. For practical freedom presupposes that although something did not occur, it yet *ought* to have occurred, and that hence the cause of this something in [the realm of] appearance was not completely determinative: not so determinative, viz., that there did not lie in our power of choice a causality for producing, independently of those natural causes and even against their force and influence, something that in the time order is determined according to empirical laws—and hence a causality whereby we can begin a series of events *entirely on our own.*

Hence what happens here—as we find in general in the conflict of a reason that ventures beyond the bounds of possible experience—is that the problem is in fact not *physiological* but *transcendental.* Hence the question of the possibility of freedom does indeed challenge psychology; but since it rests on dialectical arguments of the merely pure reason, it must, along with its solution, engage only transcendental philosophy. Now in order to enable transcendental philosophy to give a satisfactory answer to this problem, which it cannot decline to do, I must first try—by the following remark—to determine more closely the procedure of transcendental philosophy in dealing with this problem. A535/ B563

If appearances were things in themselves, and hence if space and time were forms of the existence of things themselves, then the conditions and the conditioned would always belong, as members, to one and the same series. And from this there would arise, in the present case also, the antinomy that is common to all transcendental ideas: viz., that this series would have to turn out inevitably too large or too small for the understanding. However, the dynamical concepts of reason, with which we are dealing in this and the following subsection, have the following peculiarity. Because these concepts have to do not with an object considered as a magnitude but only with the object's *existence,* we can abstract also from the magnitude of the series of conditions, and what matters in their case is merely the dynamical relation of the condition to the conditioned. Thus in the question concerning nature and freedom we already encounter the difficulty as to whether freedom is even possible at all, and, if it is possible, whether it can coexist with the universality of the natural law of causality. And hence the question arises whether the proposition that every effect in the world must arise *either* from nature *or* from freedom is a correct disjunction, or whether—rather—*both* can, with one and the same event but in different reference, take place simultaneously. As for the principle concerning the thoroughgoing connection of all events in the world of sense according to immutable natural laws, its correctness is already established as a principle of the Transcendental Analytic and tolerates no impairment. Hence the question is only whether, in regard to the same effect that is determined according to nature, freedom can nonetheless also take A536/ B564 place, or whether freedom is completely excluded by that inviolable rule. And here the deceptive, although common, presupposition of the *absolute reality* of appearances at once shows its detrimental influence of confusing our reason. For if appearances are things in themselves, then freedom cannot be saved. Nature is then the complete and in itself sufficiently determining cause of every event, and the condition of this cause is always contained only in the series of appearances—which, along with their effect, are necessary under

natural law. If, on the other hand, appearances count as nothing more than they in fact are, viz., if they count not as things in themselves but as mere presentations connected according to empirical laws, then they must themselves still have bases that are not appearances. But such an intelligible cause is not, as regards its causality, determined by appearances, although its effects appear and thus can be determined by other appearances. Hence this cause, along with its causality, is outside the series of empirical conditions, whereas its effects are encountered within the series. Hence the effect can be considered as free with regard to its intelligible cause, and yet with regard to appearances be considered simultaneously as resulting from these according to the necessity of nature. This distinction, when set forth in a universal way and quite abstractly, must appear extremely subtle and obscure, but it will become clear in its application. Here I wanted only to make the comment that since the thoroughgoing connection of all appearances in one context of nature is an inexorable law, this law would necessarily have to overturn all freedom if one were to adhere obstinately to the reality of appearances. This is also the reason why those who follow the common opinion in this matter have never succeeded in reconciling nature and freedom with each other.

Possibility of the Causality through Freedom, as Reconciled with the Universal Law of Natural Necessity

What in an object of the senses is not itself appearance I call *intelligible*. Accordingly, if what in the world of sense must be regarded as appearance has, when taken in itself, also a power which is not an object of sensible intuition but through which it can still be the cause of appearances, then the *causality* of this being can be considered from two sides: as *intelligible*, according to its action as that of a thing in itself; and as *sensible*, according to the effects of this causality as those of an appearance in the world of sense. Thus regarding such a subject's power we would frame an empirical as well as an intellectual concept of its causality, these concepts occurring together in one and the same effect. Such a twofold side from which to think the power of an object of the senses contradicts none of the concepts that we have to frame of appearances and of a possible experience. For since these appearances are not in themselves things, they must be based on a transcendental object determining them as mere presentations; and hence nothing prevents us from attributing to this transcendental object, besides the property through which it appears, also a *causality* that is not appearance although its *effect* is nonetheless encountered in appearance. Any efficient cause, however, must have a **character**, i.e., a law of its causality without which it would not be a cause at all. And thus in a subject of the world of sense we would have, first, an *empirical character*. Through this character the subject's actions, as appearances, would according to constant natural laws stand throughout in connection with other appearances and could be derived from these appearances as the actions' conditions; and thus these actions would, in combination with those other appearances, amount to members of a single series of the natural order. Second, one would have to grant to the subject also an *intelligible character*. Through this character the subject is indeed the cause of those actions as appearances, but the character itself is not subject to any conditions of sensibility and is not itself appearance. The first character could also be called the character of such a thing in [the realm of] appearance, the second the character of the thing in itself.

Now according to its intelligible character this acting subject would not stand under any conditions of time; for time is the condition only of appearances and not of things in themselves. In this subject no *action* would *arise* or *pass away*. Hence it would also not be subjected to the law of all time determination and of everything changeable, viz., that everything *that occurs* has its cause *in appearances* (those of the previous state). In a word, the subject's causality, insofar as it is intellectual, would not stand at all in the series of empirical conditions that make the event necessary in the world of sense. We could not, indeed, ever become acquainted with this intelligible character directly, because we cannot perceive anything except insofar as it appears; but we would still have to *think* it in accordance with the empirical character, just as in general we must—in thought—lay a transcendental object at the basis of

A539/
B567

A540/
B568

appearances although we know nothing about this object as to what
it is in itself.

Hence according to its empirical character this subject, as appearance, would be subjected to all laws of determination in terms of
causal linkage. To this extent the subject would be nothing but a part
of the world of sense; and its effects would, like any other appearance, flow from nature unfailingly. Just as outer appearances would
influence this subject, and as the subject's empirical character, i.e.,
the law of its causality, would be cognized through experience, so all
its actions would have to be explicable according to natural laws, and
all requirements for a complete and necessary determination of these
actions would have to be found in a possible experience.

A541/   But according to its intelligible character (although we can have
B569   nothing more of this character than just the general concept of it)
the same subject would nonetheless have to be pronounced free from
any influence of sensibility and determination by appearances. For
insofar as this subject is *noumenon*, nothing *occurs* in it and there is
found in it no change requiring dynamical time determination and
hence no connection with appearances as causes. Therefore, this ac-
tive being would to this extent be independent and free in its actions
from all natural necessity, which is found only in the world of sense.
Of this subject we would say quite correctly that it begins its effects
in the world of sense *on its own*, without the action's beginning *in the
subject* itself. And this would be valid without any consequent need
for the effects in the world of sense to begin on their own. For in that
world they are always predetermined—although only by means of
the empirical character (which is merely the appearance of the intelligible character)—by empirical conditions in the previous time, and
are possible only as a continuation of the series of natural causes.
And thus freedom and nature, each in the complete meaning of its
term, would be found in the same actions—according as these are
compared with their intelligible or with their sensible cause—simultaneously and without any conflict.

A542/   ## Elucidation of the Cosmological Idea of a Freedom in
B570   ## Combination with the Universal Natural Necessity

I thought it good to start by sketching the outline of the solution to
our transcendental problem, in order that we might better survey the
course that reason takes in solving the problem. Let us now spell out

the moments that are in fact at issue in deciding this solution, and examine each separately.

Consider the natural law that everything that occurs has a cause; that since the causality of this cause, i.e., the *action*, precedes [the effect] in time and—in regard to an effect that has *arisen*—cannot itself always have been there but must have *occurred*, this causality likewise has among appearances its cause whereby it is determined; and that, consequently, all events are determined empirically within a natural order. This law, through which appearances can first amount to a *nature* and yield objects of an experience, is a law of understanding from which we are not permitted on any pretext to deviate, nor exempt any appearance. For otherwise we would posit the appearance outside of all possible experience, but thereby would distinguish it from all objects of possible experience and thus would turn it into a mere thought-entity and chimera. A543/
B571

Thus it looks, here, as if there is only a chain of causes that in the regression to the causes' conditions permits no *absolute totality* at all. Yet this perplexity in no way detains us; for it has already been removed in our general judgment on the antinomy of reason, into which reason falls when in the series of appearances it aims at the unconditioned. If we wish to yield to the delusion of transcendental realism, then we are left with neither nature nor freedom. Here the question is only whether, if in the entire series of all events we acknowledge nothing but natural necessity, it is still possible to regard the same event, which on the one hand is a mere natural effect, as yet being on the other hand an effect arising from freedom, or whether we find between these two kinds of causality a direct contradiction.

Among the causes in [the realm of] appearance there assuredly cannot be anything that could absolutely and on its own begin a series. For here every action, as appearance, insofar as it produces an event, is itself an event or happening that presupposes another state wherein its cause is to be found; and thus everything that occurs is only a continuation of the series, and in this series no beginning that takes place on its own is possible. Hence all the actions of natural causes in the time sequence are themselves in turn effects that likewise presuppose their causes in the time series. An *original* action, through which something occurs that was not there before, is not to be expected from the causal connection of appearances. A544/
B572

But if effects are appearances, is it indeed also necessary that the causality of their cause, which (cause) itself is also appearance, must be solely empirical? And is it not possible, rather, that although every effect in [the realm of] appearance does indeed require a connection with its cause according to laws of empirical causality, yet this empirical causality itself could nonetheless, without in the least interrupting its connection with natural causes, be an effect of a causality that is not empirical but intelligible? I.e., could not the empirical causality itself be an effect of an action, original in regard to appearances, of a cause that in so far is therefore not appearance but—according to this power—intelligible, although otherwise it also must, as a link in the chain of nature, be classed entirely with the world of sense?

The principle of the causality of appearances among one another is required by us in order that for natural events we can seek and indicate natural conditions, i.e., causes in [the realm of] appearance. If this requirement is granted to us and not weakened by any exception,

then the understanding—which in its empirical use sees in all happenings nothing but nature and is, moreover, entitled to do so—has all that it can demand, and physical explanations proceed along their course unhindered. Now in this [task] the understanding is not impaired in the least if one assumes—even supposing that the assumption were, besides, to be merely invented—that among the natural causes there are also some which have a power that is only intelligible, inasmuch as this power's determination to action never rests on empirical conditions but rests on mere bases of understanding—yet rests on these in such a way that this cause's *action in [the realm of] appearance* conforms to all laws of empirical causality. For in this way the acting subject would, as *causa phaenomenon*, be linked up with nature in the unsevered dependence of all this cause's actions; and this subject's phenomenon (with all its causality in [the realm of] appearance) would only contain certain conditions that, if one wants to ascend from the empirical object to the transcendental, would have to be regarded as merely intelligible. For if we only follow the rule of nature in regard to what may be the cause among appearances, then we need not be concerned as to what sort of basis of these appearances and their connection is being thought in the transcendental subject, which is empirically unknown to us. This intelligible basis in

no way challenges the empirical questions, but concerns perhaps merely the thinking in pure understanding; and although the effects of this thinking and acting of pure understanding are found in the appearances, yet these appearances must nonetheless be capable of being explained completely, according to natural laws, from their cause in [the realm of] appearance. The appearances must be capable of being explained by pursuing, as the supreme basis of explanation, their merely empirical character, and by entirely by-passing as unknown the intelligible character that is the empirical character's transcendental cause—except insofar as this intelligible character is indicated by the empirical character as the intelligible character's sensible sign. Let us apply this to experience. The human being is one of the appearances in the world of sense, and in so far is also one of the natural causes, the causality of which must be subject to empirical laws. As such a cause he must, accordingly, also have an empirical character, as do all other things of nature. We discern this character through abilities and powers that he manifests in his effects. In inanimate nature, or in animate but merely animal nature, we find no basis for thinking any power as being other than merely sensibly conditioned. Only the human being, who otherwise is acquainted with all of nature solely through his senses, cognizes himself also through mere apperception—viz., in actions and inner determinations that he cannot class at all with any impression of the senses. And thus he is to himself, indeed, on the one hand phenom-enon, but on the other hand—viz., in regard to certain powers—a merely intelligible object, because his action cannot be classed at all with the receptivity of sensibility. We call these [specifically human] powers understanding and reason. Reason, above all, is quite particularly and primarily distinguished from all empirically conditioned abilities, because it examines its objects merely accord-ing to ideas and according to these ideas determines the under-standing, which then makes an empirical use of its own (although likewise pure) concepts. {A547/ B575}

Now, that this reason has causality, or that we at least conceive such a causality in it, is evident from the *imperatives* which, in all that is practical, we impose as rules on the performative powers. The *ought* expresses a kind of necessity and connection with bases that does not otherwise occur in all of nature. The understanding can cognize regarding nature only *what is,* or has been, or will be. That something in nature *ought to be* other than what in fact it is in all these time relations—this is impossible; indeed, the [term] ought, if we have in mind merely the course of nature, has no meaning what-soever. We cannot ask at all what ought to happen in nature, any more than what properties a circle ought to have, but can ask only what happens in nature, or what properties the circle has.

Now this *ought* expresses a possible action whose basis is nothing but a mere concept, whereas the basis of a mere action of nature must always be an appearance. Now the [concept-based] action must indeed be possible under natural conditions, if the *ought* is directed to nature; however, these natural conditions concern not the determination itself of the power of choice but only this determination's effect and result in [the realm of] appearance. No matter how many natural bases—how many sensible stimuli—impel me to *will*, they yet cannot produce the *ought;* they can produce only a willing that is far from necessary but is always conditioned, whereas the *ought* pronounced by reason opposes this conditioned willing with standard and goal—indeed, with prohibition and authority. Whether the object is one of mere sensibility (the agreeable) or even of pure reason (the good), reason does not yield to the empirically given basis and does not follow the order of things as they exhibit themselves in appearance, but with complete spontaneity makes for itself an order of its own according to ideas. Reason adapts the empirical conditions to accord with these ideas, and in conformity with these ideas declares to be necessary even such actions as in fact *have not occurred* and perhaps will not occur, but concerning which reason nonetheless presupposes that it can have causality in reference to them, since otherwise reason would not expect from its ideas effects in experience.

Let us now remain with this point and assume as at least possible that reason actually has causality with regard to appearances. In that case, despite being all reason, it must yet show itself as having an empirical character. For any cause presupposes a rule according to which certain appearances follow as effects; and any rule requires a uniformity of effects that is the basis for the concept of cause (as a power). And this concept, insofar as it must become evident from mere appearances, we may call the power's empirical character. This character is constant, whereas the effects appear in changeable shapes according to the difference in the accompanying and in part limiting conditions.

Thus every human being's power of choice has an empirical character. This character is nothing but a certain causality of his reason insofar as this causality shows in its effects in [the realm of] appearance a rule whereby one can gather, in terms of their kind and degrees, the bases and actions of his reason and thereby judge the subjective principles of his power of choice. Since this empirical character itself must be drawn from appearances, as its effect, and from the rule of these as provided to us by experience, all actions of a human being are determined in appearance on the basis of his empirical character and the other contributing causes according to the order of nature; and if we could explore all appearances of his power of choice down to the bottom, there would not be a single human action that we could not with certainty predict and cognize as necessary from its preceding conditions. In regard to this empirical character, therefore, there is no freedom; and yet only in terms of this character can we consider a human being if we seek merely to **observe** him and, as is done in anthropology, explore physiologically the motivating causes of his actions.

But if we examine the same actions in reference to reason—not, however, speculative reason in order to *explain* them in terms of their origin, but reason solely insofar as it is itself the cause *for producing* them—in a word: if we compare these actions with reason in a *practical* regard, then we find a rule and order quite different from the order of nature. For in that regard perhaps there *ought not to have occurred* all that according to nature's course yet *has occurred* and according to its own empirical bases inevitably had to occur. But sometimes we find, or at least believe that we find, that the ideas of reason have actually proved their causality in regard to human beings' actions considered as appearances, and that these actions have occurred not because they were determined by empirical causes—no: but because they were determined by bases of reason.

Now supposing one could say that reason has causality in regard to appearance: could reason's action then indeed be called free, when in reason's empirical character (the way of sensing) the action is quite exactly determined and necessary? This empirical character in turn is determined in the intelligible character (the way of thinking). We are not, however, acquainted with the intelligible character but designate it only by appearances, which, properly speaking, allow us to cognize directly only the way of sensing (empirical character).[26] Now insofar as the action is attributable to the way of thinking as its cause,

---

26. Hence the morality proper of actions (merit and guilt), even the morality of our own conduct, remains entirely hidden to us. Our imputations can be referred only to the empirical character. But no one can fathom how much of this character is a pure effect of freedom, and how much is to be ascribed to mere nature: namely, either to a defect of temperament that one has through no fault of one's own, or to one's temperament's fortunate constitution *(meritum fortunae)*. And hence no one can pass judgment in accordance with complete justice.

it yet in no way results from this way of thinking according to empirical laws, i.e., in such a way that the conditions of pure reason *precede*
the action, but only in such a way that the effects of these in [the
realm of] appearance of inner sense precede it. Pure reason, as a
merely intelligible power, is not subjected to the form of time, nor
consequently to the conditions of temporal succession. The causality
of reason in its intelligible character by no means *arises*, or starts at a
certain time, in order to produce an effect. For otherwise it would
itself be subjected to the natural law of appearances insofar as this
law determines causal series with regard to time, and the causality of
reason would then be nature, not freedom. Hence we must be entitled to say that if reason can have causality in regard to appearances,
then it is a power *through* which the sensible condition of an empirical series of effects first begins. For the condition that lies in reason
is not sensible and hence does not itself begin. Accordingly, there
takes place here what in all empirical series we were unable to find:
viz., that the *condition* of a successive series of events can itself be
empirically unconditioned. For here the condition is *outside* the series
of appearances (viz., in the intelligible) and hence is subjected to no
sensible condition and no time determination by a preceding cause.

A552/
B580

Yet in another reference the same cause belongs nonetheless also
to the series of appearances. The human being is himself an appearance. His power of choice has an empirical character that is the (empirical) cause of all his actions. There is no condition determining a
human being in accordance with this character which is not contained in the series of natural effects and which does not obey nature's law—the law according to which an unconditioned empirical
causality of what occurs in time is not to be found at all. Therefore,
no given action (since it can be perceived only as appearance) can
begin absolutely on its own. Of reason, however, one cannot say that
the state wherein it determines the power of choice is preceded by
another state wherein that state itself is determined. For since reason
itself is not an appearance and is not subjected to any conditions of
sensibility, there takes place in reason, even as concerns its causality,
no temporal succession; and hence the dynamical law of nature that
determines temporal succession according to rules cannot be applied
to reason.

A553/
B581

Hence reason is the permanent condition of all the voluntary actions under which the human being appears. Each of these actions,
even before it occurs, is predetermined in the human being's empir-

ical character. But in regard to the intelligible character, of which the empirical character is only the sensible schema, no *before* or *after* holds, and every action—regardless of its time relation to other appearances—is the direct effect of the intelligible character of pure reason. Hence pure reason acts freely, i.e., without being dynamically determined in the chain of natural causes by external or internal bases that precede the action as regards time. And this freedom of pure reason can be regarded not only negatively, as independence from empirical conditions (for the power of reason would thus cease to be a cause of appearances). Rather, this freedom can be designated also positively, as a power of reason to begin on its own a series of events. Reason begins the series in such a way that nothing begins in reason itself, but that reason, as unconditioned condition of any voluntary action, permits no conditions above itself that precede the action as regards time—although reason's effect does begin in the series of appearances, but in the series can never amount to an absolutely first beginning. A554/ B582

To illustrate the regulative principle of reason involved here by an example drawn from the principle's empirical use—not to confirm it (for such proofs by example are unsuitable for transcendental assertions)—let us take a voluntary action, e.g., a malicious lie, by means of which a person has brought a certain amount of confusion into society. And suppose that we first investigate his action as to its motivating causes from which it arose, and that thereupon we judge how the action can, along with its consequences, be imputed to him. In pursuing the first aim we search through the agent's empirical character until we come to its sources. We locate these in bad upbringing, evil company, partly also in the wickedness of a natural makeup that is insensitive to shame; and partly we put them to frivolity and rashness. Here, then, we do not ignore the occasioning causes that prompted the action. In all this we proceed as we do in general when we investigate the series of determining causes for a given natural effect. But although we believe the action to be determined by these causes, we nevertheless blame the perpetrator. We blame him not because of his unfortunate natural makeup, nor because of the circumstances influencing him—indeed, not even because of his previous way of life. For we presuppose that we can set aside entirely how this way of life was, and that we can regard the bygone series of conditions as not having occurred, and can regard this deed as entirely unconditioned with respect to the previous state, as if the perpetrator A555/ B583 starts with it a series of consequences completely on his own. This blame is based on a law of reason; and reason is regarded in this blaming as a cause that, regardless of all the mentioned empirical conditions, could and ought to have determined the person's conduct differently. And the causality of reason is by no means regarded merely as concurrence; rather, it is regarded as in itself complete, even if the sensible incentives were not at all for this causality but were even against it. The action is imputed to the agent's intelligible character: now—at the instant when he is lying—the guilt is entirely his. Hence his reason, regardless of all empirical conditions of the deed, was wholly free, and to its failure is the deed to be imputed entirely.

We can readily see from this imputing judgment that in making it we are thinking that reason is in no way affected by all that sensibility; that reason does not change (although reason's appearances— viz., the way in which reason manifests itself in its effects—do change); that in reason there is no antecedent state determining the subsequent state, and that reason therefore does not belong at all in the series of sensible conditions that make appearances necessary according to natural laws. Reason is present to, and is the same in, all actions of the human being in all circumstances of time. But reason itself is not in time, and by no means gets into a new state in which it previously was not; with regard to this state reason is *determinative,* but not *determinable.* Hence we cannot ask, Why did reason not determine *itself* differently?—but only, Why did reason not determine *appearances* differently through its causality? To this, however, no answer is possible. For a different intelligible character of reason would have given a different empirical character. And when we say that regardless of his entire previous way of life the perpetrator could still have abstained from the lie, this means only that the lie is directly subject to the force of reason, and reason is not subjected in its causality to any conditions of appearance and of the course of time. And it means, moreover, that although the difference of time can make a principal difference for appearances in regard to one another, it can make no difference for the action in reference to reason, because appearances are not things in themselves and hence are also not causes in themselves.

Hence in judging free actions with regard to their causality we can get only as far as the intelligible cause, but not *beyond it.* We can cognize that this cause determines [actions] freely, i.e., independently of sensibility, and that in this way it can be the sensibly unconditioned condition of appearances. But why the intelligible character gives precisely these appearances and this empirical character under the conditions at hand—this question far exceeds all our reason's power to answer it, indeed, all its right even to ask it; it exceeds these as far as if we asked whence it is that the transcendental object of our outer sensible intuition gives us precisely intuition in space only, and not some other intuition. However, the problem that we had to solve does not obligate us to answer that question. For that problem was only this: whether freedom conflicts with natural necessity in one and the same action; and this we have answered sufficiently. For we have shown that, because in the case of freedom a reference to a quite different kind of conditions is possible from the kind found in the case of natural necessity, the latter's law does not affect freedom, and hence both can take place independently of, and without interfering with, each other.

It must be noted carefully that by this contemplation we have not sought to establish the *actuality* of freedom as one of the powers containing the cause of the appearances of our world of sense. For not only would this contemplation then not have been a transcendental one at all, which deals merely with concepts, but this [attempt to establish the actuality of such freedom] also could not succeed; for from experience we can never infer something that must not be thought according to laws of experience at all. Furthermore, we have not even sought to prove the *possibility* of freedom; for this [attempt] also would not have succeeded, because in general we cannot from mere a priori concepts cognize the possibility of any real basis and any causality. Freedom is being treated here only as a transcendental idea whereby reason means to start absolutely the series of conditions in [the realm of] appearance by the sensibly unconditioned. In this [attempt], however, reason becomes entangled in an antinomy with its own laws, the laws that it prescribes to the empirical use of understanding. Now, to show that this antinomy rests on a mere illusion and that nature at least does *not conflict* with the causality from freedom—this was the only goal that we were able to accomplish, and it was, moreover, our one and only concern.

A558/
B586

BOOK II

ON THE DIALECTICAL INFERENCES
OF PURE REASON

Chapter III
The Ideal of Pure Reason

Section IV
On the Impossibility of an Ontological
Proof of the Existence of God

From what has been said thus far, we see that the concept of an absolutely necessary being is a pure concept of reason, i.e., a mere idea, whose objective reality is far from proved by the mere fact that reason requires this idea. Indeed, the idea only instructs us to seek a certain—although unattainable—completeness, and serves in fact more to confine the understanding than to expand it to new objects. Now here we find the strange and preposterous fact that although the inference from a given existence as such to some absolutely necessary existence seems to be compelling and correct, we nonetheless have all the conditions of the understanding entirely against us when we attempt to frame a concept of such a necessity.

People have at all times spoken of the *absolutely necessary* being, and have taken pains not so much to understand whether and how a thing of this kind can even be thought, but rather to prove its existence. Now a nominal explication of this concept is, indeed, quite easy: we can say, viz., that this being is something whose nonexistence is impossible. But this explication leaves us not a whit more informed concerning the conditions that make it necessary to regard a thing's nonexistence as absolutely unthinkable. And yet these conditions are what we want to know; i.e., we want to know whether or not we think anything at all through this concept. For if by means of the

word *unconditionally* I dismiss all the conditions that the understanding always requires in order to regard something as necessary,
this does not come close to enabling me to understand whether I
then still think something through a concept of an unconditionally
necessary being, or perhaps think through it nothing at all.

What is still more: once people had ventured to accept this concept merely haphazardly and had finally become quite familiar with
it, they even believed themselves to be explicating it by a multitude
of examples. And thus there seemed to be no need whatever for any
further inquiry as to whether the concept is understandable. People
knew that every proposition of geometry—e.g., the proposition that
a triangle has three angles—is absolutely necessary; and thus they
spoke even of an object that lies entirely outside the sphere of our
understanding as if they understood quite well what they meant by
the concept of this object.

In fact all the alleged examples are, without exception, taken from
judgments rather than from *things* and their existence. But the unconditioned necessity of judgments is not an absolute necessity of
things. For the unconditioned necessity of a judgment is only a conditioned necessity of the thing [as subject] or of the predicate in the   A594/
judgment. The above [geometric] proposition does not say that three   B622
angles are necessary absolutely; it says, rather, that under the condition that a triangle is there (i.e., is given), three angles are necessarily
also there (in it). Nonetheless, this merely logical necessity has
proved to have great power of illusion. For people framed an a priori
concept of a thing and arranged this concept in such a way that—in
their opinion—it comprised in its range also existence. Having
framed the concept in this way, they believed that they could safely
infer the being's existence. For since existence necessarily belongs to
the object of this concept—i.e., under the condition that this thing is
posited as given (existing)—the object's existence is (according to
the rule of identity) necessarily also posited. And hence this being is
itself absolutely necessary, because—in a concept that has been assumed at will—this being's existence also is thought, viz., under the
condition that the concept's object is posited.

If in an identical judgment I annul the predicate and retain the
subject, then a contradiction arises, and hence I say that the predicate belongs to the subject necessarily. But if I annul the subject
along with the predicate, then no contradiction arises, for *nothing is
left* that could be contradicted. To posit a triangle and yet to annul its

three angles is contradictory; but to annul the triangle along with its three angles is not a contradiction. And with the concept of an absolutely necessary being the situation is exactly the same. If you annul the being's existence, then you annul the thing itself with all its predicates. Whence, then, is the contradiction to come? Extrinsically there is nothing that would be contradicted, for the thing is not to be necessary extrinsically. Intrinsically to the thing there is also nothing that would be contradicted; for by annulling the thing itself you have simultaneously annulled everything intrinsic to it. God is omnipotent—this is a necessary judgment. The omnipotence cannot be annulled if you posit a deity, i.e., an infinite being, with [part of] whose concept the concept of omnipotence is identical. But if you say *God does not exist,* then neither omnipotence nor any other of his predicates is given; for they are all annulled along with the subject, and hence this thought does not manifest the least contradiction.

Thus you have seen that if I annul the predicate of a judgment together with the subject, then an intrinsic contradiction can never arise—no matter what the predicate may be. You are now left with no escape except to say that there are subjects that cannot be annulled at all and that hence must remain. This, however, would be equivalent to saying that there are absolutely necessary subjects—the very presupposition whose correctness I doubted and whose possibility you
wanted to show me. For I cannot frame the slightest concept of a thing that, if it were annulled with all its predicates, would leave a contradiction; and without a contradiction I have, through pure a priori concepts alone, no mark of impossibility.

Wishing now to argue against all these general conclusions (which no one can refuse to accept), you challenge me with a case that you put forth as a factual proof. You argue that there is indeed one concept—and, moreover, only this *one*—where the nonexistence or annulment of the concept's object is self-contradictory: viz., the concept of the maximally real being. This being, you say, has all reality, and you are entitled to assume such a being as possible. (This possibility I concede for now, although the fact that a concept does not contradict itself is far from proving the object's possibility.)[27] Now [so you

---

27. A concept is always possible if it does not contradict itself. This is the logical mark of possibility, and by this mark the concept's object is distinguished from the *nihil negativum.* But the concept may nonetheless be an empty one if the objective reality of the synthesis whereby the concept is produced is not es-

argue] *all reality* includes also existence; hence existence lies within
the concept of a possible thing. If now this thing is annulled, then the
thing's intrinsic possibility is annulled—which is contradictory. A597/
B625

I reply: You have already committed a contradiction if, in offering
the concept of a thing that you wanted to think merely as regards its
possibility, you have already brought into this concept—no matter
under what covert name—the concept of the thing's existence. If
this [move] is granted to you, then you have seemingly won your
point; but in fact you have said nothing, because you have committed
a mere tautology. I ask you: is the proposition that *this or that thing
exists* (a thing that, whatever it may be, I grant you as possible)—is
this proposition, I ask, an analytic or a synthetic one? If the proposition is analytic, then by asserting the thing's existence you add nothing to your thought of the thing. But in that case either the thought,
which is in you, would have to be the thing itself; or you have presupposed an existence as belonging to possibility, and have then allegedly inferred the thing's existence from the thing's intrinsic possibility—which is nothing but a pitiful tautology. The word *reality*,
which merely sounds different in the concept of the thing [as sub-
ject] from [the word] *existence* in the concept of the predicate, is of
no help. For even if you call all positing [of a subject] *reality* (whatever it is that you are positing), you have in the concept of the subject
already posited, and assumed as actual, the thing with all its predicates and are merely repeating it in the predicate. On the other hand,
if you admit—as any reasonable person must—that any existential
proposition is synthetic, then how can you assert that the predicate
of existence cannot be annulled without contradiction? For this su-
periority belongs only to analytic propositions as their peculiarity,
since their character rests precisely on this [necessity].

A598/
B626

I would, indeed, hope to eliminate without much ado all this med-
itative subtlety through an exact determination of the concept of existence—had I not found that the illusion arising from the confusion
of a logical with a real predicate (i.e., with the determination of a

---

tablished separately. However, as has been shown above, establishing this reality
always rests on principles of possible experience and not on the principle of
analysis (the principle of contradiction). This point is a warning that we must
not immediately infer the (real) possibility of things from the (logical) possibility of concepts.

thing) permits almost no instruction [to dispel the illusion]. Anything whatsoever can serve as a *logical predicate;* even the subject [of a proposition] can be predicated of itself; for logic abstracts from all content. But a *determination* is a predicate that is added to the subject's concept and increases it; hence it must not already be contained in that concept.

Being is obviously not a real predicate, i.e., it is not a concept of anything that can be added to the concept of a thing. It is merely the positing of a thing [in itself] or of certain determinations in themselves. In its logical use it is merely the copula of a judgment. The proposition *God is omnipotent* contains two concepts that have their objects: God and omnipotence. The little word *is* is not a further predicate over and above these two, but is only what posits the predicate *in reference* to the subject. If I now take the subject (God) together with all its predicates (to which belongs also omnipotence) and say *God is*—or, There is a God—then I posit no new predicate as added to the concept of God, but posit only the subject in itself with all its predicates; viz., I posit *the object* in reference to my *concept.* Both must contain exactly the same; and hence nothing further can be added to the concept—which expresses only the [object's] possibility—merely because (through the expression *it is*) I think this object as given absolutely. And thus the actual contains no more than the merely possible. A hundred actual thalers do not contain the least more than a hundred possible thalers. For, the possible thalers signify the concept and the actual thalers signify the object and the positing thereof in itself; hence if the object contained more than the concept, then my concept would not express the entire object and thus would also not be the concept commensurate with this object. In the state of my assets, however, there is more in the case of a hundred actual thalers than in the case of the mere concept of them (i.e., their mere possibility). For in the case of the hundred thalers' actuality the object is not merely contained analytically in my concept (which is a determination of my state), but is added synthetically to my concept; yet these thought hundred thalers themselves are not in the least augmented by their being outside my concept.

Hence no matter through which and through how many predicates I think a thing (even if I think it in its thoroughgoing determination), not the least is added to this thing by my going on to say that this thing *is.* For otherwise what exists would not be the same as I had thought in the concept, but would be more; and I could then not say

A599/
B627

A600/
B628

that exactly the object of my concept exists. Even if I think in a thing all reality except one, the missing reality is not added by my saying that such a deficient thing exists. Rather, the thing then exists as encumbered with exactly the same deficiency with which I thought it, since otherwise there would exist something other than what I thought. Now if I think a being as the supreme reality (i.e., as a being without deficiency), then there still remains the question as to whether or not this being exists. For although nothing of the possible real content of a thing as such is missing in my concept of this being, yet something is still missing in the concept's relation to my entire state of thought, viz., that the cognition of this object is possible also a posteriori. And now we find also the cause of the difficulty that prevails here. If an object of the senses were at issue, then I could not confuse the thing's existence with the mere concept of the thing. For when the object is thought through the concept, then it is thought only as agreeing with the universal conditions of a possible empirical cognition as such. But when it is thought through existence, then the object is thought as contained in the context of experience as a whole; and here the concept of the object is not in the least augmented by the connection with the content of experience as a whole, although our thinking acquires through this content another possible perception. But if we wish to think existence through the pure category alone, then we must not be surprised that we cannot indicate any mark whereby to distinguish existence from mere possibility. A601/ B629

Hence no matter what and how much our concept of an object may contain, we must yet go outside the concept in order to assign existence to the object. In the case of objects of the senses this is done through the coherence of these objects, according to empirical laws, with some one of my perceptions. But for objects of pure thought there is no means whatsoever of cognizing their existence. For their existence would have to be cognized entirely a priori. But our consciousness of any existence (whether such consciousness arises directly through perception or indirectly through inferences connecting something with perception) belongs altogether to the unity of experience. And although an existence outside this realm [of experience] cannot absolutely be declared to be impossible, it is a presupposition that we cannot justify by anything.

The concept of a supreme being is in many respects a very useful idea. But this idea, precisely because it is merely that, is quite incapable of allowing us to expand, by means of it alone, our cognition A602/ B630 regarding what exists. Even as regards possibility the idea is unable to teach us anything further. To be sure, the analytic mark of possibility, which consists in the fact that mere positings (realities) cannot generate a contradiction, cannot be denied to this concept. However, the connection of all real properties in a thing is a synthesis whose possibility we cannot judge a priori. For the realities are not given to us specifically. And even if they were, no judgment whatever in regard to them [can] take place at all. For, the mark of the possibility of synthetic cognitions must always be sought only in experience; the object of an idea, however, cannot belong to experience. Hence the illustrious *Leibniz* is far from having accomplished what he flattered himself to have achieved: viz., an a priori insight into the possibility of such an august ideal being.

Hence all effort and labor is lost if expended on the famous ontological (Cartesian) proof of the existence of a supreme being from mere concepts; and, I suppose, a human being could not from mere ideas become richer in insights any more than a merchant could become richer in assets if he tried to improve his situation by adding a few zeros to his cash balance. [...]

APPENDIX TO THE
TRANSCENDENTAL DIALECTIC

ON THE FINAL AIM OF THE
NATURAL DIALECTIC OF HUMAN
REASON

A702/
B730

[...] Thus all human cognition begins with intuitions, proceeds from there to concepts, and ends with ideas. This cognition does indeed have—with regard to all three of these elements—a priori sources of cognition that seem at first glance to defy the bounds of all experience. Yet a completed critique convinces us that all our reason in its speculative use can never—with these elements—get beyond the realm of possible experience. And the critique convinces us that the proper vocation of this highest cognitive power is to employ all the methods and principles of reason solely for tracing nature to its innermost core according to all possible principles of unity—the

foremost of which is the unity of purposes—but never to soar
beyond nature's boundary, since *for us* there is nothing but empty
space outside it. The critical investigation—as carried out in the
Transcendental Analytic—of all propositions that can expand our
cognition beyond actual experience has, to be sure, sufficiently convinced us that these propositions can never lead to anything more
than a possible experience. And if we were not distrustful of even the
clearest abstract and general doctrines, and if charming and plausible prospects did not entice us to cast off those doctrines' constraint,
then we could indeed have been spared the laborious interrogation of
all the dialectical witnesses that a transcendent reason brings forward on behalf of its claims. For even beforehand we knew with
complete certainty that all allegation of reason, although perhaps
honestly meant, must be absolutely null, because it concerns information that no human being can ever acquire. Yet there is no end of
the talking unless one uncovers the true cause of the illusion that can
trick even the most reasonable person. Moreover, resolving all our
transcendent cognition into its elements (as a study of our inner nature) is in itself of no slight value; but for the philosopher it is even a
duty. Hence not only was there a need to investigate comprehensively this entire working of speculative reason—idle though it is—
down to its primary sources. But since the dialectical illusion is here
not only deceptive in the judgment but is also enticing in the interest
that is here taken in the judgment, and since the illusion is always
natural and will remain so for the future, it was advisable for us to
draw up comprehensively the proceedings of this trial, as it were, so
as to deposit them in the archives of human reason in order to prevent future errors of a similar kind. [...]

A703/
B731

B732
A704

TRANSCENDENTAL
DOCTRINE OF METHOD

Chapter II
The Canon of Pure Reason

Human reason is humiliated by the fact that, in its pure use, it accomplishes nothing and indeed even needs a discipline to restrain its own extravagances and prevent the deceptions that these engender for it. But, on the other hand, human reason is elevated and acquires self-confidence through the fact that it can and must exercise this discipline on its own, without permitting any other verdict concerning itself; and likewise through the fact that the bounds that it is compelled to set to its own speculative use simultaneously limit the subtly reasoning claims of every opponent, so that whatever may still be left to human reason from its previously exaggerated demands can be secured by it against all attacks. Hence the greatest and perhaps only benefit of all philosophy of pure reason may be only negative. For such philosophy does not—as an organon—serve to expand [cognition], but—as a discipline—serves to determine the boundary [of cognition]; and instead of discovering truth, it has only the silent merit of preventing errors.

Yet somewhere there must nonetheless be a source of positive cognitions that belong in the domain of pure reason, and that perhaps
give rise to errors only through misunderstanding but in fact amount to the aim of reason's zeal. For to what cause could one otherwise attribute reason's indomitable desire to gain by all means a firm foothold somewhere beyond the boundary of experience? Reason there suspects objects that carry with them a great interest for it. It enters upon the path of mere speculation in order to come closer to these objects; but there they flee from it. Presumably we may hope that reason will have better fortune on the only path that still remains to it, viz., that of its *practical* use.

By a canon I mean the sum of a priori principles governing the correct use of certain cognitive powers as such. Thus general logic in its analytical part is a canon for understanding and reason as such—but only as regards form, for general logic abstracts from all content.

And thus the transcendental analytic was the canon of pure *under-standing;* for pure understanding alone is capable of having true synthetic a priori cognitions. But where no correct use of a cognitive power is possible, there is no canon. Now all synthetic cognition of pure *reason* in its speculative use is, according to all the proofs conducted thus far, entirely impossible. Hence there is no canon whatever of pure reason's speculative use (for this use is dialectical throughout), and all transcendental logic is in regard to this speculative aim nothing but discipline. Consequently, if there is a correct use of pure reason at all, in which case there must also be a *canon* of pure reason, then this canon will concern not the speculative but the *practical use of reason.* Hence we shall now investigate this use.

A797/
B825

The Canon of Pure Reason

Section I
On the Ultimate Purpose of the Pure Use of Our Reason

Reason is impelled by a propensity of its nature to go beyond its use in experience, to venture outward—in a pure use and by means of mere ideas—to the utmost bounds of all cognition, and to find rest for the first time in the completion of its sphere, i.e., in a self-subsistent systematic whole. Now, is this endeavor based merely on reason's speculative interest, or is it, rather, based solely and exclusively on its practical interest?

Let me now set aside whatever success pure reason has in regard to its speculative aim, and inquire only into the problems whose solution amounts to pure reason's ultimate purpose—the purpose which pure reason may or may not accomplish, and in regard to which all other purposes have only the value of means. These highest purposes must, according to the nature of reason, have unity in turn, in order that—as thus united—they may further that interest of humanity which is not subordinate to any higher interest.

A798/
B826

The final aim to which the speculation of reason as used transcendentally is ultimately directed concerns three objects: the freedom of the will, the immortality of the soul, and the existence of God. With regard to all three the merely speculative interest of reason is only very slight; and with this interest in view one presumably would scarcely undertake an exhausting job—which wrestles with unceasing obstacles—of transcendental investigation. For whatever discoveries one might be able to make concerning these three objects, one could still not make of these discoveries a use that would prove its benefit *in concreto,* i.e., in the investigation of nature. E.g., first, even if the will is free, this fact still can concern only the intelligible cause of our willing. For as regards the phenomena consisting of that will's manifestations, i.e., the actions, we must always—according to an inviolable basic maxim without which we could not exercise any empirically used reason at all—explain them only as we explain all the remaining appearances of nature, viz., according to immutable laws of nature. Moreover, second, even if one can have insight into the spiritual nature of the soul (and, with this nature, into the soul's immortality), one still can count on this spiritual nature neither as a basis of explanation regarding the appearances of this life, nor as shedding light on the particular character of our future state. For our concept of an incorporeal nature is merely negative; it does not in the least expand our cognition or offer suitable material for inferences—except perhaps for inferences that can be regarded only as inventions but that philosophy does not allow. Third, even if the existence of a supreme intelligence were proved, although we would indeed from this existence make comprehensible for ourselves in a general way what is purposive in the world's arrangement and order, we would by no means be entitled to derive from this existence any particular provision and order, or boldly to infer such provision or order where it is not perceived. For there is a necessary rule of the speculative use of reason, not to pass over natural causes and abandon something of which we can inform ourselves through experience, in order to take something that we know and derive it from what entirely surpasses our knowledge. In a word, for speculative reason these three propositions always remain transcendent and have no immanent use whatever, i.e., no use admissible for objects of experience and hence beneficial to us in some way; rather, when regarded in themselves, they are endeavors of our reason that are entirely futile and are even extremely difficult into the bargain.

A799/ B827

Accordingly, if these three cardinal propositions are not at all necessary to us for *knowledge* and are nonetheless urgently commended to us by our reason, then—I suppose—their importance will properly have to concern only the *practical.*

A800/ B828

Practical is everything that is possible through freedom. But if the conditions for the exercise of our free power of choice are empirical, then reason can have in this exercise none but a regulative use and can serve only to bring about the unity of empirical laws. Thus, e.g., in the doctrine of prudence, the entire business of reason consists in taking all the purposes assigned to us by our inclinations and uniting them in the one purpose, *happiness,* and in harmonizing the means for attaining this happiness. Consequently, reason can here supply none but *pragmatic* laws of free conduct that is aimed at attaining the purposes commended to us by the senses, and hence can supply no laws that are pure, i.e., determined completely a priori. By contrast, pure practical laws, the purpose of which is given completely a priori by reason and which command not in an empirically conditioned but in an absolute way, would be products of pure reason. *Moral* laws, however, are indeed such pure practical laws, and hence they alone belong to the practical use of pure reason and permit a canon.

The entire apparatus of pure reason, as considered in the treatment that may be called pure philosophy, is in fact directed only to the three mentioned problems. These problems themselves, however, have in turn their more remote aim, viz., *what is to be done* if the will is free, if there is a God, and if there is a future world. Now since this more remote aim concerns our conduct in reference to the highest purpose, the ultimate aim of nature—the nature that in the arrangement of our reason provides for us wisely—pertains properly only to what is moral. A801/ B829

But as we turn our attention to an object extraneous to transcendental philosophy, we must be cautious not to stray into digressions and violate the unity of the system, and cautious also—on the other hand—not to incur a lack of distinctness or of [power of] conviction by saying too little about our new material. I hope to accomplish both of these goals by keeping as close as possible to what is transcendental and setting aside entirely what might in this material be psychological, i.e., empirical.

And thus I must first point out that I shall for now employ the concept of freedom in its practical meaning only, and shall here set aside—as having been dealt with above—the same concept in the transcendental signification. The latter concept cannot be presupposed empirically as a basis for explaining appearances, but is itself a problem for reason. For a power of choice is merely *animal (arbitrium brutum)* if it cannot be determined otherwise than through A802/ B830

sensible impulses, i.e., *pathologically*. But the power of choice that
can be determined independently of sensible impulses and hence
through motivating causes that are presented only by reason is called
the *free power of choice (arbitrium liberum)*; and everything connected
with this free power of choice, whether as basis or as consequence, is
called *practical*. Practical freedom can be proved through experience.
For the human power of choice is determined not merely by what
stimulates, i.e., by what directly affects the senses. Rather, we have a
power of overcoming, through presentations of what is beneficial or
harmful even in a more remote way, the impressions made upon our
sensible power of desire. These deliberations, however, concerning
what is with regard to our whole state desirable, i.e., good and beneficial, rest on reason. This is also why reason gives laws that are imperatives, i.e., objective *laws of freedom*. Such laws tell us *what ought
to occur* even though perhaps it never does occur—and therein they
differ from *laws of nature*, which deal only with *what occurs*—and this
is why the laws of freedom are also called practical laws.

A803/
B831
But whether reason is not, even in these actions through which it
prescribes laws, determined in turn by other influences, and whether
what in regard to sensible impulses is called freedom may not in regard to higher and more remote efficient causes in turn be nature—
this further question does not concern us in the practical [realm].
For there we initially consult reason only concerning the *prescription*
of conduct; but that further question is a merely speculative one,
which we can set aside as long as our intention is directed to *doing* or
refraining. Hence we cognize practical freedom through experience;
we cognize it as one of the natural causes, viz., as a causality of reason [that is operative] in the determination of the will. Transcendental freedom, on the other hand, demands an independence of this
reason itself (as regards reason's causality whereby it is able to begin
a series of appearances) from all determining causes of the world of
sense; and to this extent transcendental freedom seems to be contrary to the law of nature and hence to all possible experience, and
therefore remains a problem. But this problem does not pertain to
reason in its practical use; and hence in a canon of pure reason we
deal with only two questions, which concern the practical interest of
pure reason and with regard to which a canon of this reason's use
must be possible, viz.: Is there a God? Is there a future life? The
A804/
B832
question regarding transcendental freedom concerns merely our
speculative knowledge. This question we can set aside as making no

difference whatever when our concern is what is practical; and sufficient discussion regarding it can already be found in the antinomy of pure reason.

The Canon of Pure Reason

Section II

On the Ideal of the Highest Good, As a Determining Basis of the Ultimate Purpose of Pure Reason

Reason in its speculative use led us through the realm of experiences and, since complete satisfaction can never be found for it in that realm, from there to speculative ideas. But in the end these ideas led us back again to experience, and thus they fulfilled their intent in a way that, although beneficial, did not at all conform to our expectation. This leaves us with one more attempt. Viz., we must inquire whether pure reason can be found also in reason's practical use; whether in this use it leads us to the ideas which reach the highest purposes of pure reason that we have just mentioned; and whether, therefore, pure reason cannot perhaps grant us from the viewpoint of its practical interest what it altogether denies us with regard to its speculative interest.

All my reason's interest (speculative as well as practical) is united in the following three questions:

1. *What can I know?*

2. *What ought I to do?*

3. *What may I hope?*

A805/
B833

The first question is merely speculative. We have (as I flatter myself) exhausted all possible answers to this question and have finally found the one answer with which reason must indeed content itself and, if reason does not take account of the practical, also has cause to be content. From the two great purposes, however, to which this entire endeavor of pure reason was properly directed we have remained just as distant as if we had—from love of leisure—refused this job at the very beginning. Hence if our concern is knowledge, then at least this much is certain and established: that we shall never be able to partake of knowledge regarding those two problems.

The second question is merely practical. As such it can indeed belong to pure reason; but it is then a moral rather than a transcendental question and hence cannot in itself occupy our [present] critique.

The third question—viz., If, now, I do what I ought to do, what may I then hope?—is simultaneously practical and theoretical, so that the practical [component] is only a guide that leads to the answering of the theoretical question and—if the theoretical question rises high—of the speculative question. For all *hoping* aims at happiness, and is in regard to the practical [realm] and to the moral law the same [thing] that knowing and the natural law are in regard to the theoretical cognition of things. Hoping ultimately amounts to the conclusion that there *is* something (that determines the ultimate possible purpose) *because something ought to occur;* knowing ultimately amounts to the conclusion that there is something (that acts as supreme cause) *because something does occur.*

Happiness is the satisfaction of all our inclinations (*extensively*, in terms of their manifoldness; *intensively*, in terms of their degree; and also *protensively*, in terms of their duration). The practical law issuing from the motive of *happiness* I call pragmatic (i.e., rule of prudence). But the practical law that has as its motive nothing but the *worthiness to be happy*—if there is such a law—I call moral (moral law). The pragmatic law advises [us] what we must do if we want to partake of happiness; the moral law commands how we ought to behave in order just to become worthy of happiness. The pragmatic law is based on empirical principles; for in no other way than by means of experience can I know either what inclinations there are that want to be satisfied, or what the natural causes are that can bring about the satisfaction of those inclinations. The moral law abstracts from inclinations and from the natural means for satisfying them. It considers only the freedom of a rational being as such, and the necessary conditions under which alone this freedom harmonizes with a distribution of happiness that is made in accordance with principles. Hence the moral law at least *can* rest on mere ideas of pure reason and thus be cognized a priori.

I assume that there actually are pure moral laws that determine completely a priori (without regard to empirical motives, i.e., to hap-

A806/
B834

A807/
B835

piness) the doing and the refraining, i.e., the use of the freedom of a rational being as such, and that these laws command *absolutely* (not merely hypothetically, on the presupposition of other empirical purposes) and are therefore necessary in every regard. This proposition [that there are such laws] I may rightly presuppose, by appealing not only to the proofs of the most enlightened moralists, but also to the moral judgment that every human being makes if he wishes to think such a law distinctly.

Hence pure reason contains—although not in its speculative use but still in a certain practical, viz., the moral, use—principles of the *possibility of experience*, viz., of the experience of such actions as could be encountered in accordance with moral precepts in the *history* of the human being. For since pure reason commands that such actions ought to occur, they must also be able to occur. And hence a particular kind of systematic unity must be possible, viz., moral unity. By contrast, the systematic unity of nature *according to speculative principles of reason* was incapable of being proved; for although reason has causality with regard to freedom as such, it does not have causality with regard to all of nature; and although moral principles of reason can give rise to free actions, they cannot give rise to natural laws. Accordingly, the principles of pure reason in its practical use— but specifically in its moral use—have objective reality.

A808/ B836

The world insofar as it would be in accordance with all moral laws (as, indeed, according to the *freedom* of rational beings it *can* be, and as according to the necessary laws of *morality* it *ought* to be) I call a **moral world**. The moral world is thought merely as an intelligible world, inasmuch as we abstract in it from all conditions (purposes) and even from all obstacles for morality (weakness or impurity of human nature). Therefore, to this extent the moral world is a mere idea; yet it is a practical idea that actually can and ought to have its influence on the world of sense, in order to bring this world as much as possible into accordance with the moral world. Hence the idea of a moral world has objective reality. But it has such reality not as dealing with an object of an intelligible intuition (such [a way for this idea to have objective reality] we cannot even think), but as dealing with the world of sense. However, the world of sense must here be taken as an object of pure reason in its practical use and as a *corpus mysticum* of the rational beings in it insofar as their free power of choice is, under moral laws, in thoroughgoing systematic unity both with itself and with the freedom of every other such being.

This has been the answer to the first of the two questions of pure reason that concerned its practical interest, and this answer is: *Do that whereby you become worthy to be happy*. Now the second question asks this: What if now I behave in such a way as not to be unworthy of happiness, may I also hope that I can thereby partake of happiness? In answering this question, what matters is whether the principles of pure reason that prescribe the law a priori do also connect this hope necessarily with that law.

I maintain, then, that just as moral principles are necessary according to reason in its *practical* use, so it is equally necessary also according to reason in its *theoretical* use to assume that everyone has cause to hope for happiness insofar as he has made himself worthy of it in his conduct, and hence to assume that the system of morality is linked inseparably—but only in the idea of pure reason—with the system of happiness.

Now in an intelligible world, i.e., in the moral world, in whose concept we abstract from all obstacles to morality (i.e., from inclinations), such a system of a proportionate happiness linked with morality can indeed be thought as necessary. For freedom, partly impelled and partly restricted by moral laws, would itself be the cause of general happiness; and hence rational beings, under the guidance of such principles, would themselves be originators of their own and also of other beings' lasting welfare. But this system of the morality that rewards itself is only an idea. Carrying out the idea rests on the condition that *everyone* does what he ought to do, i.e., the condition that all actions of rational beings occur as they would if they sprang from a supreme will comprising all private power of choice within itself or under itself. However, the obligation issuing from the moral law remains valid for everyone's particular use of freedom even if others were not to behave in accordance with this law. Therefore, how the consequences of these actions will relate to happiness is determined neither by the nature of the things of the world, nor by the causality of the actions themselves and their relation to morality. And thus the mentioned necessary connection of one's hope for happiness with the unceasing endeavor to make oneself worthy of happiness cannot be cognized through reason if mere nature is laid at the basis. Rather, this connection may be hoped for only if a *supreme reason* that commands according to moral laws is also laid at the basis of nature, as nature's cause.

The idea of such an intelligence wherein the morally most perfect will, combined with the highest bliss, is the cause of all happiness in the world, insofar as this happiness is exactly proportionate to one's morality (as the worthiness to be happy), I call *the ideal of the highest good*. Hence only in the ideal of the highest *original* good can pure reason find the basis of the practically necessary connection between the two elements of the highest derivative good, viz., the basis of an intelligible, i.e., *moral* world. Now, we must through reason necessarily conceive ourselves as belonging to such a world, although the senses exhibit to us nothing but a world of appearances. Hence we shall have to assume the moral world as being a consequence of our conduct in the world of sense, and—since the world of sense does not now offer us such a connection between happiness and morality—as being for us a future world. Hence God and a future life are two presuppositions that, according to principles of pure reason, are inseparable from the obligation imposed on us by that same reason.

A811/
B839

Morality in itself amounts to a system; but happiness does not, except insofar as its distribution is exactly commensurate with morality. This, however, is possible only in the intelligible world, under a wise originator and ruler. Reason finds itself compelled either to assume such a being, along with life in such a world, which we must regard as a future world; or to regard the moral laws as idle chimeras, because without this presupposition the necessary result that reason connects with these laws would have to vanish. This is, moreover, why everyone regards the moral laws as *commands;* this the moral laws could not be if they did not a priori connect with their rule commensurate consequences and thus carry with them *promises* and *threats*. But this again the moral laws cannot do unless they reside in a necessary being that, as the highest good, can alone make such a purposive unity possible.

A812/
B840

Leibniz called the world, insofar as we consider in it only the rational beings and their coherence according to moral laws under the government of the highest good, the *kingdom of grace*. And this he distinguished from the *kingdom of nature*, where these beings are indeed subject to moral laws but expect from their conduct no other results than those that occur in accordance with the course of nature in our world of sense. Therefore, seeing ourselves in the kingdom of grace, where all happiness awaits us except insofar as we ourselves limit our share therein by being unworthy of happiness, is a practically necessary idea of reason.

Practical laws insofar as they also become subjective bases of actions, i.e., subjective principles, are called *maxims*. The *judging* of morality in terms of its purity and consequences occurs according to *ideas*, the *compliance* with its laws occurs according to *maxims*.

It is necessary that our entire way of life be subjected to moral maxims. But it is at the same time impossible for this to occur unless reason connects with the moral law, which is a mere idea, an efficient cause that determines for all conduct conforming to this law an outcome, whether in this or in another life, that corresponds exactly to our highest purposes. Hence without a God and without a world that is invisible to us now but is hoped for, the splendid ideas of morality are indeed objects of approbation and admiration, but are not incentives for our resolve and for our carrying out these ideas. For they do not then fulfill the entire purpose which is natural for every rational being and which is determined a priori and made necessary by that same pure reason.

Happiness by itself is, for our reason, far from being the complete good. For happiness is not approved by our reason (however much it may be wished for by our inclination) unless this happiness is united with worthiness to be happy, i.e., with morally good conduct. But morality by itself—and with it the mere *worthiness* to be happy—is also far from being the complete good. In order for this good to be completed, the person who in his conduct has not been unworthy of happiness must be able to hope that he will partake of it. Even a reason free from any private aim and thus not taking into account an interest of its own, if it puts itself in the position of a being that had to distribute all happiness to others, cannot judge differently. For in the practical idea the two components are linked essentially—although in such a way that it is the moral attitude, as condition, that first makes possible the sharing in happiness, and not, conversely, the prospect of happiness that first makes possible the moral attitude. For in the latter case the attitude would not be moral, and hence would also not be worthy of full happiness—the happiness which in reason's view recognizes no other limitation than a limitation due to our own immoral conduct.

Hence happiness, in exact balance with the morality of rational beings whereby these beings are worthy of happiness, alone amounts to the highest good of a world into which, according to the precepts of pure but practical reason, we must definitely transfer ourselves. That world, to be sure, is only an intelligible one; for the world of sense does not promise to us, as arising from the nature of things, such systematic unity of purposes. Moreover, the reality of that intelligible world cannot be based on anything other than the presupposition of a highest original good: a good where independent reason, equipped with all the sufficiency of a supreme cause, establishes, preserves, and completes—according to the most perfect purposiveness—the order of things that is universal although very much concealed from us in the world of sense.

Now this moral theology has over speculative theology the particular advantage of leading inevitably to the concept of a *single, maximally perfect,* and *rational* original being; speculative theology does not, from objective bases, even *point* to such a being, much less is able to *convince* us [of the existence] thereof. For no matter how far reason may lead us in transcendental and in natural theology, in neither of them do we find any significant basis for assuming just a single being such that we would have sufficient cause to put this being prior to all natural causes and also to make these causes in all respects dependent on it. By contrast, if we consider from the viewpoint of moral unity, as a necessary law of the world, the cause that alone can give to this law the commensurate effect and hence also its obligating force for us, then what comprises all these laws within itself must be a single supreme will. For how could we find perfect unity of purposes among different wills? This will must be omnipotent, in order that all of nature and its reference to morality in the world may be subject to it; omniscient, in order that it may cognize the innermost core of our attitudes and their moral value; omnipresent, in order that it may be directly close to all need that the highest greatest good of the world requires [to be satisfied]; eternal, in order that this harmony of nature and freedom may at no time be lacking; etc.

A815/
B843

Thus we arrive at systematic unity of purposes in this world of intelligences—a world that as mere nature can indeed be called only the world of sense, but that as a system of freedom can be called the intelligible, i.e., the moral world *(regnum gratiae)*. But this systematic unity of purposes leads inevitably also to the purposive unity of all things making up this large whole [as a unity] according to universal natural laws, just as the unity in the world of intelligences is one according to universal and necessary moral laws; and it thus unites practical with speculative reason. The world must be presented by us as having arisen from an idea, if it is to harmonize with that use of reason without which we would consider ourselves unworthy of reason, viz., the moral use, which rests entirely on the idea of the highest good. Through this way of presenting the world, all investigation

A816/
B844

of nature acquires a direction according to the form of a system of purposes, and in its highest extension becomes physicotheology. But because physicotheology started from moral order, as a unity that has its basis in the essence of freedom and is not brought about contingently through external commands, it leads the purposiveness of nature to bases that must be inseparably connected a priori with the intrinsic possibility of things. It thereby leads nature's purposiveness to a *transcendental theology*, which adopts the ideal of the highest ontological perfection as a principle of systematic unity—a principle that connects all things according to universal and necessary natural laws because all these things have their origin in the absolute necessity of a single original being.

What sort of *use* can we make of our understanding, even as regards experience, if we do not set purposes for ourselves? But the highest purposes are those of morality, and these are purposes that only pure reason can allow us to cognize. Now even as furnished with these moral purposes and guided by them, we still cannot make any purposive use of our acquaintance with nature itself as regards cognition, if nature itself has not also laid down purposive unity. For without this unity we ourselves would not even have any reason, since we would have no school for it and no culture [of reason] through objects that would offer to it the material for such concepts of purposes. However, the moral purposive unity is necessary and has its basis in the essence of the power of choice itself. Hence the natural purposive unity, which contains the condition of the moral unity's application *in concreto*, must likewise be necessary. And thus the transcendental enhancement of our rational cognition would be not the cause but merely the effect of the practical purposiveness imposed on us by pure reason.

Thus we do indeed find, in the history of human reason, that before the moral concepts were sufficiently purified and determined, and insight gained—and this from necessary principles—into the systematic unity of purposes according to these concepts, our acquaintance with nature and even a considerable degree of the culture of reason in various other sciences [had very little theological significance; for in part they] could produce only crude and erratic concepts of the deity, and in part they left people with an amazing general indifference regarding this question. A greater treatment of moral ideas—which was made necessary by the extremely pure moral law of our religion—sharpened reason for dealing with this

A817/
B845

[divine] object, through the interest that this treatment compelled people to take in this object. And these moral ideas, without any contribution either from an expanded acquaintance with nature or from correct and reliable transcendental insights (of which there has at all times been a lack), brought about a concept of the divine being that we now regard as the correct concept; and we regard it as correct not because speculative reason convinces us of this correctness, but because the concept harmonizes perfectly with reason's moral principles. And thus in the end it is always still pure reason alone, but only in its practical use, that has the merit of connecting a cognition to our highest interest: a cognition that mere speculation can only surmise but cannot validate. And pure practical reason has the merit of thereby turning this cognition, not indeed into a demonstrated dogma, but still into an absolutely necessary presupposition linked with reason's most essential purposes.

A818/
B846

However, when practical reason has reached this high point, viz., the concept of a single original being as the highest good, it must by no means—just as if it had elevated itself beyond all empirical conditions of this concept's application and had soared to a direct acquaintance with new objects—presume to start now from this concept and to derive from it the moral laws themselves. For it was precisely these laws whose intrinsic practical necessity led us to the presupposition of an independent cause, or of a wise ruler of the world, in order to provide these laws with effect. And hence we cannot thereafter regard them in turn as contingent and as derived from a mere will, especially not from a will of which we would have no concept at all if we had not formed this concept in accordance with those laws. As far as practical reason has the right to guide us, we shall not regard actions as obligatory because they are commands of God, but shall regard them as divine commands because we are intrinsically obligated to them. We shall study freedom in terms of the purposive unity according to principles of reason, and shall believe that we conform to the divine will only insofar as we hold sacred the moral law which reason teaches us from the nature of the actions themselves; and we shall believe that we can serve this will solely by furthering in us and in others the highest good in the world. Hence moral theology is only of immanent use. It serves us, viz., to fulfill our vocation here in the world by fitting ourselves into the system of all purposes, and to keep from abandoning in a good way of life, through fanaticism or perhaps even wickedness, the guiding thread

A819/
B847

of a morally legislating reason in order to tie this thread directly to the idea of a supreme being. For doing the latter would yield a transcendent use of reason and must—just like the use of reason in mere speculation—pervert and defeat the ultimate purposes of reason.

A820/
B848

The Canon of Pure Reason

Section III
On Opinion, Knowledge, and Faith

Assent is an event in our understanding that may rest on objective bases but that also requires subjective causes in the mind of the person who is judging. If the assent is valid for everyone, provided that he has reason, then its basis is sufficient *objectively,* and the assent is then called *conviction.* If the assent has its basis only in the particular character of the subject, then it is called *persuasion.*

Persuasion is a mere illusion; for the judgment's basis, which lies in the subject, is regarded as objective. Hence such a judgment also has only private validity, and the assent cannot be communicated. Truth, however, rests on agreement with the object; consequently, in regard to the object the judgments of every understanding must be in agreement *(consentientia uni tertio, consentiunt inter se).* Thus,

A821/
B849

whether assent is conviction or mere persuasion, its touchstone externally is the possibility of communicating the assent and of finding it to be valid for every human being's reason. For then there is at least a presumption that the agreement of all the judgments, despite the difference among the subjects, will rest on the common basis, viz., the object, and that hence the judgments will all agree with the object and will thereby prove the truth of the [joint] judgment.

Accordingly, persuasion can indeed not be distinguished subjectively from conviction if the subject views the assent merely as an appearance of his own mind. But the assent's bases that are valid for us can be tested on the understanding of others, to see whether these bases have the same effect on the reason of others that they have on ours; and this test is still a means, although only a subjective one, not indeed to bring about conviction, but still to detect any merely private validity of the judgment, i.e., whatever in the judgment is mere persuasion.

If, in addition, we can unfold the judgment's subjective *causes* that we take to be objective *bases* of it, and if we can therefore explain the deceptive assent as an event in our mind without needing the object's character for this explanation, then we expose the illusion and are no longer tricked by it. But we are still to a certain degree tempted by the illusion if its subjective cause attaches to our nature.

I cannot *assert* anything—i.e., pronounce it as a judgment that is necessarily valid for everyone—unless it is something that produces conviction. Persuasion I can keep for myself if I am at ease with it, but I cannot and should not try to make it hold apart from me.   A822/ B850

Assent—or the judgment's subjective validity—in reference to conviction (which holds [subjectively and] at the same time objectively) has the following three levels: *opinion, faith,* and *knowledge. Opinion* is an assent that is consciously insufficient *both* subjectively and objectively. If the assent is sufficient only subjectively and is at the same time regarded as objectively insufficient, then it is called *faith.* Finally, assent that is sufficient both subjectively and objectively is called *knowledge.* Subjective sufficiency is called *conviction* (for myself); objective sufficiency is called *certainty* (for everyone). I shall not linger upon the elucidation of such readily comprehensible concepts.

I must never presume to hold an *opinion* without *knowing* at least something by means of which the judgment, which in itself is merely problematic, acquires a connection with truth; for truth, even when not complete, is still more than an arbitrary invention. Moreover, the law of such a connection must be certain. For if in regard to this law I again have nothing but opinion, then everything is only a play of imagination without the least reference to truth. In judgments issuing from pure reason, holding an *opinion* is not permitted at all. For such judgments are not supported by experiential bases. Rather,   A823/ where everything is necessary, there everything is to be cognized a   B851 priori. Hence there the principle of connection requires universality and necessity, and hence complete certainty; otherwise one finds in it no guidance to truth. Thus holding an opinion in pure mathematics is absurd; here one must know, or refrain from all judgment. The same applies to the principles of morality, where one must not venture upon an action on the mere opinion that something is *permitted,* but must know this to be permitted.

In the transcendental use of reason, on the other hand, holding an opinion is indeed too little, but knowing is again too much. Hence here we cannot judge at all with a merely speculative aim. For subjective bases of assent, such as those that can bring about faith, deserve no approval in the case of speculative questions, because as used independently of all empirical assistance they do not hold up, nor can be communicated in equal measure to others. [That leaves faith or belief.]

However, only in a *practical reference* can the theoretically insufficient assent be called belief at all. Now this practical [reference or] aim is either one of *skill* or of *morality*—of skill for optional and contingent purposes, of morality for absolutely necessary purposes.

Once a purpose has been set, the conditions for attaining it are hypothetically necessary. This necessity is subjectively sufficient—yet it is so only comparatively if I do not know any other conditions whatever under which the purpose could be attained. But the necessity is sufficient absolutely and for everyone if I know with certainty that no one can be acquainted with any other conditions leading to the set purpose. In the first case my presupposition and the assent to certain conditions is a merely contingent belief, but in the second case it is a necessary belief. A physician must do something for a patient who is in danger, but is not acquainted with the nature of the patient's illness. He observes the phenomena and then judges, not knowing anything better to conclude, that the disease is consumption. His belief, even in his own judgment, is merely contingent; another belief might perhaps hit it better. Such belief, which is contingent but underlies our actual use of the means for certain actions, I call *pragmatic belief*.

A824/
B852

The usual touchstone as to whether something asserted by someone is mere persuasion, or at least subjective conviction—i.e., firm belief—is *betting*. Often someone pronounces his propositions with such confident and intractable defiance that he seems to have entirely shed all worry about error. A bet startles him. Sometimes the persuasion which he owns turns out to be sufficient to be assessed at one ducat, but not at ten. For although he may indeed risk the first ducat, at ten ducats he first becomes aware of what he previously failed to notice, viz., that he might possibly have erred after all. If we conceive in our thoughts the possibility of betting our whole life's happiness on something, then our triumphant judgment dwindles very much indeed; we then become extremely timid and thus discover for the first time that our belief does not reach this far. Thus pragmatic belief has merely a degree, which according to the difference of the interest involved may be large but may also be small.

A825/
B853

Even if we cannot undertake anything at all concerning an object, and the assent regarding it is therefore merely theoretical, we can still in many cases conceive and imagine an undertaking for which we suppose ourselves to have sufficient bases if there were a means of establishing the certainty of the matter. And thus there is in merely theoretical judgments an *analogue* of *practical* judgments, and for an assent to such judgments the word *faith* is appropriate. We may call this a *doctrinal faith*. I would indeed bet all that I own—if this matter could be established through some experience—that there are inhabitants on at least one of the planets that we see. Hence I say that this view—that there are inhabitants also on other worlds—is not a mere opinion but a strong faith (on whose correctness I would surely risk many of life's advantages).

Now, we must admit that the doctrine of the existence of God be- A826/ longs to doctrinal faith. To be sure, as regards theoretical cognition B854 of the world I have nothing *available* that necessarily presupposes this thought as a condition for my explanations of the world's appearances; rather, I am obligated to employ my reason as if everything were mere nature. Yet purposive unity is such a major condition for applying reason to nature that I cannot pass it by—[especially] since experience also provides me richly with examples of this unity. But I know no other condition for this unity that would make it my guide for the investigation of nature except the presupposition that a supreme intelligence has arranged everything in this way in accordance with the wisest purposes. Hence presupposing a wise originator of the world is a condition for an aim that is indeed contingent but still not unimportant, viz., to have guidance in the investigation of nature. Moreover, so often is this presupposition's usefulness confirmed by the outcome of my attempts, while nothing can be adduced against the presupposition in a decisive way, that I would say far too little if I wanted to call my assent merely an opinion. Rather, even in this theoretical relation we may say that I A827/ have firm faith in a God. But this faith is then still not practical in a B855 strict meaning of this term; rather, it must be called a doctrinal faith, to which the *theology* of nature (physicotheology) must necessarily give rise everywhere. With regard to the same wisdom, and in view of the superb endowment of human nature and the shortness of life that is so incommensurate with this endowment, we can likewise find a sufficient basis for a doctrinal faith in the future life of the human soul.

The expression *faith* is in such cases an expression of modesty from an *objective* point of view, but simultaneously of firmness of confidence from a *subjective* point of view. If I here wanted to call the merely theoretical assent even just a hypothesis that I am entitled to assume, I would already be promising to have a fuller concept of the character of a world cause and of the character of another world than I can actually show. For if I assume something even just as a hypothesis, then I must know at least so much about its properties that I need to invent *not its concept* but *only its existence*. The word *faith*, however, applies here only to the guidance that an idea gives to me, and to the idea's subjective influence on the furtherance of my acts of reason—the furtherance that keeps me attached to the idea even though I am unable to account for it from a speculative point of view.

The merely doctrinal faith, however, has something shaky about it; for the difficulties encountered in speculation often drive one away from this faith, although inevitably one always returns to it again.

The situation is quite different with *moral faith*. For here there is an absolute necessity that something must occur, viz., that I comply in all points with the moral law. Here the purpose is inescapably established, and—according to all the insight I have—only a single condition is possible under which this purpose coheres with the entirety of all purposes and thereby has practical validity, viz., the condition that there is a God and a future world. I also know with complete certainty that no one else is acquainted with other conditions that lead to the same unity of purposes under the moral law. But since the moral precept is thus simultaneously my maxim (as, indeed, reason commands), I shall inevitably have faith in the existence of God and in a future life. And I am sure that nothing can shake this faith; for that would overturn my moral principles themselves, which I cannot renounce without being detestable in my own eyes.

In this way, even after all the ambitious aims of a reason roaming beyond the bounds of experience have been defeated, we are still left with enough in order to have cause to be satisfied from a practical point of view. No one, indeed, will be able to boast that he *knows* that
there is a God and that there is a future life; for if he knows this, then he is just the man that I have been looking for all along. All knowledge (if it concerns an object of mere reason) can be communicated, and hence I could then hope that I might through his instruction see my own knowledge extended in such a marvelous degree. No, the conviction is not a logical but a *moral* certainty; and because it rests

CHAPTER II, SECTION III

on subjective bases (of the moral attitude), I must not even say, *It is* morally certain that there is a God, etc., but must say, *I am* morally certain, etc. In other words, the faith in a God and in another world is so interwoven with my moral attitude that, as little as I am in danger of losing my moral attitude, so little am I worried that my faith could ever be torn from me.

The only precariousness to be found in this is the fact that this rational faith is based on the presupposition of moral attitudes. If we abandon this presupposition and assume someone who is entirely indifferent with regard to moral laws, then the question posed by reason becomes merely a problem for speculation; and it can indeed still be supported then by strong bases taken from analogy, but not by bases to which the most obstinate skepticism would have to yield. But in these questions no human being is free of all interest. For although he may be separated from moral interest through a lack of good attitudes, yet enough remains even in this case to make him *fear* a divine existence and a future life. For this requires nothing more than the fact that at least he cannot plead any *certainty* that *no* such being and *no* future life are to be found. This [negative proposition]—since it would have to be proved through mere reason and hence apodeictically—he could prove only by establishing that both such a being and such a future life are impossible; and certainly no reasonable human being can undertake to do that. This [faith based on fear] would be a *negative* faith; and although it could not bring about morality and good attitudes, it could still bring about their analogue, viz., a powerful restraint on the eruption of evil attitudes.

But, it will be said, is this all that pure reason accomplishes in opening up prospects beyond the bounds of experience? Nothing more than two articles of faith? Even the common understanding could presumably have accomplished as much without consulting philosophers about it!

In reply, I do not here want to extol what merit philosophy has on behalf of human reason through the laborious endeavor of its critique, even supposing that this merit were in the upshot deemed to be merely negative; for I shall say something more about this in the following section. But do you indeed demand that a cognition which concerns all human beings should surpass the common understanding and be revealed to you only by philosophers? Precisely the point which you rebuke is the best confirmation that the assertions made thus far are correct. For it reveals what one could not have foreseen

A830/
B858

A831/
B859

at the outset: viz., that in matters of concern to all human beings, without distinction, nature cannot be accused of partiality in the distribution of its gifts; and that with regard to the essential purposes of human nature the highest philosophy cannot get further than can the guidance that nature has bestowed even upon the commonest understanding.

INDEX